PRAISE FOR
Evolutionary Ideas

"Sam Tatam connects theory with practical illustrations to make a case for the vital role of behavioural science in modern innovation. A wonderfully valuable book!"

—Nir Eyal, author of *Hooked* and *Indistractable*

"A provocative case for the role of behavioural science in contemporary innovation."

—Dilip Soman, Canada Research Chair in Behavioural Science and Economics at University of Toronto,
author of *The Last Mile*

"This book is fabulous and fascinating, teeming with insights about the psychology of innovation, not least that most innovation is not revolutionary but evolutionary."

—Matt Ridley, author of *How Innovation Works*

"*Evolutionary Ideas* is a hothouse of fresh insights, ready to invade your brain and take a life on their own. Every innovator should read it."

—Chiara Varazzani, Lead Behavioural Scientist, OECD

"A wonderful mix of fresh stories and robust experiments that helps explain the world around us. A must-read for anyone interested in out-innovating their competition."

—Richard Shotton, author of *The Choice Factory*

"Sam lays out the case for an evolutionary approach to innovation and problem solving in an engaging, accessible and – most importantly – usable way. In short, evolution is a way of thinking about innovation that can be applied to any area of human endeavour and *Evolutionary Ideas* gives you the tools and strategies to get started, now."

—Eaon Pritchard, Brand Strategist and author of *Where Did It All Go Wrong?* and *Shot By Both Sides*

"Why invent a revolutionary solution with so many existing solutions out there, in our society and in nature alike, that can easily evolve to fit the problem? Sam Tatam not only makes a compelling case for using evolutionary ideas, he also packs this book with examples and, more importantly, inspiration for anyone who needs to solve a problem."

—Koen Smets, Adjunct Assistant Professor at Saint Louis University

"People are always searching for the next revolutionary idea. But, as Sam Tatam shows in this captivating tour of *evolutionary* ideas, the best ways of generating solutions may be right in front of us. The engaging real-life examples in this book make getting a new dimension to your thinking effortless!"

—Michael Hallsworth, PhD, Managing Director, BIT Americas

"With the explosion of demand for behaviour change programmes, many of us struggle: we feel we should design behaviour change interventions from scratch. Sam shows why and how to use what already exists. Smart, sharp and very timely. Read this and steal!"

—Mark Earls, author of *HERD* and *Copy Copy Copy*

Evolutionary
Ideas

Every owner of a physical copy of this edition of

EVOLUTIONARY
IDEAS

can download the eBook for free direct from us at
Harriman House, in a DRM-free format that can be read on any
eReader, tablet or smartphone.

Simply head to:

ebooks.harriman-house.com/evolutionaryideas

to get your copy now.

Evolutionary Ideas

Unlocking ancient innovation to solve tomorrow's challenges

Sam Tatam

Foreword by
RORY SUTHERLAND

HARRIMAN HOUSE LTD
3 Viceroy Court
Bedford Road
Petersfield
Hampshire
GU32 3LJ
GREAT BRITAIN
Tel: +44 (0)1730 233870

Email: enquiries@harriman-house.com
Website: harriman.house

Paperback ISBN: 978-0-85719-787-0
eBook ISBN: 978-0-85719-788-7

British Library Cataloguing in Publication Data
A CIP catalogue record for this book can be obtained from the British Library.

For Mila and Riley,
our greatest creations

CONTENTS

FOREWORD
BY RORY SUTHERLAND

IMAGINE JUST FOR a moment that you're in a party of 100 people setting off to climb a high and distant mountain. You have no satellite imagery. You have no relief map of the mountain, nor much in the way of information on its shape, other than what you can see at a distance from one side. You certainly don't know where the gullies are, you don't know where the rivulets are, the glaciers, the impenetrable cliffs.

Well, one sensible approach might be something like this: you would all break up into different parties and approach the mountain from different sides. Some of you, perhaps, would try approaching the north face, others might try the south col or the northeast ridge.

You would then remain in rough contact with each other, occasionally shouting to Bob, "I think there's a path over here," or "Jane, I think I might have found a better ascension on the face 200 yards to the west." Some parties would give up entirely, finding themselves in an impassable bind or facing an unexpected cliff. At which point they would retrace their steps or even return to base camp to start the climb afresh from a new angle, based on what they have seen and heard.

Eventually, someone will make it to the top.

And it's at this point that two things will immediately happen.

Everybody will remember the name of the person who first made it to the top, and credit him or her with some special power of genius. They will, equally certainly, very quickly forget the other unfortunates who, though their approaches were perhaps no less worthy, had ended up sidetracked, wrong footed or stymied through no fault of their own.

It may even be that the success of the first person to reach the summit was ultimately dependent on inherited learning from people who had visibly failed, or who had succeeded disproportionately well lower down the mountain, and who had passed on the lower route to the victor before being sidetracked into a crevasse themselves.

(The British award, the OBE, has often been jokingly said to stand for *Other Buggers' Efforts*.)

But all those failures will be quickly forgotten, with all the focus now on the ultimate victor, and the effective, though not necessarily optimal, series of decisions that led them to succeed first.

And then the second thing happens.

Once you're at the top, of course, with the benefit of altitude and a new perspective, the best route up the mountain is completely obvious to you. Looking down from your new vantage point, the route up presents itself *as though it was obvious all along*.

And so you forget about all the wrong turns and the sidetracks. And the misdirected effort. You forget about the wrong turns you yourself made in making it to the top, and even more about the exploratory work done by your fellow climbers who ultimately failed.

In time, the story becomes rewritten to suggest that the perfect route, now self-evident in retrospect, was the route you took all along. There were no failures, there were no sidetracks, and no one was unexpectedly kiboshed through a sensible but ultimately inescapable turn into an impassable gulley. You, and you alone, made it from the bottom to the top via the only plausible route as a product of your own conscious and deliberate actions and nothing more than that. It was a triumph of reason, nothing else.

And that is why we always give the evolutionary mechanism far too little credit for its importance.

It's the same reason why there are far too few famous Belgians. Or Canadians.

You see, when a Canadian becomes famous everyone assumes they are an American; when a Belgian becomes famous, everyone assumes they are French or Dutch.

And whenever evolutionary processes pay off, their spectacular and irreplaceable contribution to success is misattributed in hindsight to acts of intentional design.

For some reason, perhaps itself a product of evolutionary psychology, it is very difficult to get people to see the world this way.

Sir John Harington, the Elizabethan courtier and poet (and, for trivia buffs, inventor of the toilet and ancestor of the actor Kit Harington, who played John Snow in *Game of Thrones*) spotted something of this asymmetry of attribution when he wrote:

Treason doth never prosper? What's the reason?
For if it prosper, none dare call it treason.

What Harington spotted is that there are very few documented cases of successful treason, because when treason is successful it is always called something else afterwards: for instance it might be rebranded as a war of independence, or a revolution.

If you have an American to hand, you can even try this experiment for yourself. If you explain that the American War of Independence was a narrow uprising based on grievances confected by a small number of rich, slave-owning plantation owners and other land-hungry men, motivated in large part by greed, and entirely lacking in democratic legitimacy,* you will be stating a perfectly arguable position (and one where there is even a happy counterfactual, in the shape of Canada, to suggest what *might* have happened otherwise). Yet, interestingly, you will be met not with any counter-argument, but by a mix of annoyance and complete bemusement. I'm not blaming Americans for this at all – all countries have their own explanatory self-serving narratives constructed after the events they describe, my own more than most. It's simply revealing how difficult it is to provide alternative explanations once a palatable and believable narrative has taken hold in an individual or group.

And for some reason the evolutionary narrative, once simplified by one thinker as "Things are the way they are because they got that way," always loses out to a narrative centred around deliberate, conscious intention and design.

I think this mixture of narrative bias and survivorship bias explains what we so often get wrong about most human progress. The process in reality involves much more experimentation and failure than we ever like to acknowledge in retrospect.

Again, once we've made some kind of breakthrough, the pathway becomes clear in retrospect as though it was clear all along: hindsight is always 20:20. There is the *successful* route, and all other routes are rapidly forgotten or disparaged as self-evidently wrong-headed, the names of the people who took them often lost to history.

Yet successes may not arise from intention at all: often they may be the fortunate survivors of, and the only visible participants in, a random process of variation and selection.

Is there a parallel universe where, owing to a few quirks of timing, The Beatles ended up being a smaller band than The Kinks? I think it's entirely plausible that an all-knowing God

---

* Notably the native and enslaved population, who had no say in the revolution, overwhelmingly supported the Crown.

who happened to be a big Ray Davies fan might engineer such an outcome. Just don't try arguing that to a Beatles fan. And don't go to someone involved in planning and strategy and suggest that their successes may sometimes be the unintended consequences of things they never predicted or devised. They really won't like it.

Yet understanding this distinction, and the asymmetric way we are inclined to see it, matters a great deal. For if we misunderstand the origins of progress, we will misdirect our efforts in attempting to create more of it.

This book is a perfect companion to an earlier book, by Matt Ridley, called *How Innovation Works*. Ridley is by background a biologist. And he understands that, actually, variation and selection with a mechanism for rewarding success and weeding out failure, or eradicating it as quickly as possible, is a far better mechanism for the advancement and development of technologies than deliberate directed investment, based on certain possibly wrongheaded preconceptions.

Ridley makes the point that evolutionary processes play a much greater part in advances than we properly acknowledge. And he also explains how this stochastic process, over time, can produce outcomes that planned intent could never obtain. There are mountains climbed by evolution which are unclimbable by other means.

But what my friend Sam Tatam does in this book is to take it one stage further.

For one thing, through his study of biomimicry, he makes the point that we can translate evolutionary progress in one sphere of activity into seemingly unrelated areas. Following the system of TRIZ, which is explained in this book, he documents some of the recurring patterns which are found in successful problem solving, and provides a template not for replacing evolutionary processes but for amplifying them and replicating them.

But he also does something else which I welcome wholeheartedly. He makes the point that the same recurring patterns of evolved intelligence can be found and reproduced in the psychological aspects of innovation just as they are in the technological aspects of innovation.

Why does this matter? Because just as we tend to downplay in hindsight the role that variation and selection play in the development of any new invention, we also grossly underestimate the role played by marketing, presentation, advertising, persuasion and salesmanship in encouraging people to adopt a new technology in the first place.

Once we are persuaded to adopt a new technology, we tend to supply reasons of our own as to why we adopted it, and the role of the external persuasion is completely forgotten. In the aftermath of a purchase, we forget that we were sold something, and rebrand it as a *choice*. It's that famous Belgian problem all over again.

To put it another way, do I think it a coincidence that Edison, Jobs, Ford and Musk are spectacular hucksters as much as they are (or were) inventors? No, I do not.

Now, I would say this, wouldn't I? I work in advertising, as does the author of this fabulous book. But I think it's a point worth making, that the role of marketing and advertising – which is also a game of experimentation, variation and selection – is an essential and often ignored handmaiden to innovation.

Successes in marketing seem obvious in retrospect, but are rarely obvious at the time. It is for this reason that we not only need to experiment more, but also benefit from evolutionary pattern recognition in deciding what to test. Evolution does not repeat itself, but it does rhyme.

Evolution does not repeat itself, but it does rhyme.

And here, I think things become particularly interesting, because I think behavioural science, as Sam has spotted, doesn't always provide you with right answers but it does provide you with sensible – and often unexpected – things to test in the psychological domain.

I suspect many great technological successes are really marketing successes in disguise. The genius of Uber, for example, lies in the app's map and its reapplication of an extraordinary psychological insight – that people often care about the uncertainty of waiting far more than about the duration. An engineer would measure the time of a wait – a psychologist would consider the mental state of the person waiting. The map, by solving the uncertainty problem through psychological means, contributes far more to Uber's success than the technologists behind it would probably like to acknowledge.

This same discovery had been made years before in train departure information systems. But no one had thought of documenting the finding and applying it to taxis.

Aided by Sam's approach, I think that in the next 10 to 20 years advances in psychology may prove to be just as important to the improvement of the human condition as technology is today. And as such, I think, by taking what is a focused but still evolutionary approach, and translating it into the sphere of perception, psychology and phenomenology, the following pages provide us not with a rulebook but a signpost to better directed experimentation – and a faster, more human kind of progress.

RORY SUTHERLAND
London, 2021

PROLOGUE

I CAN STILL REMEMBER when I was first exposed to what I now know as psychology.

I would have been about nine or ten when I was given a homework project from school. The task was to write a simple *how-to* guide. Today, I would call this an *open brief*. Over the following days I can remember other kids confidently returning with elaborate recipes for delicious pancakes, impressive paper aeroplanes and wondrous ant-farms. I, on the other hand, was a bit lost.

Going home for some inspiration, I asked my parents for some ideas. My dad (an accountant by profession who should really have worked in a more creative field) considered the challenge and gave me what at the time was a confusing response.

"Why don't you teach people how to make a crowd?"

(Head scratch.)

"How?" I asked.

"All you need to do is look up," he said.

Now I was even more confused. "Well, if you look up, someone behind you will stop to see what you're looking at. If two people are looking up, next thing you know, there'll be three..."

Unlike the other kids, this recipe needed no eggs, no flour

or milk. There was no paper or soil. It cost nothing yet had the potential to influence others through this simple appreciation of innate human behaviour.

It was magic.

Ever since, I have been interested in these kinds of ideas and how understanding human psychology can conjure up value from virtually nowhere. Today, I'm lucky to make a living in a business where ideas and creativity are our product – and psychology is our core ingredient. By training, I'm an Organisational Psychologist. For a decade I've worked at the coal face of applied behavioural science within one of the greatest creative networks on the planet. From Sydney to Silicon Valley, New York to Nigeria, I've been fortunate to experience how the combination of behavioural science and creativity can help us address some of the most interesting and challenging problems we all face.

I decided to write this book to illuminate the vast opportunities the fields of behavioural science and evolutionary psychology offer contemporary innovation. Through this book, my ambition is to help us spend less time developing expensive and high-risk solutions and more time embracing, and imaginatively executing, psychological solutions that have been road tested over time.

I will share a process that can be learned, yet still applied magically.

You're about to embark on a journey to identify patterns of evolved psychological solutions. You will see that, once you know what you're looking for, these solutions can be consciously redeployed to solve some of the most important challenges you face.

Through them, you will find a faster, more efficient, and more effective approach to innovate creatively.

THE PATH WE'LL TAKE

This book is structured in two parts. The first will arm you with the tools required for *Evolutionary Ideas* and the second will teach you how to generate them.

In the first part we'll see that, when faced with novel challenges, despite our tendency to seek radical and revolutionary innovation, better ideas exist in nature. From *biology* and *technology* to our evolved *psychology*, we'll learn that there are patterns of existing solutions all around us. In fact, many of the world's greatest innovations are themselves adaptations. We'll see that the process of creativity can be systematic and that the classification of behavioural science can be our playbook. By asking more powerful questions we'll learn that we can accelerate innovation through conscious adaptation, *breeding* new ideas from those that already exist.

In the second half of the book we will learn how you can apply this thinking to solve five of the most fundamental challenges faced in business, innovation and behaviour change. We'll explore how evolved psychological solutions can be creatively applied to (1) reinforce trust, (2) aid decision making, (3) trigger action, (4) boost loyalty and (5) improve experiences. We will focus on the process and the raw ingredients of innovation – those that can be transported and utilised elsewhere, not just the specific execution or the scale of the outcome.

ITSELF AN ADAPTATION

This book is for problem solvers. While I work in the creative field, it's not just a book for advertisers or marketing departments (although it's extremely useful there). Its aim is to provide prompts for people looking to solve old problems in new ways (or indeed, new problems in old ways).

Some may ask "why another book on behavioural science?" It's true, much has been written on the subject and this book is, itself, an adaptation. It has been made possible by the many brilliant minds from behavioural science, evolutionary psychology and innovation strategy – authors who have penned their thoughts and research before me. My role has been one of observation and orchestration.

In addition, while I have endeavoured to represent the latest research in the field, this is neither a strict piece of academic thinking, nor an exhaustive playbook of psychological solutions for the challenges this book identifies. There will, undoubtedly, be some who read this book and view it as an over-simplification. Others may argue it's too complex. At different stages of the book, it's probably both. On some occasions we will willingly approach concepts in an over-simplistic fashion to make their value more pragmatic and creatively applicable.

My ambition is that *Evolutionary Ideas* adds to society by providing new ways of thinking about applied behavioural science and the vast opportunity this discipline brings innovation today. This book shares the foundations of a systematic model of psychological innovation, albeit a philosophy more than a mechanical rulebook. My hope is that it provides a starting point to organise this theory in a way which will enable more creative solutions in the future.

Welcome to *Evolutionary Ideas.*

INTRODUCTION

I N A SECRET laboratory hidden deep within Silicon Valley, a revolutionary idea is born.

Nurtured by a small team of rockstar scientists and shrouded in secrecy, it is an innovation with the potential to transform technology and human interaction with it.

Decades ahead of its time, on 4 April 2012, when the project was first announced, it was heralded as such.

Time magazine would go on to declare it product of the year, with everyone from celebrities and CEOs to presidents and global royalty wanting a piece of it. *The Simpsons* dedicated an entire episode to it and *Vogue* even gave it a 12-page spread. It was an innovation that captured the imagination.

This is a story about one of the most highly anticipated technology breakthroughs of all time.

When first demonstrated publicly, it was revealed as courageously as the innovation itself. Brought to life by sky divers jumping from a zeppelin, roof-top bikers, and abseilers down the side of the Moscone exhibition complex in San Francisco, no expense was spared. On 27 June pre-orders were offered to a select few, and from Spring 2013 it was made available to the public – but even then, not the open market. Enthusiastic shoppers were asked to pledge their case on Twitter to buy it (at a $1,500 price tag, no less). Two years later it was made available to all. Then came the biggest announcement yet.

As quickly as it arrived, it was going away.

This is the story of Google Glass. A dream so many believed in, left shattered.

What went wrong?

Despite Google's best attempts to ensure Glass didn't become a Segway for your face, it was seen as over-hyped and impractical. The public's disappointment was instantaneous. A wearable computer strapped to a pair of glasses, it was stuck in a strange paradox of celebrities wanting it, and everyday consumers not really understanding why they would ever need it. While it had several clever functions, critics argued none of them worked particularly well – offering little to compete against existing smartphones and watches. Glass was clunky. It was heavy and had terrible battery life.

And it looked weird.

The thought of having cameras wrapped around everyone's faces made people feel uneasy. Society was genuinely afraid of it – it was creepy. The *New York Times* ran a front-page story questioning whether it might put an end to privacy as we know it. Banks, bars, cinemas and strip clubs(!) soon began to ban it. Before long, Glass's early adopters, branded *Explorers* by Google, were relabelled as *Glassholes* by the public. Google's requirement to change social etiquette for the product to survive was just too heavy a lift. While there were some technical queries, ultimately it was social trepidation that sealed its fate.

The promise of Glass was to create technology that worked for us. In the end, it seems you can have the might of Google and all the sky divers in the world, but if there's a small risk of you live-streaming your next trip to the bathroom, that's pretty much the end of it.

In their excitement to revolutionise the industry and create an innovation the world had never seen, Google failed to identify the uniquely human challenge that stood in their way. Although an impressive device, people didn't really know what to do with it, nor feel comfortable with it once they did. Never truly adopted, it was destined to be an invention in search of a problem.

Just because it glitters, it isn't necessarily gold.

Google Glass isn't the first casualty of this sort of revolutionary thinking, and it won't be the last. While the story of Glass is one of very public disappointment, the unfortunate truth is that this is more common than we would care to think. Harvard Business School professor Clayton Christensen explained that the world of innovation remains "painfully hit and miss."[1] Of the 30,000 new products introduced every year, an estimated 95% flop.[2]

We live in a competitive environment. Good ideas, stable businesses and powerful campaigns survive; the bad ones die out. In this selective game of innovation we could reasonably assume that our success would eventually improve over time. Sadly, that improvement remains elusive. The *Wall Street Journal*[3] approximates that three of four start-ups go bust and not only do 70% of organisational transformations fail, *Forbes*[4] tells us this figure is *increasing*. Despite the efforts of brands, governments and entrepreneurs across the globe, the collateral damage of well-intended revolutionary thinking is astonishing.

> *"Radical innovation is what many people seek, for it is the big, spectacular form of change."*
> —DON NORMAN

When you first saw the cover of this book, you may be forgiven for having read it as *Revolutionary Ideas*. Our brains have a habit of seeing what they expect – and with our modern-day culture's fetish for the radical and novel we end up expecting little else. In life and business, our obsessions are a similar search for the radical and revolutionary. From weight-loss miracles and viral campaigns to the launches of mega-brands and the search for (venture capital) unicorns, we are hungry for novel and game-changing ideas. The field of marketing remains particularly obsessed with the big and the new. It's believed, almost universally, that radical and revolutionary innovation is what it takes to compete and win.

But chasing revolutions is high-risk business. We assume organisations underspend on it, but what if leaders are actually doing too much of it? In the pursuit of breakthrough innovations, many businesses adopt the strategy of funding a large selection of innovative projects hoping for a rare success to pay for the remaining failures. In their *Harvard Business Review* article on the subject, Noubar Afeyan and Gary Pisano describe this as "the shots-on-goal" fallacy.[5] That is, the belief that by the laws of probability – or sheer luck – you'll eventually score.

For many, when it comes to innovation, it's as if we're rolling the dice.

This book introduces a new way of approaching innovation. But before we get there, to truly embrace the alternative, it's helpful for us to first unpack our insatiable appetite for the *revolutionary*. Why is a 'creationist mindset' and the allure of the big, novel and radical so strong (particularly when modern corporate culture so openly supports concepts like marginal gains and adaptability)? Why do we continue to be blinded by the prospect of the revolutionary? Underpinning this is a dangerous concoction of our obsession with intention and status, as well as a desire for psychological 'coherence' (we'll learn more about this in a moment), all washed down with a generous serving of optimism – the belief that *this time it will be different.*

THE LONE GENIUS

From Archimedes and Leonardo da Vinci to Marie Curie and Steve Jobs, history has been taught in terms of legendary visionaries and lone mavericks. Across cultures we continue to celebrate an exclusive trophy cabinet of individuals who have changed our path through their bravery or genius – their 'moon-shot' discoveries and inventions single-handedly changing the world.

Human history, argues biologist and best-selling author Matt Ridley, has a misleading emphasis on planning, direction and design. We have an infatuation with human intentionality and are obsessed by this myth of a lone genius receiving a blinding flash of inspiration or wisdom. We find it hard to imagine it any other way. In the words of Ridley, "A battle is won, so a general must have won it."[6] This expectation of revolutionary outcomes, unlocked by individual mastery and intention, is then expected of organisational leadership.

Imagine for a moment you're the CEO of BMW. In such a prestigious role, it's understandable to perceive your remit as making significant impacts by exposing new and exciting opportunities for growth: the blue sky. Getting involved with something seemingly inconsequential, like optimising the process of signing up for a test drive, may seem below your level of status. But these can actually be the kinds of activities that have the greatest impact on an organisation's performance. In many cases, the incremental and trivial is delegated to the junior. It's beneath our dignity.

In a similar vein, when in a position of leadership, we're often too ashamed to suggest minor or adapted solutions to challenges, considering them too small or obvious to make a difference. If a leader isn't making big, bold, radical decisions, are they even a leader at all?

BRING A KNIFE TO A KNIFE FIGHT

A little while ago I was watching my young daughter (she was two at the time) watering some plants. There were two: a small pot plant and a large one. She had a single watering can. As I watched, she walked up to the small pot and gave it a tiny drop then, without missing a beat, continued to empty the rest of the water into the larger pot. Even at such a young age she had determined that the small plant only needed a little water, and the big plant needed the rest. Sometimes known as a *proportionality bias*, this pervasive mental short-cut leads us to particularly dangerous territory when it comes to innovation.

By creating a persistent instinct that solutions need to match the size and shape of their problem, the proportionality bias has wrought havoc across a number of human domains – as documented by psychologists and sociologists.[7,8] Throughout human history, individuals have selected cures that are proportionate to the nature of a specific illness. In ancient Chinese medicine, the visually impaired were fed ground bat in the belief that bats had particularly keen vision. It's also been known for ancient physicians to prescribe the lungs of the fox (known for their endurance) to asthmatics. This proportionality bias has been recognised in the emergence of conspiracy theories ("How is it possible for a lone gunman to assassinate the President?") and helping us to explain our difficulty comprehending the explosive impact of epidemics ("There's no way a tiny mosquito could lead to something as devastating as yellow fever!").

Here, the inputs simply don't equal their outputs.

A fascinating illustration of proportionality has been further identified when observing craps shooters – the famous casino dice game.[9] In these scenarios, astonishingly, people tend to roll the dice gently when looking for a low number and more forcefully when hoping for a high one. It seems we have a habit of searching for solutions (the forcefulness of the roll) that feel like they match our desired outcome (a high or low figure).

The same can be true of innovation. The more surprising, complex, or significant a problem, the bigger and more extravagant we feel the solution needs to be. Big problems need big ideas and new problems need new ideas. When faced with a challenge we've never seen before, we feel we also need a solution the world has never seen.

When it comes to innovation, now we're not only just rolling the dice, we're rolling them *hard*.

THE GLASS IS HALF FULL

A final explanation for our dogged pursuit of the revolutionary is an inherent overconfidence we all share. Be it underestimating our chances of divorce to overestimating career success, the human brain is wired to be unrealistically optimistic. Every year, millions of people flock to Las Vegas, a city filled with vast casinos and hotels built on the spoils of gambling. Even here, with the odds being stacked against us (and the evidence all around us), we believe that *we* will be the exception. This optimism bias is recognised as one of the most consistent and robust predispositions in psychology.[10] From an evolutionary perspective, it makes a lot of sense too. It's important that we've evolved to remain optimistic and engaged with life, even when faced with adversity. Unfortunately, while this positive outlook may help us *deal* with failure, it doesn't help us *prevent* it. On the contrary. Often this overconfidence can lead us to throw caution to the wind and blissfully engage in risky behaviours, like driving without a seatbelt, failing to wear sunscreen, ignoring social distancing policies, or skipping that annual doctor's appointment... again.

> *"The four most expensive words in the English language are, 'this time it's different'."*
> —JOHN TEMPLETON, BRITISH INVESTOR

Both to our advantage and potential demise, we're biased to believe that we are *luckier* than those around us. Where they failed, we will succeed. This same optimistic challenge exists when it comes to the anticipated success of revolutionary ideas and *out of the box* innovation. The reality is that the prospect of hitting that home run is not so rosy.

In fact, the revolutionary glass isn't even half full. It's virtually empty.

JAWS IN SPACE

At midnight on 25 May 1979, a category-defining sci-fi-blockbuster was premiered in Seattle.

Met by critical acclaim, it was a box-office smash, grossing almost $80 million in its first run in the US.* The film catapulted the careers of its leading cast and spawned the production of comic books, video games and franchise films. To this day it's considered one of the greatest films of all time, still holding an impressive 97% on famed review website Rotten Tomatoes.

---

* Approximately $300m in today's money.

But what does it take to create such a breakthrough film? How does one approach the origination of such an iconic movie? How do you even sell the concept? Well, as the legend goes, echoed in the book with the very same title, once upon a time its two writers walked into a Hollywood producer's office to sell the script. Their killer pitch was just three words: "Jaws in Space."

This was the original studio pitch for *Alien*.

The traditional view of creativity is that it doesn't follow patterns. We hold the belief that we need to go wild or travel off the grid to generate ideas that have never existed. In fact, we're so in love with the myth of the revolutionary and creating that iconic "I've got it!" moment in a dark garage somewhere, we often misattribute innovation that occurs through adaptation, derivatives and spotting patterns. For example, the technology for James Dyson's much celebrated bagless vacuums was actually borrowed from large industrial cyclones he noticed at a local sawmill. Inspired by a visit to Swift & Company's slaughterhouse in Chicago, Henry Ford's revolutionary assembly line was also just a butcher's *disassembly line* in reverse.* We consider a movie like *Alien* as one that threw the rules away to start from scratch. That it's a true revolution. But it's really just *Jaws in Space*.

In almost every category, there are patterns of existing ideas just like this. When you stop to look, the reality is that true revolutions are far rarer than you think. Ironically, one of the most thorough investigations into the genuine scarcity of truly radical ideas was conducted during a particularly revolutionary period of human history, early 20th century Communist USSR.

In a fascinating analysis, a team of engineers reviewed a staggering 200,000 of the world's most successful technical patents, categorising them into different degrees of inventiveness

---

* Swift & Company's butchers would stand at fixed stations with a pulley system bringing the meat to each worker.

and uniqueness. Astonishingly, despite reviewing inventions that had all received legal patents, they found that 95% of the problems that engineers faced had already been solved within their industry. Roughly a third (32%) were deemed to be "obvious solutions,"* almost half (45%) were considered "small improvements to an existing system,"† under one-fifth (18%) were categorised as "significantly improving the existing system,"‡ and about 5% of innovations were described as solutions "found in science, not in technology."§ The highest classification of innovation, a selection representing a mere 1% of the patents analysed, were considered *true* innovations.[11]

Even the invention of the lightbulb, the symbolic icon of innovation cementing Thomas Edison as a hero in engineering history, is itself a story of gradual innovation arrived at by multiple inventors. In fact, as Ridley outlines, "twenty-one different people can lay claim to have independently designed or critically improved incandescent light bulbs by the end of the 1870s, mostly independent of each other."[12]

So, armed with a fetish for intention and individual genius, a tendency to seek proportionality and an unrealistically rosy view of our prospects, we set out in a chaotic search of exceptional "*eureka!*" moments. We roll the dice. The problem is, as we've just seen, revolutionary innovation is much rarer than you might think. In fact, in more instances than we would like to admit, looking to address our problems with a creationist mindset means we'll be running to stand still.

What's even worse, when we go out of our way to produce the

---

* Like increasing the thickness of a wall to improve its insulation.
† Like creating an adjustable steering column so that people of all body types can drive the same car.
‡ Like replacing the standard transmission of a car with automatic transmission.
§ Like cleaning surfaces using ultrasound technology.

unprecedented, we lose sight of something far more useful: the answer that has already *evolved*.

EVOLUTIONARY IDEAS

We tend to think of evolution in terms of biology. For many of us, the word naturally summons images of dinosaurs and apes – millipedes and marsupials. What's often less considered is the role of evolutionary processes in shaping our culture, our ideas and our innovations. While we might not appreciate it, evolution is all around us. As Ridley argues, it's "far more common, and far more influential, than most people recognise."[13]

In competitive environments, only the adapted prevail.

Over the course of human history, while this is of course true of our biology, it is also true of our psychology. The more our ancestors made decisions that increased their chances of survival, the more likely it was that these underlying mechanisms would be passed on. Over time, our ideas have also evolved based on their success or failure within their environment. As French philosopher Alain (Émile) Chartier writes in *Propos d'un Normande*, "It is the sea herself who fashions the boats."[14] Bad ideas are sunk and the good ideas sail. Just as homo sapiens didn't magically appear through the late-night coffee-fuelled genius of a single intelligent designer, innovation is also an evolutionary phenomenon.

Today, armed with an enhanced understanding of our evolved psychology, and how this has informed some of our most effective solutions, we can more successfully disrupt some of the classic myths of *revolutionary* innovation.

INNOVATION MYTH 1:
BIG PROBLEMS NEED BIG SOLUTIONS

When we consider our daily experience with the physical world, it mostly makes sense to believe that "something doesn't come from nothing."

When we bend a stick too far, it breaks. If we drop a plate, it smashes. If we want a loud bang, we must hit it, well, hard... In the physical realm, in most instances this proportionality adds up. Here, it largely makes sense to *magnitude match*. In fact, if someone was to argue the opposite, we might find this quite concerning. The problem is, we bring this very same mentality when it comes to innovation. The bigger the problem the harder we roll the dice. We fail to see that, particularly when developing psychological solutions, the rules are different. The subtle, small and incremental can have unexpectedly significant impacts.

In perception, for example, something literally *can* come from nothing (never underestimate the power of placebos). When innovating to change behaviour, getting debt-free doesn't always mean cutting major costs, improving your long-term health can begin with small changes, and boosting the performance of an online business can be as simple as tweaking the check-out page. In the words of Stanford habit expert Professor BJ Fogg, when it comes to behaviour change, the "tiny is mighty."[15]

Although the journey we're about to take in this book will feature small and subtle ideas, like tweaks to a campaign message, a product experience or environment, this isn't a story focused on how trivial or incremental changes can have big effects (while true, this is now well established in the field of innovation and applied behavioural science). Instead, the central goal of this book will be to focus on the second myth in our revolutionary conundrum – our tendency to throw out the rule book in search of the novel and new.

INNOVATION MYTH 2:
NEW PROBLEMS NEED NEW SOLUTIONS

Even though the underlying mechanisms of human behaviour have remained relatively stable (certainly in our recent history), it's all too common for individuals and organisations to see their problems as unique, seeking fresh thinking and revolutionary ideas to achieve their outcomes.

As we have just learnt, like our biology, many of the ideas we have instinctively generated and passed down across generations have also undergone an adaptive process. In his book, *Learning from the Octopus*, Marine Ecologist Rafe Sagarin writes, "good ideas in evolution are identified because they appear nearly exactly the same across many different organisms."[16] Just as we can see patterns in biological solutions in nature (like the evolution of the dorsal fin across different species), similar patterns exist in evolved psychological solutions when viewed across time, cultures and categories.

Today, fuelled by advances in neuroscience and normalised by the now mainstream field of behavioural economics (and its umbrella discipline, behavioural science), many of us have become familiar with new and sophisticated ways of thinking about evolved human behaviour. We're in the midst of a movement ignited by the identification of a rich classification system, a contemporary language, helping us to see and better organise these patterns of our evolved psychology.

Challenging the view that innovation is the result of isolated mavericks, rare visionaries and flashes of inspiration, this book will illustrate that, because of the classification of behavioural science, we can now more easily implement existing psychological solutions to address some of the shared challenges we all face. This isn't a book about shouting louder or rolling the dice harder, but taking a *sideways view* inspired by ideas that already exist (more like jujutsu than boxing). As opposed to invention-centric thinking, this is also, understandably, more human-centric by nature.

To help, we'll explore a more systematic approach to innovation and creativity – a method of consciously *breeding* ideas from those that have already survived the test of time. By first exploring the application of evolved *biological* solutions (our first tool) then evolved *technical* solutions (our second tool), we'll see that, once we know what we're looking for, there's an abundance of untapped evolved *psychological* potential around us just waiting to be redeployed (our third tool).

> *"Your idea needs to be original only in its adaptation to your problem."*
> —THOMAS EDISON

Importantly, an adaptive and systematic approach to innovation doesn't mean we're deprioritising or discounting the role of creativity. In fact, it's quite the opposite. At its core, creativity can be defined as bringing into being something which didn't exist before in the exact form (just like *Alien*). *Evolutionary Ideas* will reveal an approach to achieving even more creative outcomes by helping to consciously redefine the problems you face or the category you're in. By identifying patterns of evolved solutions across disparate domains and industries, you will be armed with entirely new frames of reference and the ability to connect ideas that would otherwise never have met. While you might inform public policy, manage internal stakeholders, or sell TVs, we all face shared psychological challenges every day. Why not learn from each other?

*"An idea is nothing more nor less than a new
combination of old elements."*
—JAMES WEBB YOUNG

By the end of this book, just as we've learnt not to ignore herds of animals running uphill from the ocean (an evolved response before a tidal wave), my hope is that we'll also no longer be tempted to start from scratch when it comes to innovation. We'll find that there's a more systematic way to think creatively across industries, with our evolved psychology, and the classifications of contemporary behavioural science, providing the connective tissue.

Rather than endorsing costly and risky innovation processes in the hope for something the world has never seen, we will see how we can innovate more purposefully and more effectively by creatively adapting from what already exists. We'll see that evolutionary advantages don't always occur slowly, accidentally and incrementally. We'll learn they can be identified rapidly, applied systematically and that their impacts can be transformational. We'll discover there is a way of thinking that can be learnt, yet still applied *magically*.

By the end, I hope we'll all be less focused on doing different things than on finding the right things to do differently. We'll no longer ask, "How are we going to solve this?" But rather, be excited to start with, "How have we solved it before?"

In short:

- Revolutionary thinking is an expensive and high-risk strategy.

- Evolutionary ideas offer a more efficient and human-centric approach to innovation.

- There's a method we can all use.

Part 1
GETTING THE TOOLS

CHAPTER 1
Swapping Spiders
for Sweets

EVOLVED BIOLOGICAL SOLUTIONS

WHEN YOUR GREAT grandfather 125 million generations removed stumbled across a hairy spider on his morning walk, he didn't run away or swipe at it with a rolled-up newspaper, he ate it. To understand how we could possibly be related to these insect-enjoying ancestors, we need to follow a critical path – one laid out in direct opposition to creationist or revolutionary thinking. If we're going to appreciate evolutionary ideas, we first need to understand a few things about, well, evolution.

To help us on this whistle-stop tour, we turn of course to Charles Darwin.

At its core, Darwin's famous theory outlines evolution as the result of slight and random variations in an organism's genetic make-up that, through the currency of biological fitness, is amplified by natural selection. In other words, if a mutation gives an organism a competitive advantage to survive and reproduce, it's passed on. If it doesn't, well, that's that.

In the past, animals that enjoyed the taste of fats and sugars experienced reproductive success because of the benefits these nutrients provided them (juicy spider anyone?). As a result, today the world is filled with organisms with taste buds adapted to detect calories, and an almost universal preference for sweetness.

Over time, evolution can result in entirely new species; dinosaurs evolved into birds (just look at their feet), amphibious mammals into whales (it's true) and our ancestor apes into modern-day humans (I'm hoping there's no convincing needed here). This type of evolution, where one species evolves into another, is called *macroevolution*; a process requiring fossil records to track, typically occurring over millennia.

Critically, natural selection can also occur *within* a species over more rapid timeframes, enabling a population to change in size, shape or colour in a matter of generations. This is called *microevolution*. To appreciate why these adapted solutions succeed, we need to first understand the environmental constraints an organism is under.

CREATIVE CONSTRAINTS

In 1836, when Darwin returned from his global expedition, he brought hundreds of specimens home for investigation. Amongst all of his collection, he was particularly puzzled by his assortment of finches from the Galapagos Islands.

When comparing the birds, he noticed that their anatomical features seemed related, appearing to have descended from a common ancestor.* However, despite their similarity, the finches

---

* Now believed to have originated in mainland Central America.

varied in the size and shape of their beaks and claws. Some of the finches, like the warbler, presented with long thin beaks and sharp claws, most suitable for spearing insects. Others, like the ground finch, displayed large, powerful beaks helping them to crack nuts. These differences were attributed to the unique environmental constraints and selective pressures each of the birds evolved to face on the different islands of the Galapagos.

Darwin's finches have since become a prime example of a concept known as *adaptive radiation,* a type of microevolution illustrating how different animals within the same species can evolve to benefit from particular ecological niches, all the while sharing the same parent or ancestor. More interesting still, these cunning adaptations don't just take place within a species, they occur across species too. That is, under similar evolutionary constraints, two completely different species can arrive at the same adaptive solution.

For example, while physically similar (terrifyingly so with your legs dangling off a surfboard), you may be surprised to hear that sharks and dolphins are categorically different species. The shark is a fish, and the dolphin is a mammal. The shark extracts oxygen through its gills, while dolphins need to surface to breathe. A shark's skeleton is made of flexible cartilage while a dolphin's is made of bone. One might as well compare a racehorse with a seahorse.

However, despite being utterly different species, both dolphins and sharks have evolved similar traits, including streamlined bodies, dorsal fins and flippers. This process, where different species arrive at similar adaptive solutions, is known as *convergent evolution.* Just take a quick walk outside and see how wing-like features have developed independently across several species, from insects and birds, to flying fish and bats (you may need to walk a little further for these).

Evolution is nature's problem solver. Over time, it's offered insulation against harsh arctic chills and cooling from oppressive equatorial heat. When faced with common constraints, like swimming quickly through the ocean or escaping the pull of gravity, convergent evolution shows us how different species, from every corner of the globe, can arrive at shared evolutionary conclusions.

As we'll soon see, being able to identify these patterns in evolved solutions doesn't just help us to understand the shared constraints an organism may have faced in its past, it offers a variety of solutions that humans can implement when faced with the same environmental constraints ourselves.

In other words, we can convergently evolve, on *purpose*.

To survive in nature, organisms converge on winning solutions. There's more than one route to the same good idea.

THREE BIRDS AND A BULLET TRAIN

In 1990, Eiji Nakatsu saw a tiny notice in his local newspaper announcing an upcoming lecture about birds by an aviation engineer at the Osaka branch of the Wild Bird Society in Japan. Both a passionate engineer and avid bird watcher, Nakatsu decided to attend and hear what a fellow engineer had to say about two of his favourite topics. What started as an oblique intersection of interests soon turned into a momentous occasion for both Nakatsu and the Tokaido Shinkansen, the 515km stretch of rail that connects Tokyo and Osaka.

When the challenge was set to move passengers the distance of the Tokaido Shinkansen in two and a half hours, it was

Nakatsu, the general manager of technical development at West Japan Railway, who was tasked with the job. Interestingly, reaching the necessary speed to achieve this didn't prove to be the biggest challenge (the company's experimental 6-car train could already reach the required speed). The problem was that the faster the train travelled, the more noise it made, with levels far exceeding the standards permitted in Japan. Reducing noise, not increasing the speed, became the real challenge.

So where was all the noise coming from?

At full speed, analysis demonstrated that rushing air hitting the train's pantographs (an element of the train that connects the carriage to the overhead wires) was creating most of the noise. A second issue, an environmental constraint, was caused by the many tunnels of the Tokaido Shinkansen. At the time, approaching these tunnels at great speeds produced a gun-shot-sounding shockwave (or tunnel boom), due to the compressed blast of air these created (a bit like firing a bullet from a pistol). Worryingly for the team, every unit increase in speed produced an increase in force to the power of three!

Puzzled as to how to solve this cacophony of acoustic challenges, the technical development team was at a deadlock until Nakatsu recalled his lecture at the Wild Bird Society. Surprised by how much both past and present aircraft technology was related to the functions and structures of birds, he was convinced that further studying the flight and physiology of these animals could help solve his team's problems and accelerate his train into the future.

In the end, to the astonishment of many, the solutions to the team's challenges didn't lie in the further study of enhanced physics, or even the discovery of specific technical innovations, but in a richer understanding of the evolved biology of three unique birds. The owl, the Adélie penguin and the kingfisher.

The owl

The owl is an impressive predator. These nocturnal hunters can fly just inches from their prey without being detected. While air typically rushes over a standard wing, creating a *whooshing* noise, the owl's feathers have adapted to reduce this turbulence via small noise-dampening serrations on the surface. This has the effect of chopping up the flow of air into smaller 'micro-turbulences,' making them whisper-quiet in flight. Going so far as to borrow a stuffed specimen from the local zoo, Nakatsu's team began studying the owl and how its specific adaptations might help the Shinkansen 500-Series. Guided by their findings, the engineers made structural changes to the top of the pantograph, and, after a series of air tunnel experiments, their efforts appeared to have paid off. Micro-serrations made to the pantograph, breaking bigger vortexes of air into smaller ones, produced far less turbulence and ultimately reduced the noise. This was a big win for Nakatsu's team.

The penguin

The second avian influence on the 500-Series train was the Adélie penguin. If you've ever seen footage of a penguin rocketing around the Antarctic, typically avoiding the jagged teeth of a leopard seal, it's likely to be the Adélie. Energy-efficient hunters, these tuxedo-wearing flashes are impressively quick, known to sustain swimming speeds up to 8km per hour and, in short bursts, can move twice this fast.[1]

One of the factors enabling this agility is the smooth, spindle-shaped body of the Adélie. Borrowing from the Adélie's physique, Nakatsu's engineers began experimenting with the shape of the pantograph, embracing a rounded 'spindle' body to slide through the air more efficiently. To the team's delight,

Image 1 – The evolutionary inspiration for the 500-Series Shinkansen bullet train: (top) the owl; (middle) the Adélie penguin; (bottom) the kingfisher.

after further tests the new design reduced wind resistance and minimised the noise even further.

With pantograph turbulence now muted, it was only the tunnel boom challenge that remained for the team. Enter, the kingfisher.

The kingfisher

From his birdwatching days, Nakatsu remembered a bird that plunged at high speed from the air into the water (a substance 800 times denser), barely making a splash. Faced with a similar challenge of penetrating different densities of air across the Tokaido Shinkansen, it struck him that the long, sharp and pointed bill of the kingfisher was worthy of closer investigation.

The kingfisher's bill is particularly unusual. Not only does its sharp and streamlined shape gradually increase in diameter from the tip to the head, but, when closed, both the upper and lower beaks create triangular cross-sections, forming a "squashed diamond shape,"[2] allowing the bird to effortlessly cut through the water and skewer its prey when diving from a great height.

To test the noise-reduction potential of the kingfisher bill, Nakatsu and his team ran another series of experiments, including shooting bullets of various shapes into a pipe to measure the differences in pressure waves (from a traditional bullet shape to one modelled after the kingfisher). Their data showed that the ideal shape for the 500 series was almost identical to that of a kingfisher's beak.

The boom was busted.

In 1997, the 500-Series bullet trains sped into service with a break-neck speed of 300 km/h. On the open track, they were quieter, experienced no tunnel booms and even consumed 15% less electricity than before, all thanks to some creative thinking inspired by the infinite wisdom of biological evolution.[3] Most importantly for our story, to achieve these results, Nakatsu's team didn't start from scratch. They carefully *bred* their solution by borrowing existing adaptations from the wild.

BORROWING FROM BIOLOGY

The idea of borrowing from the natural kingdom isn't new.

For thousands of years, early humans developed knives and hooks inspired by the teeth and claws of animals. Similarly, in attempts to increase the difficulty of estimating the range, speed and shape of US naval ships during World War I, dazzling camouflage, like that of the zebra, has also been called upon.*

Today, modern technology has bestowed upon us an even greater understanding of the intricacies of biology, and with this the ability to embed nature into some of the world's most exciting innovations; from painless needles mimicking mosquitoes and water purification systems based on fish gills, to cooling technology imitating the unique ears and blood flow of the hare. Even the bumps (known as tubercles) on the flippers of humpback whales have spawned an industry of efficient wind turbines.

This burgeoning field is known as biomimicry – it's our first innovation tool. Michael Pawlyn, an awarded biomimic architect, explained "Biomimicry helps us escape our normal frame of reference. We can get so used to thinking about the same problems with the same frames."[4] It's here that the adaptive nature of evolution is most critical. "There's a mountain of things we can learn from biology because there are so many different adaptations to so many different functional constraints," says Pawlyn. "We essentially ask, 'what's the most applicable strategy from biology that can be applied to this challenge?'"

---

* Evidence regarding the effectiveness of this approach is mixed.

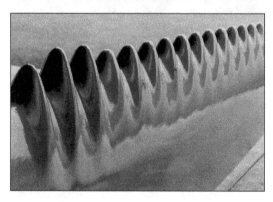

Image 2 – Biomimicry in action: (top) SS West Mahomet in dazzle camouflage, 1918; (middle) the 500-Series Shinkansen; (bottom) WhalePower's Tubercle Technology helping wind turbines to be more efficient and reliable.

The philosophy of biomimicry is simple. After billions of years, failures are fossils, and that which has remained is the secret to survival.[5] If you think about it, everything in the natural world today has already passed 3.8 billion years of rigorous testing. If it hadn't, it simply wouldn't be here. As Sagarin writes, "there is no technical solution that can prepare us for the risks of a highly variable and unpredictable world as well as the ancient natural process of adaptation."[6] Even if only in a tiny way, every species alive today is a success story.

Biomimicry connects human problems with evolved biological solutions. It helps us to accelerate innovation by escaping our normal frame of reference.

The field of biomimicry is an essential tool for *Evolutionary Ideas*, and the development of the 500-Series bullet train is a striking example.

For the 500-Series, the evolved adaptations of three different birds were intentionally drawn upon to accelerate the innovation process. Biomimicry acted as a means of conscious and deliberate convergent evolution (as though borrowing from the dolphin to make a shark). Rather than waiting for natural selection, human intelligence allowed us to consciously apply the wisdom of biological evolution *across* industry. Instead of waiting for successive genetic mutations over thousands of years, it can now be consciously initiated in a matter of days.

For the bullet train, our enhanced understanding and classification of concepts from physics, like gravity, drag and lift, helped to connect the natural intelligence of highly evolved beaks and feathers, with the distinctively human world of iron and steel. This book shares the belief that many of life's challenges have already been solved by someone, somewhere. However, in this book, rather than being inspired by evolved *biological* solutions, our focus is on how innovation can be accelerated by better understanding our evolved *psychological* solutions.

But before we get there, we need to unveil our second innovation tool, the application of evolved *technical* solutions. For this, we explore a ground-breaking theory of inventive problem solving.

If nothing else, remember this:

- Despite the appeal of new ideas, better solutions often exist in nature.

- We can accelerate innovation through the conscious adaptation of evolved solutions.

- Evolved differences between species (like the owl and the kingfisher) can unlock ground-breaking innovation.

CHAPTER 2
Innovation
Impossible

EVOLVED TECHNICAL SOLUTIONS

WE'VE JUST SEEN the power of embracing evolved biological solutions when innovating to solve distinctively human problems. We've learnt that, rather than relying on lone genius and flashes of inspiration, existing evolutionary solutions can be applied on purpose, across multiple domains, to help us to innovate.

But how can these insights be applied systematically? What does it take to remove the sword from the stone and extract its value today? We find our next clue in Soviet Russia, triggered by a somewhat misjudged letter to Joseph Stalin.

In December 1948, troubled by the incompetent nature of the Soviet approach to innovation following World War II, a confident young lieutenant sent a personal letter to "Comrade Stalin."[1]

In his note he outlined the chaos and inefficiencies he had experienced in the navy, explaining that there was a new way of thinking that could help any engineer to invent. He believed this process could revolutionise the technological world.

Well, this went down as well as you might expect and in 1949 the young man was arrested, interrogated and tortured. Following his supposed confession he was sentenced to 25 years in the notorious Vorkuta labour camp just above the Arctic Circle.

During his imprisonment the young man was placed on an interrogation conveyor, where he was questioned all night and prevented from sleeping during the day. Realising he couldn't survive this for long, he asked himself, "How can I *sleep* and *not sleep* at the same time?" This contradiction meant his eyes needed to be both open and closed at the same time.

"Impossible!" you say? Well, working with a fellow prisoner, the lieutenant found that sticking two pieces of paper to his closed eyelids, cunningly fashioned from a cigarette packet with charred pupils drawn on each, was enough to convince the guards that his eyes were open as he peacefully slept.

With this, he solved an almost impossible contradiction and, in the process, stumbled across one of the defining elements of his historic theory of innovation.

The man who wrote the letter was Genrich Altshuller.

AN EVOLUTIONARY ENGINEER

Growing up in 1930s Soviet Russia, Genrich Altshuller was recognised from a young age for his uniquely inventive brain. He received his first Russian patent – for an underwater diving apparatus – while a primary student, and by tenth grade he had developed a carbide-fuelled rocket boat. In his twenties, Altshuller enlisted in the army and soon developed what many consider to be his first mature invention, a method for escaping an immobilised submarine without diving gear. Both this design and its designer were hastily snapped up by the Russian military, his invention was classified as a military secret, and Altshuller quickly landed a position at the navy's innovation centre.

During his navy service Altshuller found himself faced with an unusually tricky challenge: how to help others to innovate. It was a task he found increasingly frustrating, especially during a time when the scientific and innovation communities believed that the creative leaps of invention were the result of accidents, mood and even blood type. "Inventions always come late," Altshuller noted.[2] "Sailors can draw maps of reefs and shallow waters that others can follow, but inventors have no such maps. Each beginner goes along making the same mistakes." When charged with scaling the navy's creativity without a structured methodology, Altshuller committed himself to making one.

Surrounded by patents at the naval innovation centre, Altshuller threw himself into the interrogation of a potential science behind problem solving, an exploration that led him to his most significant discovery. Through reviewing many hundreds of patents, Altshuller uncovered that inventors were unknowingly using the same solutions over and over again, with the same fundamental question in one area being addressed by multiple technical inventions in another (it was Altshuller and his colleagues who assessed the 200,000 patents we have already discussed). For the navy, this meant they had been funding expensive, long, low probability projects, when in reality, a vast majority of their problems had already been solved.

He had stumbled across the existence of a universal pattern of technical problem solving – and the implications were huge.

TRIZ: A THEORY OF INVENTIVE PROBLEM SOLVING

Buried in Altshuller's now-infamous note to Stalin was the beginning of a theory that would change the world of technical innovation.

His study of thousands of patents didn't just expose the scarcity of genuinely revolutionary thinking, it unearthed a logic for systematic innovation, later to be known as TRIZ (a Russian acronym for the 'Theory of Inventive Problem Solving').[*] Through TRIZ, Altshuller was now able to demonstrate the science behind creative innovation, not only paving the way for new breakthroughs in technology but establishing a framework of immense value to countless other fields.

To innovate with *Evolutionary Ideas,* there are three important elements we need to learn from TRIZ:

1. It's been solved before.

2. There are consistent patterns of solutions.

3. Solving contradictions creates breakthrough innovation.

It's been solved before

TRIZ works to formalise the belief that somebody, somewhere has already solved your problem. Just as different species have converged upon similar biological solutions when faced with shared environmental constraints (like the dorsal fin helping both dolphins and sharks thrive in the ocean), TRIZ helps us

---

[*]   Theoria Resheneyva Isobretatelskehuh Zadach

recognise engineering strategies that have converged across categories and industries, when faced with shared technical constraints. While biology classifies different families and species of animal based on the similarities of these adapted features (like the presence of a spinal cord or gills), in TRIZ, these patterns of solutions are classified based on their related technical features. These are known as *inventive principles*. In total, the TRIZ methodology recognises that there are 40 inventive principles that can be drawn upon to inspire innovation.

There are consistent patterns of solutions

If you were to ever jump out of a plane, it pays to have a parachute (and a back-up, for that matter!). When we fly, we also do so with life jackets under our seats and spare oxygen overhead. Likewise, irrespective of the impressive talents of Formula 1 drivers, we can all agree that it's unwise to travel at 350km/h without a few tyres around the edges of our route... just in case. In TRIZ, these patterns of solutions are known as *beforehand cushioning* – the integration of features which cushion or mediate a surge or sudden change. They all represent inventive principle number 11.

TRIZ's inventive principles, these identified patterns of solutions, include concepts such as *segmentation* (no. 1): describing solutions that break up an object into its independent parts (like modular furniture or Venetian blinds). *Do it in reverse* (no. 13) is another favourite, in which the movable part of an object or environment is held stationary, and the stationary part made moveable (like a swimming training pool where the water moves, not the swimmer). The inventive principle *nested doll* (no. 7) classifies patterns of solutions that place one object inside another (like the typical Russian doll), helping to represent an array of adaptations from several technical categories. A nail polish brush that's screwed inside its own bottle is an example of a nested doll. So too are the Kinder Surprise, stacked measuring cups, telescopic lenses and the retraction mechanisms of many tape measures.

"You can wait a hundred years for enlightenment, or you can solve the problem in 15 minutes with these principles."
—GENRICH ALTSHULLER

Similar to biomimicry, which benefits from a millennia of biological evolution, TRIZ inherently draws on the past knowledge and resourcefulness of many thousands of engineers. By classifying technical solutions based on their shared features, their commonalities, stacked measuring cups, telescopic lenses and retractable tape measures are now all able to serve as suitable inspiration when looking to solve nested doll-shaped problems. Like in biomimicry, we're once again able to escape our normal domain – our traditional frame of reference – when looking to solve problems.

Although *nested doll* is just one inventive principle, it represents, and helps us better connect, hundreds of engineering solutions that have convergently evolved in the wild.

Solving contradictions creates breakthrough innovation

During his time in prison, Altshuller recognised one of the most important concepts of TRIZ. That is, to create breakthrough inventions, one must overcome a contradiction (or trade-off), just like the challenge of needing to sleep, while not sleep.

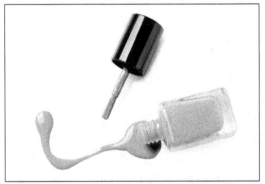

Image 3 – TRIZ inventive principle no. 7, nested doll: (top) retractable tape measure; (middle) nail polish bottle and brush; (bottom) telescopic camera lenses.

However, rather than solving the contradiction of "How do I hold my eyes *open* and *closed* at the same time?" TRIZ helps to address challenges like "How might we make a bullet-proof jacket *stronger* without it becoming *heavier*?" or "How might we make an umbrella *big enough* to cover a human body but *not so large* it doesn't fit in a handbag?"

Following his studies, Altshuller concluded that there were about 1,500 standard engineering contradictions which he then summarised into a contradiction matrix comprising 39 parameters. These parameters include physical constraints (like weight and shape), performance parameters (think speed, power and stability) and efficiency limitations (like time, temperature and information). For each contradiction identified in the matrix, TRIZ then maps the most relevant inventive principles for a solution. For example, when using TRIZ's contradiction matrix, the inventive principle *nested doll* can be used to address contradictions like "How might we increase the *amount* of a substance without increasing its *volume*?" or "How might we increase the *length* of an object without changing its *shape*?"

Let's look at an example.

According to the Centers for Disease Control and Prevention, every 40 seconds an American will have a heart attack.[3] Heart attacks occur when an artery carrying blood and oxygen becomes blocked. To fix this, and help people recover, tiny devices called stents are used to keep arteries open, allowing the flow of blood and oxygen to travel more smoothly. Stents are tubular in shape and tend to be made from a very fine metal mesh. The challenge with these metal stents is that, after too long in the body, they risk tissue forming on the stent, creating a danger of further clotting. So, while stents are an effective and reliable solution, using a metal one can become costly through the requirement for multiple surgeries. To innovate in the face of this challenge, one might ask, "How might we increase *reliability* without reducing *ease* of operation?" Well, if you were to look at this contradiction via the TRIZ matrix, it maps three inventive principles for you to explore:

1. Inventive principle no. 17: *another dimension*
2. Inventive principle no. 27: *cheap, short-living objects*
3. Inventive principle no. 40: *composite materials*

Let's start with inventive principle no. 27: cheap, short-living objects. Examples of this pattern of solution include paper cups and disposable diapers. If we were to look even further afield for convergent 'specimens' of this principle, we may discover an innovative plastic product developed to replace single-use packaging. Made from polylactic acid, its special quality is that it dissolves in water. Fast forward a few years, and with the first polymer stent gaining FDA approval in 2016 the dominance of the field of polylactic (or bioresorbable) stents is set to increase continually. When compared to a permanent metal stent, these bioresorbable alternatives are found to improve arterial recovery while reducing the risks of further clotting.[4] Inventive principle no. 27 to the rescue!

By identifying a contradiction, mapping TRIZ's inventive principles and borrowing from existing solutions in the wild, just as biomimicry fast-tracked the innovation of the 500-Series bullet train, the TRIZ methodology helps to short-cut costly reinvention processes so prevalent today. From the development of anti-vibration technology for Ford, to pioneering refuelling systems for Boeing, it is a form of adaptive problem solving that's embraced by some of the world's most influential companies.

I hope we have now grasped the benefits of methodically applying evolved solutions (in both biology and technology) to solve distinctively human challenges. Soon we'll see that there is another world of contradictions begging to be solved – one that has less to do with environmental or technical constraints and more to do with psychological ones. We will see how we can begin to apply the thinking of our first two tools, biomimicry and TRIZ, to address the most fundamental challenges we face today.

We are now able to meet the hero of this story and explore our final innovation tool: our evolved psychology.

To quickly recap:

1. Chances are, your problem has been solved before.

2. TRIZ identifies patterns in existing solutions. Akin to the classification of a biological species, these are called *inventive principles.*

3. By systematically applying *inventive principles* and borrowing from existing solutions in the world around us, TRIZ methodically resolves contradictions to create breakthrough innovation.

CHAPTER 3

The Quick and the Dead

EVOLVED PSYCHOLOGICAL SOLUTIONS

I T'S TIME TO unlock our final tool, the contemporary fields of behavioural science and evolutionary psychology. If you feel you already have a sophisticated understanding of these disciplines and want to skip ahead, we'll see you again at Chapter 4.

For the rest of us, here we go.

Take a look at Image 4. The A square and the B square have something in common. What is it?

Image 4 – The Adelson Checkerboard: while they may appear different, the A and B squares are exactly the same shade of grey.

Yes, they are both grey, but the fun fact is, believe it or not, both the A and B squares are precisely the same shade (you can see this for yourself on the right-hand side, where the boxes are removed from their illusory context). Don't worry, your mind isn't broken. This famous illusion was developed by American neuroscientist Professor Edward Adelson, a certified 'brain bender' from MIT.[1]

Although I've seen this hundreds of times before, my eyes – or more accurately, my brain – still tell me they're totally different shades (with the A square darker than the B square). So, what's happening here? Why is our perception thrown so radically by this? And what's the significance for us? Well, Adelson's checkerboard provides an essential insight into the evolved human brain, and as we will soon see, its relevance for innovation remains virtually untapped.

The first element at play in Adelson's checkerboard is a concept known as *simultaneous contrast effect*.[2] Our visual system isn't a physical light meter. We don't navigate the world viewing information perfectly, nor calculating colour values

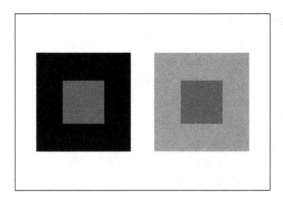

Image 5 – Simultaneous contrast effect: the two enclosed squares have the same luminance, but they do not appear equally bright.

like a printer. Instead, the context we see things within heavily influences our perception. A light grey patch will appear darker when placed on a bright background and brighter when placed on a dark background (see Image 5). In Adelson's illusion, when surrounded by four darker squares the B square appears to be lighter by comparison.

A second factor shaping our perception in Adelson's checkerboard is an idea called *lightness constancy*.[3] Here, objects that we know are white (like a fridge) will remain cognitively white, even in a dimly lit room. Because of the ingenuity of lightness constancy, when observing Adelson's checkerboard we overlay meaning – that the boxes in shadow should also be lighter than they appear (a bit like seeing our fridge in the dark), and our perceptual experience adjusts itself accordingly.

Why am I sharing Adelson's illusion and the slightly complex (but hopefully interesting) rationale behind it? Our brain isn't, nor has it ever needed to be, a perfect photometer or rational calculator. Instead, in a world where we make thousands of judgements every day, the survival of our species has relied on our ability to respond quickly enough, correctly enough, *most* of the time.

As a result, our evolved perception is heavily influenced by expectations, our previous experiences and the way information is presented. While sometimes it may feel like these short-cuts mean that we're inherently broken or faulty (like our experience with the checkerboard), how our imperfect and often lazy brain solves problems is truly extraordinary. The way evolutionary processes have shaped the human mind is something we should work with and learn from, not wish away.

Your brain isn't broken.
It's just great at taking short-cuts.

THE BRAIN THAT LIVED

The evolved human brain is the most remarkable organ on earth. It's estimated that the brain contains around 100 billion neurons (outnumbering the number of stars in the galaxy)[4] and is home to more than 100,000 km of interconnections.[5] From a computational perspective, it's reported that your mind can take in an astronomical 11,000,000 pieces of information at any given moment.[6]

You might have guessed that there's a *but...* coming. Sadly, the most generous evaluation is that we can only consciously process 40 of these pieces of information at any one time. To get where we are today, it's clear we've needed to cut some corners.

From an evolutionary perspective, both the speed and nature of our response to the events above are critical for our survival. In

Adelson's checkerboard, rather than accurately calculate the raw information, our brain has evolved to make mental compressions (like JPEGs) of the data available, resulting in quick, intuitive and often automatic responses, sometimes referred to as biases or heuristics. We jump when we hear a loud bang. When we see empty shelves of toilet paper and only one left, our evolved brain urges us to grab it. Thankfully, when we touch a hot stove, our hand is ripped away before we're even able to process "that's flipping hot!"

A helpful (albeit reductionist) way to understand our evolved decision making is to consider our brain as being composed of two different systems:

- *System 1*: related to fast, intuitive judgement and automatic perception (like Adelson's checkerboard, jumping when we hear a loud bang, or quickly removing our hand from a hot stove).

- *System 2*: responsible for slower, more deliberate and conscious reasoning tasks (think learning a new language, solving complex mathematics or playing *Trivial Pursuit*).

This concept was popularised by psychologist and Nobel laureate Daniel Kahneman in his best-selling book, *Thinking, Fast and Slow*.[7] To elaborate on the interplay between these two systems, our 'fast' (evolutionarily old System 1) and 'slow' (evolutionarily more recent System 2), psychologist Jonathan Haidt provides a helpful metaphor.[8] He describes it like a rider (System 2) atop an elephant (System 1). While the deluded rider might *think* he's in control, all that's needed is to go near a bucket of peanuts or ride too close to a cliff's edge and it becomes clear who's really in charge.

When we observe human decision making in the real world, we see similar predictable patterns in our decisions and actions as we might expect from this elephant and rider scenario. We see our propensity to follow the crowd, over-eat and fail to save; with many of these decisions deviating from what might be considered more rational decision-making models, like economics. We see the control of the elephant. Nobel laureate Richard Thaler describes these as *anomalies*.[9]

It's been found, for example, that humans have an almost universal tendency to choose a smaller immediate reward over a more substantial and delayed one (blowing our salary on short-term fun rather than saving for a home deposit). This is now classified in behavioural science as *temporal discounting*.[10] While this behaviour may be unhelpful today, in the primitive environment in which our brains evolved, with little opportunity to accumulate wealth over time, having a lack of self-control might actually have been a successful adaptive trait.[11] Our ancient ancestors rarely faced choices that required them to calculate discounted rates or time-based trade-offs, like being charged $10 for something now compared to a discounted $8 in the future. More often, the goal was to eat it now, or it'll run away! In short, these aren't failures or glitches – they're evolved *features*.

The problem is, the world has moved on.

Just as humans have inherited biological solutions like goosebumps or hiccups (believed to have helped our longer-haired relatives keep warm and our amphibious ancestors gulp for air, respectively), many of our evolved psychological solutions are now mismatched with our modern environment.[12] We're experiencing a psychological *lag*.

As opposed to our ancient past, in modern society it can be beneficial to plan for retirement and not squander our savings on short-term thrills. Despite the convenience and availability of high-calorie meals, we also really shouldn't just go around eating from every burger joint we see on a walk down the high street. Over the last twenty years, the field of psychology has provided an invaluable lens through which we can view and analyse these miss-matches between our evolved response and rational economic expectations, laying the foundation of modern-day behavioural economics.

A discipline rapidly gaining momentum within organisations and governments across the globe today, behavioural economics (and more broadly the field of behavioural science) is enabling us to harness and work with our evolved traits to make sounder decisions in a world quite different to the one in which these strategies originated. From combating climate change to vaccine hesitancy, behavioural insights are now regularly drawn upon to help address some of the most significant challenges our species has ever faced.

Despite the current interest, however, it must be recognised that many of the solutions behavioural science now offers are not new. When we look closely, we can see they've been here all along.

ORGANISING OUR INTUITION

To survive, compete and reproduce, humans have been unconsciously perfecting solutions to many of life's challenges over the course of aeons.

In the words of David Halpern, chief executive of the Behavioural Insights Team (the UK Government's 'Nudge Unit'), "people have been 'nudging' each other for as long as mankind has existed."[13] From closing-down sales and limited deals (while stocks last), to slashing recommended retail prices (RRPs), and the practice of restaurateurs seating their venues from the front windows backwards to make them seem more popular, humans have always stumbled upon ideas that just *work*. Akin to the convergent adaptation of biological solutions (like the evolution of the dorsal fin) and shared technical solutions (like the inventive principle, *nested doll*), human problem solving has also converged on the most successful psychological solutions when addressing common constraints and contradictions.

Remember, "It is the sea herself who fashions the boats."

Since biblical times, much of this Darwinian wisdom has been observed, identified and passed down in the form of religion, parable and folklore.

Consider Luke (6:38), "Give and ye shall receive." This is a beautiful articulation of the behavioural science principle of *reciprocity* (when someone is generous to us, we feel obliged to return the favour in kind).[14] Before we had developed terms like *certainty effect* (a tendency to feel disproportionately better about a certain outcome than those that are probable or possible), someone told us that "A bird in the hand is worth two in the bush."[15] The saying, "There's safety in numbers" articulates *social proof* or *herd bias*.[16] "No pain, no gain" summarises what's now known as the *effort heuristic*.[17] Even the kitchen wisdom of "A watched pot never boils" fittingly digests the fact that unoccupied time feels longer than occupied time.[18]

The work of academia and government to identify these consistent patterns, and scientifically classify them, has not only helped to develop a shared language for us to discuss, compare and unite behind, it's crystallised what we've instinctively known for centuries. As has occurred in other fields of innovation (like the development of vaccines) instinct and observation often precede science. Much of the value of the field of behavioural science, therefore, is in aiding us to more easily recognise and organise these facets of our intuition.

In the next section we will see that having a language for concepts, creating this classification system, doesn't just help us to collect and categorise evolved solutions – it fundamentally allows us to see and apply them more readily. Unlike beaks and fins, these solutions have largely been invisible, until now. What we say, we can see, and what we see, we can apply.

That was a lot... Here's a little less:

- Our psychology and decision making is a product of evolutionary processes.

- Behavioural science has identified and classified consistent patterns in evolved human decision making and behaviour.

- This classification is now helping us to predict and address some of the most significant challenges our species has ever faced.

CHAPTER 4
Seeing with
New Eyes

YOU WON'T FIND a polar bear in the desert. You're also unlikely to see a camel in the jungle. Yet, despite our origins on the African savanna, humans have been able to occupy virtually every habitat on Earth. The evolution of language has been recognised as a critical factor in our species' global domination.[1] It has armed us with a high-fidelity code to transmit information, helping us to produce tools, construct shelter and create clothing suitable for navigating and surviving the extremities of nature.

It has allowed us to share ideas.

Importantly, the words we use don't only help our species to coordinate, the language we create also informs how we see the world around us. As a prime example, the enhanced classification of our psychology is now helping us to see, and draw connections between, ideas that we never would have before.

*"The limits of my language mean
the limits of my world."*
—LUDWIG WITTGENSTEIN

Consider for a moment the humble banana. We don't see this potassium-packed beauty as a *long, bent, yellow, slippery morning staple.* Instead, we immediately identify it as a *banana* and this classification conjures a rich diversity of additional associations like its feel, taste and smell. In her TED talk on the topic, Lera Boroditsky, an associate professor from the University of California, San Diego, argues that language not only helps to build concepts (like *banana*) but actually opens up new cognitive realms that inform our world.[2] It appears that having a language to articulate concepts helps us to see and identify things more readily and easily.

Given the shared physiology of vision across humankind, exploring the language used to describe colour is a compelling way of seeing this relationship between language and cognition. For example, Greek and Russian speakers have two distinct classifications (and words) for both light and dark blue. In Greek, the darker shade is called *ble* and the lighter shade called *ghalazio*; in Russian, light blue is *goluboy*, and dark blue, *siniy*. English and German speakers have a single label for each (they're both categorically *blue*). Deprived of these finer colour distinctions, research has found that English and German speakers are comparatively slower and less accurate than their Greek and Russian counterparts when asked to identify various shades of blue.[3,4] Boroditsky reports that when we look at people's brains as they perceive shifts in these colour ranges, those with a richer vernacular for shades of blue will react with surprise, as if something has categorically changed. This response isn't shared by English speakers, who don't make this distinction at all. For these audiences, argues Boroditsky, it's as if nothing is categorically changing.

While the absence of richer (and clearer) classifications for colour might make life tricky for an English and Russian couple agreeing on the shade of a new sofa, the implications of this underlying insight can be far more serious. For instance, rather than distinctions in colour, some languages also differ in the way they encode time. To predict the rain, a German speaker can do so in the present tense, saying "It rains tomorrow." In contrast, an English speaker is required to use a future marker like "it *shall*" or "it *is going to.*" Fascinatingly, it has been empirically shown that speakers of languages with obligatory future-time references (like English) actually engage in less future-oriented behaviour, while those with more present-focused languages (like German) are likely to save more, retire with more wealth, smoke less, practise safer sex and become less obese.[5]

It's been argued that roughly two-thirds of Americans make sub-optimal financial decisions in part because they lack a clear understanding of the vocabulary related to compound interest and how this can help or hurt their future finances.[6] As a further disturbing example, a third of people suffering from type 2 diabetes can remain unaware of the disease, therefore taking no health precautions, because they're missing an overarching concept helping them to piece together the disparate symptoms.[7] In this instance, diabetes isn't recognised as a single concept (like *banana*), it's still a collection of disparate elements yet to make sense (*long, bent, yellow, slippery*).

Language doesn't just influence perception, it shapes behaviour. Having access to vocabulary opens new doors.

What we say, we can see, and what we see, we can *apply*.

TRY THE BANANA

In 2007, IBM partnered with advertising agency Ogilvy to develop a commercial for their *Stop Talking, Start Doing* campaign. The advert opens on a group of colleagues gathered before a team meeting. "These innovation meetings are killing us..." explains one. "The hype, the jargon!" adds another. They hand out scorecards. "It's Buzzword Bingo. Every time you hear one, you mark it down." The advert cuts to a business leader on stage. "In short," he says, "we are 100% committed to facilitating a culture of out-of-the-box, goal-oriented, value-added, disruptive, web—"

"*BINGO!*" is excitedly shouted from the crowd.

> *"To be a good diagnostician, a physician needs to acquire a large set of labels for diseases."*
> —DANIEL KAHNEMAN

Often, it can be hard to defend the volume and complexity of behavioural science's vernacular. Using terms like *choice paralysis* might seem a fancy way of saying *too many options*, or *idiosyncratic fit* just a complex way of recognising an offer that uniquely benefits a particular individual or group (discounted health care for accountants, for example). That said, in a world where Canadian Inuits have 53 words to describe snow, it also strikes me as a missed opportunity that the language of business, communication and innovation more generally remains so unnuanced.

Just like in the IBM advert, there's only so many times you can hear the terms *surprise and delight, trust, value-added, experience* and *loyalty*. These are the common buzzwords we use but cannot *truly* realise without a finer, richer vernacular.

In the same way advances in biology and physics have armed us with the language of genomes and thermal dynamics, concepts propelling their fields forwards, contemporary behavioural science has gifted us with a means of more precisely classifying the realm of the psychological. We now have a deeper understanding of the elements that contribute to these buzzwords (a more granular understanding of what might constitute loyalty, for example), as well as a means of creating ideas and innovations that address them.

The language and classification of behavioural science has enriched our vernacular and, as a consequence, our opportunity for innovation.

Whether working to enhance a loyalty programme or implement a behaviour change campaign, we can now more easily see that there are many different types of psychological solutions that can be implemented to achieve our objectives. Without the language of physics, including finer concepts like lift and drag, Eiji Nakatsu would never have connected the kingfisher with a bullet train. Similarly, without the classification of TRIZ's inventive principles, we couldn't work to rapidly resolve technical contradictions by likening a tape measure to a camera lens. Applying a similar nomenclature to TRIZ, evolved patterns in psychological solutions – classified by contemporary behavioural science – can now become our **psychological inventive principles** (from here on, simply **psychological principles**). These are the connective tissue between evolved solutions 'in the wild' and the challenges we can solve today.

At this juncture, despite the promise it shows, it's important to also caution against a blind over-reliance on the classification and biases of behavioural science, which risks underestimating the complexity of behaviour change. Not everything is reducible to a single, addressable bias or principle and unfurling a long list of heuristics is not itself a winning innovation strategy. As we will explore further at the end of the book, context and individual differences can heavily shape our responses. All of this is undoubtedly true. However, for *Evolutionary Ideas* I welcome an additive view. Imagine for a moment that innovation and behaviour change were a little like making a fruit salad. As we prepare, would it be easier for us to say, "Let's try the long, bent, yellow, highly slippery morning staple?" or just go with, "Shall we try the banana?"

If you skimmed that bit, know this:

- Language provides an efficient shortcut to reality. It informs how we see the world and, on occasion, shapes our behaviour.

- The richer language of behavioural science helps us to identify greater opportunities for innovation.

- What we say we can see. What we see, we can *apply*.

CHAPTER 5
Psychological TRIZ

SEVERAL YEARS AGO, I worked on a classic retail challenge. Our client was running a quarterly promotion for one of its high-value items and we were tasked with increasing the attractiveness of the offer and boosting sales. It could be said that our challenge was: "How can we change the *perceived value* of the product without changing the *price?*"

By the end of the promotion period, sales had risen by 56%.

When faced with a conundrum like this and knowing that we couldn't make the product any cheaper or modify it in any way, a traditional approach might have been to generate a new way to tell people about the offer's high value and quality. It could have even been to reinforce the product's competitive attributes. Instead, like TRIZ, we set out to find the types of solutions that had naturally evolved to solve this psychological conundrum in the past.

These patterns of evolved solutions included psychological principles like *scarcity* (making the offer feel limited or scarce) and *social proof* (illustrating existing consumption to reinforce trust in the product's quality). We tested several innovative campaigns via social media to determine their effectiveness.

One of our trial results stood out from the rest – an evolved solution used successfully in the past to sell more Campbell's soup.

In 1998, three Iowa supermarkets took part in a field study.[1] In each store, end-aisle displays were created featuring tins of Campbell's soup with a modest 10c discount (from 89c per can to 79c). The research team made one small tweak on each of three consecutive evenings. They advertised three different purchase limits on the discounted soup: no limit per person, a limit of four per person, and finally a limit of twelve per person. At the end of the experiment, the researchers found that these purchase limits increased product sales. When limited to twelve, people bought significantly more (an average of seven cans) than both the limit of four and no limit conditions (3.5 and 3.3 cans respectively). By providing a purchase limit, they had anchored behaviour.

Quantity limitations, like those showcased in the Iowa study, are often considered a deficiency within an offer. Because of this they're frequently shied away from, buried in a disclaimer. This was indeed the case for our client at the time. For every piece of communication we had previously made for this promotion, the disclaimer *maximum of four per customer* had sat in the bottom right hand corner in near-microscopic typeface. Now, liberated by behavioural science's classification – the psychological principle of *quantity anchoring* – we were able to innovate to solve this familiar value conundrum. This limitation was, in fact, the most valuable element of the offer.

Our most successful campaign applied a quantity anchor in the headline *maximum of four per customer,* and the product virtually sold itself. Without changing the product or the price, we were able to springboard our innovation and unlock new growth opportunities for our client. Through this process, we didn't just communicate our client's value, we *created* it.

We increased perceptions of value *without* changing the price.

SYSTEMATIC CREATIVITY

Imagine an uncharacteristically foggy morning for the New York summer. At 7.33 am, Delta DL 970 prepares to take off from JFK airport and begin its flight to Denver.

"He loses everything," jokes Captain Kim Gibson to one of her cabin crew as her co-pilot, Eric Wu, heads back into the cabin to find his mobile phone. "Alright," she announces on his return. "Services and shocks?"

Slightly rattled, Wu looks across the Boeing's expansive dashboard, covered in dials and switches. "Um, checked."

"Landing gear leaver?" prompts Captain Gibson.

"Yep, it's down."

"Oxygen?"

"Tested, 100%."

At this same moment, in the emergency ward of Mount Sinai Hospital, on the other side of the city, following surgical protocol Dr Vinod Kumar makes his first incision down his patient's chest. To access her heart, he first needs to get to the breastbone and rib. With little time to spare, his surgery is underway.

"Looking at our destination altitude," announces Co-Pilot Wu, "We're going to Denver, so that's 5,400 feet."

"Yep, great. Parking brake," instructs Gibson.

"Off."

With limited visibility still, the huge aircraft rolls onto the runway.

By 11.45 am, just over four hours later, Delta DL 970 has safely landed in Denver and Dr Kumar's patient is in the recovery ward. It has been a successful morning. But not by accident.

I used to hate checklists. They reminded me of being swamped with work, long shopping lists and household chores. It's a good thing that I've never received an early morning call to conduct open-heart surgery or been tasked with landing a Boeing 737 in an ugly crosswind. In complex scenarios such as these, where thousands of factors can cause a catastrophe, checklists are crucial.

In creative pursuits, it tends not to be an avoidance of tragedy we're most concerned about. Instead, our primary fear is leaving great ideas off the table. The problem is, to many of us checklists, templates and a systematic approach to creativity sound directly opposed to achieving it. Yet regardless of whether we recognise it or not, there's already a hidden structure to most creative endeavours – even the most awarded advertising.

In 1999, researchers from the Jerusalem School of Business Administration compiled 200 highly evaluated print ads from award-winning contests.[2] When analysed, the team found that 89% of these successful adverts could be accounted for by six creative templates (just like TRIZ's inventive principles) which had been previously identified. For example, there is the template of *pictorial analogy* (like a Nike Air sneaker being depicted as a fire fighter's jumping sheet) or *extreme situation* (a Jeep driving underneath the snow to prove its all-weather driving capacity). In a second study, a group of less successful adverts were then assessed via the same process and structure. Interestingly, for this group, only 2.5% could be classified against the templates. In short, the researchers found that adverts awarded for their creativity were actually *more* predictable and formulaic than their uncreative counterparts.

Creativity, the research shows, follows tried and tested patterns (let's not forget *Jaws in Space*).

*"The production of ideas is just as definite a process
as the production of Fords."*

—JAMES WEBB YOUNG

From advertising royalty to The Beatles, some of the world's most creative minds admittedly follow a templated or consistent process when executing their craft. In their book *Inside the Box*, Drew Boyd and Jacob Goldenberg deconstruct the success of crime novelist Agatha Christie (neck and neck with William Shakespeare as best-selling author of all time).[3] For Christie, there was a clear process and structure to her novels: "a dead body is discovered; a detective examines the crime scene, collects clues, interviews suspects, and only at the very end reveals the killer – the person you least suspected!" While we might think that this structure would limit Christie's imagination, or indeed lessen our enjoyment as readers, sixty-six detective novels later, it's a process that helped to constrain and focus her thinking. This structure *fuelled* her creativity.

By creating checklists and templates for our own innovation and problem solving, we can begin to systematically conduct what is an implicit process for many.

Behavioural science's classification of evolved solutions, our psychological principles, naturally create an order by which innovation checklists can be generated. Instead of starting with a blank page, jumping to conclusions, or praying for a revolutionary spark, they provide immediate access to the instinctive thought processes of many thousands of problem solvers before us. Rather than assume creativity is the dominion of a lone genius, these checklists help us to approach innovation more like a disciplined surgeon or pilot. As opposed to avoiding a thousand potential disasters, like TRIZ, this structure helps us to identify the relatively few ideas that really, really work.

PRICK THEM WITH A PIN

I was at a family gathering one sunny afternoon in Sydney when I overheard my partner's cousin retelling the story of the time she was pregnant with her second baby.

She reminded the table that only she, her husband and their existing young daughter, Ava, had known the sex of the unborn child. No one else in the family was in on the secret and they were keen for it to stay that way.

As you might imagine, everyone began to interrogate poor young Ava. For months she was cross-examined but, to her absolute credit, she kept tight-lipped. Ava didn't spill the beans. She was repeatedly posed questions like "Is it a boy or a girl?" and "What's the sex of the baby going to be?" To this, she said nothing. Her alarm bells were ringing, and her conscious (System 2) barriers were engaged.

Then one day someone asked a slightly different question. Approaching it creatively and obliquely, rather than asking if the baby was a boy or a girl, the interrogator asked, "So, Ava, what's the *name* of the baby going to be?"*

To this, she proudly replied, "Sophia."

The role of a good psychologist isn't to generate the answers to problems but to enable the real experts, those closest to the experience, to find answers for themselves. The same is true when writing good creative checklists to help unlock powerful ideas. In ideation, the more effective the question (and occasionally the less direct), the better the answer can be.

---

* I've since learned that another great question may have been "what *colour* is the nursery?"

As they say, don't ask someone to say *"ouch,"* prick them with a pin.

So, where do we find these powerful questions for our checklists, and how can we approach our challenges obliquely or laterally? Well, as you might expect by now, the answer is all around us.

There's a structure to creativity. By asking better questions, we'll generate more creative answers.

MISSING BULLET HOLES

During World War II the United States armed forces faced a dilemma when their bomber planes continually returned riddled with bullet holes. It was clear to the military that extra protection was needed – the only question was, "where?" To help devise their strategy, the US military gathered as much data as they could (including mapping the bullet-hole distribution on the returning planes) and engaged a high-powered research agency, the Statistical Research Group, to determine where reinforcements should be made. The initial directive was for these to be placed on the fuselage, where the plane was being hit most frequently.

While at first this seems a logical suggestion, insightfully, statistician Abraham Wald argued that the armour should be placed where the bullets were *not*. It was in fact the planes that never returned that they needed to better understand. As Harvard Professor Gary Pisano argues, "The problem for most companies is not where they look for ideas; rather, it is where they do not look for them."[4] Just like the US military, when faced with a challenge it's all too common for us to be blinded by the data most readily available or to look to our direct, or literal, competitive set. It's easy to be captivated by the information we most easily recognise. But to out-innovate those around us, we need to look *laterally*. We need to explore the places we otherwise wouldn't have considered.

We need to search for the missing bullet holes.

As with the convergent adaptation of the dorsal fin (an evolved biological solution across entirely different species) and the inventive principles of TRIZ (evolved technical solutions across industry), there's an abundance of evolved psychological solutions (our psychological principles) surrounding us every day. Because of their adaptive nature we can also see these solutions working successfully across species, as well as converging across category and industry. (Recall Sagarin, "Good ideas in evolution are identified because they appear nearly exactly the same across many different organisms.") For example, what connects the owl butterfly and cow? *Watchful eyes*, it appears.

Through millennia of adaptation, the owl butterfly has evolved to mimic the high-contrast eyes of predators on its wings. While the exact mechanism behind its effectiveness is still debated, these markings help to deter predators while the butterfly rests and feeds. Similarly, to reduce the tendency of free-roaming livestock to be picked off by lions and leopards, a comparable solution was employed in 2020 by an innovative project in Botswana. Here, painting eyes on the rumps of cattle

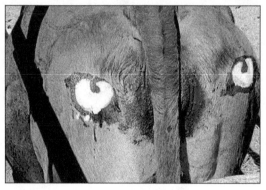

Image 6 – Convergent solutions across species: (top) owl butterfly; (bottom) Botswana conservation project.

was found to be a cost-effective tool to reduce livestock predation without harming the apex predators.[5]

When viewed across industry or domain, we see similar convergences in evolved psychological solutions: just look at the complexity-reduction adaptation across both remote controls and Qatar Airline's tickets in Image 7.

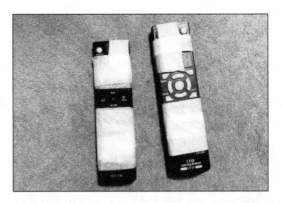

Image 7 – Convergent psychological solutions across domains: (top) a similar complexity reduction innovation for a remote control 'hack'; (bottom) and a Qatar Airways plane ticket.

As with the convergent adaptation of the dorsal fin, there is an abundance of convergent psychological solutions surrounding us every day.

Today, armed with our psychological principles, it's now easier for us to see these examples of convergent evolution in the wild, even across brands as different as, say, BMW and Domino's pizza. These are two brands that, in any other universe, would almost never be connected (unless you went to pick up your pizza in a 4-Series). But, for one thing, both brands offer 'build your own,' an example of the psychological principle known as the *IKEA effect* (evidence suggests this can increase a product's perceived value).[6] They are also noticeably transparent in their operations (you can watch your car being delivered from Munich just as you can track your pizza from the oven to your door). These are both examples of the psychological principle, *operational transparency*.[7]

In the same way biomimicry enables us to borrow from a penguin to innovate a 16-car bullet train, establishing patterns in psychological solutions helps us to deploy these evolved ideas *across* categories to achieve similar outcomes (from charity and banking, to workplace safety and product design). Because of this, the pool of creative inspiration is now also infinitely wider, and truly cross-category. We can avoid fixating on our existing competitive set or the data most readily available (like the challenge of the World War II bombers) and reframe our opportunity by borrowing from categories we typically wouldn't explore. We can learn from both Dominos and BMW, fast food and luxury cars, when reinforcing the nature of a diagnosis at a local hospital, say, where as much as 70% of diagnoses come from the pathology lab hidden away in the basement or off-site.[8]

Importantly, again analogous to both biomimicry and TRIZ, the innovative power of our psychological principles is infinitely richer when supported by their nuanced adaptations in the wild. Let's not forget, it was the specific evolved *differences* of the owl, Adélie penguin and kingfisher that enabled the innovation of the Shinkansen 500. It wasn't just finding any old bird, wing, or beak and strapping it to a train.

The question is, "What can we learn from the different ways that Domino's and BMW implement *operational transparency?*"

By exploring these differences to generate better innovation questions, we'll not only avoid the pitfalls of limiting our frame of reference – like reinforcing the fuselage – we'll also get better answers.

INNOVATION CHECKLISTS

What we say, we can see and what we see, we can *apply.*

Through adopting behavioural science's classification of evolved solutions, we can now more easily spot these elusive creatures, and their differences, in the wild. For instance, we can now more clearly identify that Katz's deli in New York has employed *anchoring* to its tip jars. Either through intuition or conscious design, Katz's 'cutters' have adapted to organise their tips, leading our eyes from $10, to $5, to $1, theoretically boosting customer tips by anchoring on the higher reference point (the $10 note). Better still, by converting it into an innovation question, we can now apply this idea in other contexts, for example: "How might we make a request *feel smaller* by first setting it in the context of *something bigger?*" By converting these observed adapted solutions into questions, allowing them to be more abstract and hence more widely applicable, we can begin to generate powerful innovation checklists.

Image 8 – Cutters at Katz's deli, New York: the process of arranging tips in a way that leads the eyes from a higher reference point to a lower one ($10, to $5, to $1), is known as anchoring in behavioural science.

As another example, let's consider the psychological principle of *social proof.* Research shows that illustrating the actions of others can influence our own perception and behaviour (for example, referencing an individual's energy use compared to their neighbours' to reduce over-consumption).[9] Knowing this facet of our psychology, we might ask ourselves the innovation question: "How might we communicate what *most people* are doing?" This direct approach is the social proof equivalent of asking Ava, "Is it a boy or a girl?" It's not wrong, but it's also not as strong as it *could* be.

Better armed with the ability to spot patterns of psychological solutions in the wild, we can now learn from countless, more nuanced, examples of social proof that have convergently evolved in nature. Let's look at this evolved social proof specimen from Sydney, Australia – it's the regulars' wall at a local café.

Image 9 – Social proof 'in the wild': regulars' wall, café, Sydney, Australia.

As you can see, the café's wall is plastered with its customers' loyalty cards. From one perspective, it's a practical solution. It ensures those who visit regularly always have their loyalty cards available, never missing out on a free coffee. However, from a psychological perspective, it's also a powerful example of social proof. It *proves* that the café is popular.

This coffee card adaptation provides us with a more useful checklist question – a more creative jumping-off point – when compared to a more straight, predictable or bullish social proof provocation. It sparks questions like, "How might we *tally* or *visualise* previous behaviour?" Or, "How might we enable people to *signal* their preferences to others?" These oblique approaches get us closer to "What's the *name* of the baby going to be?" Just as it took an indirect approach to get Ava to spill the beans, lateral questioning can help us to liberate more unexpected and effective solutions.

By identifying convergent adaptations of our psychological principles in the wild, like that of Katz's deli or the regulars' wall, then converting them into more nuanced questions, we're able to reapply their value in foreign contexts (just like adding the micro-serrations of an owl to the 500-Series' pantograph).

Soon, as we explore five of the most common, complex and important challenges faced in business, innovation and behaviour change today, we will be asking some of the most powerful questions that can help us solve them. At the end of each section, and then again at the end of the book, you'll see a collection of these questions in an innovation checklist. This list is by no means exhaustive. They provide a starting point from which we can conduct a form of psychological TRIZ and, over time, you may even begin to internalise these questions yourself.

Eventually they will become implicit.

Rather than starting from scratch every time we're faced with a challenge, this approach helps us to translate the value of existing solutions, *breeding* new ideas from those that have already survived the test of time. As our friend Altshuller writes, "There is no magic formula after all, but there are procedures that are sufficient in most cases."[10]

Whoever said innovators always need to sound like Richard Branson?

SOLVING PSYCHOLOGICAL CONTRADICTIONS

"The future will be psychological, not technological."
—RORY SUTHERLAND

In a hostile and competitive environment, creating and holding an advantage via conventional *economic* or *technological* approaches is harder than ever. Continually pressured to do more with less, for many businesses, the threat of extinction is real.

In contrast to the shrinking playing field offered via traditional economic and technical approaches, the world of psychology is expanding like never before. Over the past 30 years we've learnt more about the human brain than in the previous 3,000. Advances in disciplines like economics and physics are being dwarfed by comparative leaps occurring in psychology and, as behavioural science is repeatedly demonstrating, "value can be created in the mind just as it can be in the physical world."[11] As a result, Rory Sutherland argues, our evolved psychology is one of the few remaining places where untapped and unexpected monopoly advantage still lies. But to truly exploit this opportunity, we need to think differently.

As a start, we need to recognise the limitations of measuring success on straightforward physical or engineering metrics, like *speed, weight, drag, temperature, cost* and *duration*. Although these are attractively quantifiable (and might work for the Shinkansen 500-Series or TRIZ methodology), they limit our ability to benefit from the psychological renaissance occurring under our noses. In this new world we compete for richer and arguably more abundant psychological outcomes, like *satisfaction, preference, joy* and even experiences *remembered.*

Embracing this mindset also presents a fresh spectrum of *psychological contradictions* for us to resolve. No longer constrained to the realms of the technical or physical world (as might be prioritised in TRIZ) we can now innovate to solve psychological contradictions just like the one we saw at the beginning of this chapter ("increasing the *perceived value* without changing the *price*"). By starting here, we also naturally prioritise psychological solutions, creating value in a way that requires far fewer costly resources (like time, money and material).

No kingfisher required.

In the next part of the book, we'll investigate five of the most common psychological contradictions shared across business, innovation and behaviour change. They're vitally important challenges to solve, yet often the most difficult to 'crack'.

First, we'll explore the development of **trust**, a cornerstone of human cooperation. While a critical underpinning of mutually profitable trade, today trust is threatened by increasingly accessible misinformation and the obscurity of otherwise valuable honest signals.

We'll then turn our attention to **decision making**. Faced with an estimated 35,000 choices every day, we will identify patterns of solutions that have evolved to help people choose more quickly and accurately, without reducing the choices available.

From helping to save water and switch off the lights, to washing our hands, we then explore the importance of **triggering action**. We'll see that, although a disproportionate amount of energy is still spent on the early stages of the value creation process (like the corporate vision, strategy and even advertising), evolved solutions can help us to close this last mile, triggering action without forcing a response.

With action commenced, we move to **loyalty**. More than 90% of companies in the US invest in loyalty programmes, yet evidence illustrates these can have minimal to negative commercial impacts. We explore a suite of evolved solutions that can be drawn upon to **boost loyalty** and secure commitment.

Finally, we disentangle the psychology of **experience**. We interrogate a critical distinction between **clock time** and **brain time**, appreciating the commercial and customer implications of mistaking the two. Whether it's tourism or travel, banking or baking, we'll see that the way we develop and deliver our products and services can significantly impact our moment-by-moment experiences and, even more importantly, our longer-lasting memory of them.

Because of the frequency of these challenges in modern business, they not only offer a commensurately large potential impact if we can resolve them but, due to their near-universal relevance, a rich array of solutions by which to solve them has already evolved across industry. You can use these existing solutions to inspire your future innovation.

Here are our five *psychological contradictions*:

1. Reinforcing Trust *Without* Altering the Truth

2. Aiding Decisions *Without* Limiting Choice

3. Triggering Action *Without* Forcing a Response

4. Boosting Loyalty *Without* Increasing Rewards

5. Improving Experience *Without* Changing Duration

You may be reading this thinking "But I don't have a loyalty programme; this won't be necessary for me…"

Think again.

This isn't about frequent flyer points, filling tables or selling sneakers, it's about understanding *deeper* solutions; the psychological opportunity that lies beneath these tactics (but ultimately informs them). As advertising legend Bill Bernbach expresses, we will be exploring the soul, not just the flesh and bones.[12] We'll be interrogating the ideas.

When faced with challenges like these, while we might be tempted to start from scratch or throw away the rule book, in the next section we will see how these challenges can be solved by reapplying the value that already exists. We'll learn **"Where has it been solved before?"** and how we can apply it today.

A final reminder before we switch gears:

- Despite our fondness for the radical and revolutionary, the answer to your challenge has likely already evolved, somewhere.

- The classification and language of behavioural science helps us to see evolved patterns of solutions all around us. We will call these patterns of solutions **psychological principles**.

- By generating powerful questions, we can systematically resolve **psychological contradictions**, connecting solutions across categories and breeding better ideas on purpose.

Part 2
APPLYING THE TOOLS

CONTRADICTION 1:
REINFORCING TRUST
Without
ALTERING THE TRUTH

CHAPTER 6
Talk Is Cheap

DURING THE DARKEST part of the night, a lone vampire bat quietly laps at a cow's ankle. With the ability to spot warm blood flowing under its victim's skin, armed with razor-sharp teeth and an anticoagulant in its saliva, this notorious mammal is superbly adapted to extract and feed almost exclusively on blood.

While a vampire bat's meal of choice may not be so shocking, what you might be surprised to hear is that if a bat misses two meals in a row, it will starve. Vampire bats need to know where the next meal is coming from, even if there isn't a cow at hand. Bats and humans alike cannot survive and thrive in the wild without one invaluable resource: trust.

Whether deciding who to disclose our deepest secrets to, choosing a babysitter, or selecting a candidate for a new job, trust is a cornerstone of human cooperation. From healthcare and education to financial investment, the success of many industries relies on trust. Trust allows people to live and work together, helping us to feel safe and accepted within social groups. When trust is present, things go well. When it's lost, we're not just skating on thin ice, we've already fallen through it.

In the animal kingdom, because of their need to feed so regularly, it's common for vampire bats to regurgitate a portion of their most recent feast to those unfortunates who have not scored a meal. While this is an amazing gesture, bats are not alone in offering such complex forms of reciprocal altruism. In several bird species, breeding pairs will receive help raising their young. The vervet monkey also sounds alarms to warn others if a predator is nearby, despite the unnecessary attention (and risk) this brings. At some point during these altruistic acts, particularly when there is incomplete information (what academia calls *information asymmetry*), an organism needs to willingly volunteer to behave this way.

To start the cycle of reciprocity, it's a matter of regurgitate first, ask questions later.

As with the vampire bat, the cultivation of trust is critical for the survival of our species. Humans are naturally sensitive to cues and signals that reinforce trust, as well as those that might cause us to question it. For example, akin to the social bonding that occurs during the grooming of higher-order chimps, when we receive a massage from a loved one it doesn't just ease pain, it strengthens relationships.

Psychologist Dacher Keltner has shown that even the subtleties of physical touch can help develop trust between people.[1] Under experimental conditions, those who received a quick touch from an experimenter were more likely to cooperate with others in a game. Our evaluation of trustworthiness is virtually instantaneous (within 100 milliseconds), with additional studies showing that the perceived trustworthiness of a website can also be informed by even the briefest exposure to it.[2,3,4] While these cues of trust may be subtle, as a species we're clearly highly adapted to receiving, encoding and acting on them in near immediate fashion.

Through advances in technology and the explosion of social media, untrustworthy information is now travelling faster and further than ever before. In fact, Pew Research Center estimates that less than half of the health and medical information available online has been reviewed by doctors![5] When faced with information-rich environments, our ability to navigate sources in search of the truth, and create effective truthful messages ourselves, is more important than ever.

ENGINEERING TRUST

In a world where it's not so easy to change the trustworthiness of our face or the warmth of our handshake, fortunately, we *can* inform other important signals of credibility, integrity and reliability. Luckily, there are several evolved psychological solutions that we can employ to efficiently reinforce trustworthiness.

By donning a stethoscope a doctor can signal their authority, and in doing so improve confidence and trust in their medical diagnosis.[6] This is just one example of the messenger effect at work – where the perceived integrity of the individual delivering a message can be just as critical as the message itself, with signals of status and competence reinforcing trust.

Interestingly, just as we can be persuaded by the perceived authority of a messenger, we can also be influenced by the subjective virtues of a message, like its aesthetic qualities, when making judgements of truth or accuracy.

For instance, consider the following sayings:

- An apple a day keeps the doctor away.

- Haste makes waste.

- Woes unite foes.

- Will is no replacement for skill.

If you're like most people, these statements have a ring of truth to them, certainly more so than the clumsy, yet comparable, "Woes unite *enemies*," or "*Determination* is no replacement for skill." While the content of these claims should be considered distinct to their form, research[7] shows people base judgements of statement accuracy on their prosodic qualities.* That is, rhyme isn't incidental to the trustworthiness of a message – it's central to it. (Let's not forget, "If the gloves don't fit, you must acquit.")

As information trustworthiness becomes harder to establish, and the proliferation of untrustworthy information expands exponentially, we're all in need of clearer signals of honesty.

By understanding our evolved responses to the cues and signals that reinforce trust, we can hopefully succeed at being more honest, by producing more effective honesty signals, rather than modifying the facts in the hope of being more persuasive.

While there are multiple psychological solutions that have evolved to help reinforce trust, we will now explore just a few in greater detail, including examples of their adaptations across industries and categories.

If we know how to best communicate the truth, an honest solution – even if it's not the perfect solution – can be our strongest asset.

We can reinforce trust, without altering the truth.

---

* This mental shortcut is commonly known as the Keats heuristic, a reference to the poet's famous assertion that "Beauty is truth, truth beauty."

To sum up:

- The success of civilisation relies on trust.

- Untrustworthy information is now travelling faster and further than ever before.

- By understanding our evolved psychological solutions, we can learn how to reinforce trust through powerful 'honest' signals.

CHAPTER 7
If It Looks Like a Duck

PSYCHOLOGICAL PRINCIPLE:
SIGNALLING

WHY DO WE spend so much on extravagant engagement rings?

Why did Van Halen create their "no brown M&Ms" clause?

Why did a group of gamers relish in the excitement of shrinking horse testicles (nope, not a typo)?

How can we learn from these evolved ideas to accelerate our own innovation today?

To understand, let's first look to nature.

THAT LOOKS EXPENSIVE

In biology, signals have evolved to help organisms communicate otherwise unobservable characteristics. Take the black and yellow colours of a poison dart frog. This distinctive visual signal, in brazen disregard of its camouflage, has been favoured by natural selection because it accurately indicates the frog's toxicity. ("Go on, eat me if you dare!")

Similarly, a springbok's energetic *stott*, bounding into the air and lifting all four feet simultaneously, is a reliable signal that it's young and fit, so not worth chasing. Then we have the famed peacock, which illustrates its fitness through its dazzling and extravagant tail, or train. This expensive handicap serves no other purpose than to signal that a healthy male has resources to burn, boosting his attractiveness as a mate. Signals like these are favoured by natural selection so long as the costs are offset by the benefits (a little energy spent stotting has the potential to prevent the springbok from being chased at all).

Critically, it is the cost or risk associated with this signal that is the most reliable way of confirming its truthfulness. If an old and tired springbok (a low-quality signaller) attempts to fake enthusiastic stotting (a high-quality signal), they will exhaust themselves, becoming vulnerable. As a result, low cost signals that are easy to fake are often unreliable cues of trustworthiness. Consistent with this, the eye-catchingly bright colouration of frogs has been found to correlate almost perfectly with their toxicity.[1] Peacocks also don't just strut around telling peahens "I'm rich!" Any old bird can do that - they need to show it.

When it comes to trust, talk is cheap.

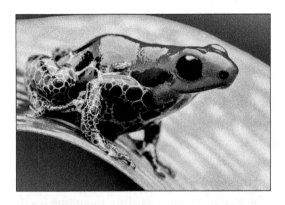

Image 10 – Costly signals in biology: (top) the colouration of the poison dart frog provides an honest signal of its toxicity, warning off predators; (middle) by stotting, a springbok signals that it's young and fit, therefore not worth trying to chase down; (bottom) the peacock signals its reproductive fitness through its extravagant, resource-expensive train.

The Wild West videogame *Red Dead Redemption* 2 was one of the most highly anticipated media launches of all time. It opened with one of the largest weekends in the history of entertainment, grossing over $725 million in revenue in three days.[2] It was hailed by critics as setting a new benchmark in adventure gaming. However, in the weeks leading to its release, reports noted a surprising absence of detail regarding the game itself.

With so little for the media to go on, how did *Red Dead Redemption* 2 drum up so much hype?

> "Red Dead Redemption 2 *will blow it out of the water. How do I know this? Balls. Horse balls, specifically.*"
>
> —RAE JOHNSTON, *JUNKEE*

"*Red Dead Redemption 2* will be so realistic, horse's balls shrink in the cold," wrote another industry headline.[3] Capturing the attention of gamers across the globe were reports that the game's engine was so powerful, and the graphics so realistic, that the testicles of the male horses had been programmed to shrink in cold weather (and expand in warm). The leak of this otherwise insignificant feature became a powerful signal of the game's brilliance. It helped inflame interest and reinforce trust in the game's quality.

The investment in this one small feature (well, depending on the weather, of course) signalled quality, integrity and the game's extraordinary dedication to craft. Merely *feeling* expensive can also be a powerful cue of quality. Just like the peacock's tail, wasteful displays of advertising have been found to act as a signal of product quality, with expensive-looking advertising being more effective than cheaper alternatives when saying the exact same thing.[4] We trust expensive messages because they help us to access otherwise unobservable information about the messenger: "We're already successful enough to have resources to burn."

Consciously and unconsciously, we're continually creating signals to reinforce our own credibility and trust. There are evolved examples all around us. College recruiters drive around in flashy cars embellished with the school's logo to signal the resource-rich environment awaiting their recruits (though when they're only leased, this might be considered a dishonest signal). Governments and banks signal their legitimacy through impressive stone buildings and costly architecture. While a bank's operations could be conducted in modest surroundings (your money isn't really behind those walls), these signals indicate financial stability and the organisation's confidence in their permanency (we would be a little less enthusiastic trusting our money at a market stall).

At the personal level, extravagant gifts and expensive engagement rings can also act to enhance trust ("If this was a short-term fling, I wouldn't have spent so much on the diamond!"). Sacrifice in obtaining these items signals our intentions, providing security in relationships. Duke University psychologist and author of *Predictably Irrational*, Dan Ariely, arms us with an additional perspective on how personal sacrifice can reinforce trust. Imagine for a moment that you're dining with friends, he describes.[5] When ordering the meal, the first person asks for the fish. The waiter responds, "Don't take the fish, it's too expensive and it's not so good. Take the chicken. The chicken is cheaper and better." What then happens to the waiter's recommendations for everyone else? It receives their trust. Argues Ariely, showing that we have the other person's interest in mind, and we are willing to sacrifice some of our utility for theirs, is a trust-creating exercise.

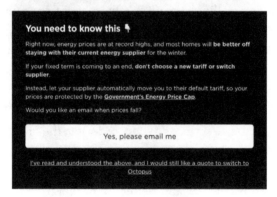

Image 11 – Sacrifice and costs to utility: (top) grand façade of The Commonwealth Bank in Sydney reinforces trust in the bank's security and longevity; (middle) expensive stones and engagement rings signal our long-term intentions to a partner; (bottom) Octopus Energy counter-intuitively advises prospective customers *not* to switch to them before the winter.

Following a similar strategy, during record-level UK energy prices in 2021, specialist sustainable energy company Octopus Energy Group advised would-be customers *not* to switch suppliers for the winter. Their website communicated, "Right now, energy prices are at record highs, and most homes will be better off staying with their current energy supplier for the winter." Just like the honest waiter, this sacrifice acted as a powerful signal that Octopus wasn't there for short-term gain alone, providing an indicator of their future intentions. Acts like these are met, in return, with trust.

Now we're back full circle to our regurgitating vampire bats.

REINFORCING TRUST: INNOVATION CHECKLIST

1. What expense or cost would demonstrate our trustworthiness?

2. How might we illustrate the sacrifice we're willing to make for others?

3. What investment or waste would show our confidence in our product or service?

CANARY IN THE COALMINE

To fly at altitudes that would make you or me sick, the canary requires immense quantities of oxygen. To attain this, its anatomy has evolved air sacs allowing it to take in air both when inhaling and exhaling. Essentially, it is able to get a double dose. While this is wonderful for our canary when flying high over a beautiful mountain range, it's not so great when there's poisonous gas all around as he squeezes into a small dark tunnel 100 metres underground.

In situations of uncertainty, observable signals provide insight into otherwise unobservable characteristics ("Look, I'm not sure about the whole game, but if the horse's balls are anything to go by..."). From coal mining to rock music and even heavyweight boxing, across industry, patterns of psychological solutions have evolved to help reinforce our trust and safety in certain scenarios.

For instance, from the early 1900s until the 1980s, knowing that canaries were particularly vulnerable to airborne poisons, coal miners in several countries used them as an early warning system to detect gases like carbon monoxide. Their rapid breathing rate, small size and adaptive double-dosing of the air around them meant that canaries would be impacted by the gas much faster than the miners themselves. Their health acted as a clear signal of whether a shaft was trustworthy or poisoned. If the animal became ill or died, miners knew it was time to run. It was a valuable innovation for the miners, albeit a bad one for the canary.

In the 1970s, while canaries were still being taken down mines, the band Van Halen stumbled across a similarly inspired solution to signal otherwise unobservable information. They created their own early warning device to protect the group from disaster (without harming any animals in the process).

When hired to play at a venue, like many bands Van Halen provided the promoter with a contract (or rider) outlining specific requests for the performance (including things like security requests, lighting instructions and backline equipment). To be confident the promoter had followed the instructions accurately, something the band wouldn't otherwise be able to check themselves until it was too late, they created a "no brown M&M's" clause. These instructions called for a bowl of M&Ms

to be left backstage, with all the brown M&Ms removed. In his memoir, lead singer David Lee Roth shares, "When I would walk backstage, if I saw a brown M&M in that bowl, well, we'd line-check the entire production. Guaranteed you're going to arrive at a technical error... Guaranteed you'd run into a problem."[6] Through their "no brown M&Ms" clause, Van Halen had bred their own canary. They had created an observable cue indicating the unseen risks that awaited them. To protect the band from catastrophe, they generated a reliable signal of trustworthiness.

Still in Madison Square Garden, but this time relating to heavyweight fighters rather than listening to heavy metal music, signals of trustworthiness have also evolved in the boxing ring. While there are many ways to cheat in boxing, this dishonest behaviour can often be easier to detect when it happens 'below the belt' than when it occurs 'beneath the gloves.' Here, while removing padding from the gloves (an illegal act in boxing) can lead to considerable damage to your opponent, adding elements can be even more horrifying. If officials aren't vigilant, plaster of Paris has been known to be mixed into hand-wraps. As the bout goes on, and the fighter sweats, this can cause the plaster to harden. Before you know it, the boxer has hands of concrete.*

To help assess the trustworthiness of boxers, it's customary for referees to inspect the taping and gloves of each fighter – sanctioning that the boxer's hands haven't been tampered with. When the gloves are wrapped, the tape used to do this is then signed by the referee. Akin to the unique wax seals used by bishops and monarchs to secure documents in centuries past (if the seal is cracked, you'll know something is awry). If the signature disappears or looks broken in any way, the referee can easily detect foul play. Without wearing a punch themselves, they'll see the boxer is hard-handed.

---

* Boxer Antonio Margarito was caught doing exactly this before his fight with Shane Mosley.

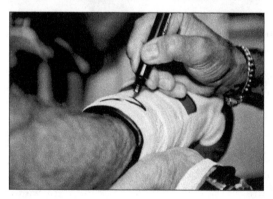

Image 12 – Creating signals of trust: (top) canary in coalmine; (middle) Van Halen's "No brown M&Ms" clause; (bottom) referee-signed boxer's gloves.

When we can't immediately assess the trustworthiness or safety of a scenario or person, alternative signals have evolved across industry to help identify otherwise unobservable information. Whether it's a canary down a coal mine, a brown M&M or the simplicity of a signature – identifying early, salient or hard to fake cues not only ensures that dishonesty is detected, it can help us to reinforce our own trustworthiness as an individual, brand, product or service.

REINFORCING TRUST: INNOVATION CHECKLIST

1. How might we create a clear signal of otherwise-unseen trust-affirming activities?

2. What detail is hard to fake yet telling of the honesty of the offer?

3. How might we focus on one specific feature to increase confidence in the whole?

MORE TO LOSE

Once, on my way to a family holiday in Cornwall, I met with Vikki and Jack – two employees at a local Tesco store.

After I had noticed a few things about their staff uniform, the pair kindly spoke to me in the carpark during their break. I introduced myself and began to explain the reason for my request. "Well, from what I can see, Vikki is more trustworthy than Jack," I said. Vikki grinned. In fact, neither seemed to disagree with my provocation. While I of course wasn't serious – I had only known them for about thirty seconds and there are far more creative ways to be beaten up in a carpark – there was a subtle difference between Vikki and Jack that helped me to justify my position.

Throughout evolution there's been significant selective pressure to develop strategies helping to detect dishonest signals. As we've seen, the expense of a signal, the personal sacrifice or cost to utility, is one way of achieving this. An additional expense that reinforces the honesty of a signal is its potential reputational cost. For example, a signal might be considered costly when there's a greater risk that a dishonest signaller will receive a penalty as a result. The most powerful signals in nature aren't directed one-to-one: the brightly coloured poison dart frog, the extravagant tail of the peacock and the athletic stott of the springbok – these are for *all* to see. The more witnesses of a signal, the higher the stakes are for a dishonest signaller.

Interestingly, the arrival of digital communications (specifically targeted ads online), is limiting this reputational risk, theoretically reducing the impact of a communicator's signal. Writer Don Marti hypothesises that, in communications, "targeting breaks signalling."[7] This means that when you see an advertisement that's targeting you alone, it's more like a cold call than a public message. It doesn't carry the same credible information about the seller's intentions because it's free of reputational cost. It's maybe no surprise that deceptive sellers and scammers have far more success online than through more public communication channels. To build trust, often it's not just about seeing the message, it's knowing that other people have seen it too (an implicit social proof, as we will learn more about in Chapter 9).

For example, to help counter concerns regarding

misinformation, at key stages during the Covid-19 pandemic, some adverts were shared simultaneously on all key UK channels reinforcing the significance, validity and, subsequently, trustworthiness of the message. (They can't all be lying to us!)

By communicating 'out of platform' in conspicuous public channels, many digital brands also work to reinforce trust in their promises and claims. If we look at Uber, they do this not just through their *message* ("Safety Never Stops") but also the *medium* – a very public billboard in Dubai. This same approach is consistently used by digital giants like Google and Facebook. Although these brands have humongous digital footprints, by delivering important claims (particularly those regarding security and safety) via traditional media, they expose themselves to greater public scrutiny and, as a result, greater reputational risks if found to be dishonest. This reputational cost works to reinforce the message's perceived trustworthiness.

So why was I able to make such a bold statement when I met with Vikki and Jack? Why didn't Jack thump me there and then? Well, as part of their staff uniform and name badges, Tesco includes selected personal information (like an interest in floristry or football). They also share their employees' starting dates. A powerful signal reinforcing trust, not only does this show us that Vikki has been working with Tesco for decades (therefore she's probably not done anything so horrendous as to be sacked over this time), but because of her time employed, she likely risks a higher reputational cost from mistreating a customer. She has more to lose. Jack, on the other hand, is a lesser-known quantity. With fewer years of proven performance and far less investment behind Tesco, whether to trust Jack or not could almost be anyone's guess (I write this with a smile. He was lovely... but you never know).

Image 13 – Signalling risks to reputation: (top) Vikki and Jack from Tesco; (middle) Uber advertising their safety commitments on a public billboard in Dubai; (bottom) unprecedented all-channel Covid-19 advert, UK.

REINFORCING TRUST: INNOVATION CHECKLIST

1. What cues would illustrate that there is 'reputation' at stake?

2. How might we ensure broad viewership to enhance reputational costs?

3. How might we communicate promises publicly to reinforce message trustworthiness? (See also Commitment, Chapter 20.)

CHAPTER 8

I'll Believe It When I See It

PSYCHOLOGICAL PRINCIPLES:
OPERATIONAL TRANSPARENCY
& THE LABOUR ILLUSION

" **I** STILL REMEMBER THE night we were gathered around my laptop computer in a third-floor apartment in Cambridge, Massachusetts," Harvard Business School's Professor Ryan Buell tells me. "This was going to be the moment that we were to hit the button, *create book.*"

Working with a colleague during his grad school years, Buell was developing a collaborative online platform, in the form of a book where friends could gather during important life moments to share stories and pictures. For months the pair had worked on the venture, and they were finally ready to turn their hard work into their first book. "I knew what was going on in the background," Buell recalls, "There were all of the images and the text to pull, the program needed to size the images, arrange the pagination and get all of the customisation right. Then it needed to convert it into a pdf and present it for someone so they could page through it." The pair had spent weeks coding and building the book for one of their professors. They hit the button and, magically, it worked. "It was beautiful." Buell was elated, and then, "immediately depressed."

Something about it just didn't feel right.

TOO GOOD TO BE TRUE

As the legend goes, Picasso was sitting in a restaurant when he was interrupted by a star-struck fan. Sheepishly, the admirer asked Picasso if he would do a quick sketch on a paper napkin as a keepsake. Picasso politely agreed and began to draw. When finished, the fan reached out to collect the drawing. At this point, Picasso withheld it. "You owe me $10,000," Picasso said. The fan was gobsmacked.

"How can you ask for so much? It only took you a minute to draw."

To which Picasso replied, "No, it took me 40 years."

The concept that effort can influence our perception is an old and important one in social psychology (you'll recall the proportionality bias from the introduction). However, our reliance on this mental short-cut to ascertain value is particularly strong when the actual quality of a product or service is otherwise obscured.[1] *

"If I can't see it, how can I trust it?"

To improve customer service and increase efficiencies, it's common for organisations to intentionally prevent clientele from

---

* Dan Ariely calls this the locksmith's paradox. He refers to a locksmith who becomes more efficient at opening doors the more experienced he becomes, only to be perceived as providing less value for money.

observing their efforts (either via physical distance or through automated technology). In many instances, this can lead to enormous improvements in service speed, as well as reductions in staff costs and waiting times.[2] However, as a detrimental by-product, it can detach customers from business operations, limiting their ability to see the effort behind them. Just like the story of Picasso's admirer, when we can't see the work conducted on our behalf, we may actually be less satisfied, less willing to pay and less trusting. When customers use ATMs more and branch tellers less, rather than leaving the bank relieved, their overall level of satisfaction with the bank actually goes *down*.[3]

Fascinatingly, it seems the reverse can also be true. That is, the more effort we see, the more we value and trust it.

Following his disappointment when weeks of work resulted in his book's seemingly effortless production, Buell began coding again straight away. With a small tweak he created an interstitial message. Now, instead of clicking the button and receiving an instant response, it said, "We're going to produce your book. It will take about 20 minutes. We will email it to you when we're done."

With a wry smile, Buell recalls, "This felt better." The quality of the experience was being improved by conveying the work being conducted on their behalf and, somewhat counter-intuitively, slowing it down.

Just a few years later Professor Ryan Buell and fellow Harvard Business School Professor Michael Norton turned these observations into a ground-breaking experiment.[4] They established that when people can see the work that's done on their behalf, they perceive more effort going into its delivery, believing the service provider has more expertise. Further still, provided you show what you're doing, people can even prefer outcomes if you make them wait.[5] They called this observed pattern *operational transparency*. In their paper, Buell and Norton report that travel website Kayak.com is beloved in part because of this psychological principle. When searching for a holiday, the site laboriously illustrates which airline is being examined, providing visual updates of results throughout the search rather than offering an instantaneous reveal. They show how hard they're working for us, making us wait until it's finished. As a result, the pair found that we trust Kayak.com to deliver a better outcome for us, the traveller.

Astonishingly, even the mere appearance of effort can reinforce perceptions of trust, a psychological principle the pair classified as the *labour illusion*. They report this approach being demonstrated in a diversity of service environments, for example, in automated voice response systems that play pre-recorded typing in the background (giving the impression that a digital operator is busily typing your query), and even ATMs that animate your bills being carefully counted before a transaction. By providing cues of effort during automated processes like these, we can effectively reinforce perceptions of quality and trust.

Despite the attraction of automation and the appealing efficiency of big batch production, there's an abundance of evolved solutions helping people to 'see the work' or signal the labour involved in producing a product or providing a service – even when that work happens behind closed doors. It's a solution that's evolved to reinforce trust in a range of products and services, from cider and orange juice to restaurants and dishwashing capsules.

SORRY ABOUT THE TWIGS

In 2012, Monteith's Brewing Company apologised to the whole of New Zealand: "Sorry about the twigs, folks!"

For weeks, thirsty customers across the land of the long white cloud had been finding twigs in their cartons of Monteith's apple cider – and they were none too happy about it. Bewildered queries and complaints flooded in from their customers. "Some fruit picker's probably going to get in trouble for this one," reported a local radio station.[6]

The strange thing is, Monteith's did it on purpose.

To reinforce trust in their honest claim of using freshly crushed apples and pears in their famous cider, the Monteith's team took twigs from their orchard and slipped them into every box. They created a cue of their production process, increasing operational transparency. Climaxing in a national apology, this simple idea helped to validate their claim "not from concentrate," strengthening consumer trust and helping Monteith's grow a whopping 43% that year.[7] While finding something unexpected in our drink isn't normally a cause for celebration, and *putting* something unexpected into someone's drink doesn't normally shout "Trust me!" if we understand *why* it works, it can.

For Monteith's, trust in their claim of "real apples and pears" was critical for their brand distinction and quality credentials. For orange juice brands, more often than not, it's trust in the claim of being freshly squeezed. To achieve this, rather than planting twigs from the orchard, French supermarket chain Intermarché found an alternative, yet highly creative, way to signal the effort in their operations. Their solution was to develop "The freshest fresh orange juice brand ever created," making a new brand for each bottle of juice with the exact time it was squeezed – every bottle, every minute (just like 8:36, 8:54 and 10:15 below).

Through accident or design, similar signals of operational transparency have convergently evolved in businesses across the globe. At my local farmers' market when living in Queens Park, London, the carrots are sold for nearly three times the price of the local Sainsbury's (just a five-minute walk away). The market carrots actually benefit by being rationally worse than those at Sainsbury's. How so? They're still dirty. Just like twigs in a carton

Image 14 – Cues providing operational transparency: (top) Monteith's "Sorry about the twigs, folks!"; (bottom) Intermarché's "The freshest fresh orange juice brand ever created."

of Monteith's, the soil provides a window into the production process, reinforcing the link between paddock and plate and underlining our trust in their freshness. In a slightly different adaptation, American burger franchise Five Guys are known for stocking their Idaho potatoes at the restaurant front door, signalling their 'made from scratch' fries (a process we otherwise may never have witnessed, nor believed as a message alone).

This is a solution that has convergently evolved in other restaurants, too. For example, a pasta-house I noticed in Paris.

Here, rather than Idaho potatoes, bags of flour are stored by the doorway to signal "We make our pasta on site." From Paris to Hoosick, New York, a final evolved idea we can learn from occurs at Berle Farm. This farm produces everything from certified organic vegetables and eggs to yoghurt (even the odd apple cider). In celebration of their generous cows (and reinforcing the farm's dedication to healthy farming practices), each jar of Berle's Certified Organic Cow Milk Yoghurt contains the names of the cows that helped to produce it. While certainly a lovely touch, it also provides an important cue of the farm's operations and the yoghurt's provenance. Just ask Myrtle.

To improve efficiencies and customer experience, modern business is increasingly distancing its customers from its operations. Armed with the classification and psychological principle of *operational transparency*, we can see that there are evolved solutions helping us to combat this everywhere. By showing the work and providing cues of labour, we can reinforce the quality of our offer and boost trust in our claims, without altering the truth. We can help people *see it to believe it.*

REINFORCING TRUST: INNOVATION CHECKLIST

1. How might we open the doors to help people see behind the scenes?

2. How might we cue elements of our production in the product itself?

3. What is an unseen element of our offer which would reinforce trust if noticeable?

Image 15 - Transparent cues of production: (top) dirty carrots in Queens Park, London; (middle) raw ingredients stored at the door at Five Guys & Parisian pasta house; (bottom) crediting the cows at Berle Farm, NY.

HARDWORKING PRODUCTS

What do washing detergent, toothpaste and cough lozenges have in common? Yes, they all clean, but even more than that, they're all products that need to work *hard*. With their advertised claims to scrub AND shine AND degrease, clear your nose AND soothe your throat, while providing you with stronger teeth AND fresher breath AND healthier gums, these are some dizzyingly impressive claims for products as elemental as the aforementioned to be making (I'm still not completely convinced that NASA isn't involved somewhere).

But with such sophisticated and hard-working promises, in what are reasonably low-involvement categories, how do these brands convince us they're telling the truth? Once again, companies need to do more than tell us, they need to *show us*.

We have just seen *operational transparency* in action for campaigns like Monteith's "Sorry about the twigs" and Intermarché's "the freshest fresh orange juice brand ever created." Similar evolved solutions are also apparent in the design of consumer products themselves. Here, a product's format can help to reinforce the effort that it puts in, helping us to focus our attention on its active features; the parts that work hardest for us.

For example, the bright red *Powerball* in Finish dishwashing tablets, as well as the salient red centre of Anticol's medicated throat lozenges, illustrates "this is the hardworking bit." When we see these products there's no question in our minds where the unique value or effort is. They're practically radioactive. As Rory Sutherland writes in *Alchemy*, the same is true of striped toothpaste.[8] Psychologically, the red, blue and white coloured stripes give us a clear signal that the toothpaste is performing more than one function, aiding the belief that this single toothpaste can offer the trifecta of strong teeth, fresh breath *and*

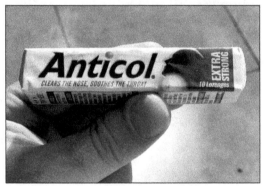

Image 16 – Hardworking products: (top) The red centre of Finish *Powerball* and Anticol losenges (middle) help us see the 'active' ingredients working hardest for us; (bottom) striped toothpaste helps us believe claims of strong teeth, fresh breath *and* healthy gums.

healthy gums. It helps us to trust a claim far harder to believe when this effort is disguised in an undifferentiated white paste. For these products, it's the format itself, not the messaging or peripheral services, that reinforces trust in product quality or claim. Now we know this, it's easier to see that the bright red colour of the *Powerball* is not for the grease, *it's for you.*

The bright red colour of the Powerball *isn't for the grease, it's for you.*

It's critical to note that this is not about making up claims, distorting facts or lying to customers through the development of signals of labour. We can't just make it seem like we're working hard or adding active ingredients when there's no truth to it. As Buell emphasizes, 'There's lots of research that shows that when customers catch an organisation in a manipulation attempt, or they feel like they are being manipulated, it completely undermines the relationship."[9] All it takes is a bat to feign blood once and it's out of the colony. By appreciating and honestly deploying the power of the labour illusion, we can ensure that a product's engineered superiority can be more readily identified and trusted by those required.

REINFORCING TRUST: INNOVATION CHECKLIST

1. How might we visualise how complex technology works?

2. How might we 'deconstruct' our product to highlight its 'hardest working' elements?

3. What unique name might we provide to the 'hardworking' components (i.e., *Powerball*)?

CHAPTER 9
Safety in Numbers

PSYCHOLOGICAL PRINCIPLE:
SOCIAL PROOF

" **A** ND NOW THE sea begins to boil."

Deep in the ocean, the BBC's *Blue Planet* pans out to reveal thousands of anchoveta swimming tightly together. Herded by beasts from the deep, the school binds to form an impressive silvery mass that heaves and contracts with the waves, just beneath the surface. "At first, the sheer scale of the 'bait-ball' seems to daunt the predators," narrates Sir David Attenborough. The school continues to pulse with the waves. Before long, bonito tuna, drawn to the shallows by the swirling soup, commence their strike. The anchoveta bind tightly together, remaining safe. "Still, the bait-ball holds together."

Before long, the yellowfins arrive. These piscine freight trains commence their attack, hitting with such ferocity that dozens of anchoveta splinter away from the densely packed main group (the bait-ball). The water is alive with action. Again and again, a yellow-finned assault fragments the school. With the bait-ball

Image 17 – Using communications to infer the social norm: "Take your litter home with you – others do!"

now broken, the mass of anchoveta disintegrates. "In just fifteen minutes," continues Attenborough, "all that is left is a silvery confetti of scales."

Like the anchoveta, humans also seek safety in numbers when deciding how to act, particularly when faced with conditions of uncertainty. To help decide what's risky and what's safe, who's trustworthy and who's not, we look for *social evidence*.[1] From an evolutionary perspective, conforming to this herd mentality is almost always positive for our prospects of survival. "If everyone's doing it, it must be a sensible thing to do," explains renowned psychologist and best selling author of *Influence*, Robert Cialdini.[2] While we can frequently see this today in customer testimonials and product reviews, even subtler cues within the environment can signal trustworthiness. Consider this: when you visit a local restaurant, are they busy? Is there a line outside or is it easy to find a seat? While a hassle to wait, a line can be a powerful cue that the food's tasty, and these seats are in demand. More often than not, it's good to adopt the practices of those around you. Writes professor of psychology Steve Stewart-Williams, "For one thing, the people around you aren't dead. If you do what they do – eat what they eat; avoid the dark alleys they avoid – you might continue not being dead as well."[3] Before our first bite, social proof helps to tell us that it's a restaurant that is safe and worth visiting. It says it's trustworthy.

BENDING NATURE

Centuries before mobile phones and GPS, the natural environment held crucial clues of trusted and safe routes, often signalled by prominent landmarks or existing trails. For hundreds of years we were led by the sun and the stars. However, in what's now the United States of America, Indigenous peoples developed a particularly novel solution to navigate safe passage. They shaped nature for their own means, leaving a mark for others to see. They created social proof to illustrate a trusted route.

Whether it's a stairwell sunken by the footsteps of a thousand years, or the blessed right foot of St Peter worn away by millions of pilgrims' hands at the Vatican, evidence of expected and trusted behaviour is all around us. While this social proof can include the unintended wear and tear of high-frequency interactions at particular locations, it can also include the manipulation, addition or removal of items from a context, providing social proof of certain behaviours, making it feel like the normal or trusted response.

For Indigenous Americans, this social evidence for safe passage came in the form of carefully shaped *marker trees*, most commonly white oaks with an abrupt bend several feet from the base. The prominent theory is that saplings were bent by local tribes at various intervals, forcing them to grow in unnatural shapes to communicate important messages like safe crossing points, mineral deposits or the burial sites of their ancestors.

As a physical representation of safe passage, these marker trees provided *decisional shortcuts*, which researcher Dennis Downes outlines "could mean the difference between life and death, between eating and starving, between crossing the river correctly or incorrectly."[4]

Today, akin to the marker trees of North America, adding something within an environment can still provide social proof. By seeing the behaviour of others before us, we learn that this is the normal or trusted response. A pile of cigarettes tells smokers where it's safe or accepted to smoke. Accordingly, it's commonly reported that littering is more likely in littered environments when compared to a clean setting.[5] Studies have even shown how nuanced our responses can be in these circumstances. For example, when a transparent donation box was pre-filled with lots of coins, many small donations were received.[6] However, when a box was filled with fewer, larger bills, more infrequent larger donations were recorded. We are immensely observant of our surroundings and diligently follow cues illustrating what's expected, normal and safe.

With reports of up to 4.5 billion 'Likes' a day, Facebook is arguably the world's most powerful modern-day social proof engine (poor St Peter wouldn't stand a chance). Fascinatingly, the Like button is itself an evolved adaptation. StumbleUpon featured a 'thumbs-up' mechanism in the early 2000s and Vimeo was using the term "Like" four years before Facebook introduced it in February 2009. Today, social behemoths like Instagram, Twitter and LinkedIn all embed social proof as central to their user experience, with e-commerce platforms like Amazon creating further opportunities for social proof through star ratings and testimonials. They have created persuasive reputational systems that work to reinforce our trust – while also keeping the signaller (seller) honest.

From the Appalachian Trail to the Amazon check-out, we have not only evolved to follow the behaviours and cues of others

Image 18 – Evidence of social proof: (top) Indigenous American marker tree; (middle) a pile of cigarettes near a local office illustrating where it's 'safe' to smoke; (bottom) online social proof via Facebook Likes.

to decrease our chances of dying but also to signal actions which are trustworthy and valuable for those around us. Be it marker trees or star ratings, by creating social evidence and providing social proof, we make it easier for people to navigate uncharted waters and make decisions in uncertainty. We can reinforce trust of a particular route or option, without changing the truth.

REINFORCING TRUST: INNOVATION CHECKLIST

1. What would illustrate that others have conducted the behaviour before?

2. What might we leave behind to show it's a normal or safe response?

3. How might we enable others to rate the trustworthiness of an actor or offer?

WHAT'S TAKEN AWAY?

I recently visited a café looking for a few coffees and snacks on a trip to the Cotswolds. Realising it was close to the end of their day, I peered inside to check for key signs of life. Someone was at the counter (check). The coffee machine was still on (double-check). There looked to be a selection of food under the glass counter (triple-check). I wandered in and began to place my coffee order with a young staff member. Turning my attention to the food, I perused the selection of pastries on offer. "We still have these vegetarian ones left," she said as I peered below.

Aha... I thought to myself, sucking my teeth. While not normally opposed to a vegetarian option, when contrasted with the gaping hole left by the other choices that had clearly been snapped up during the day, the perfect line-up of vegetarian pastries created an inkling of concern. They were untouched. "Just the coffee thanks."

While it may be more obvious to see things that are *left* within an environment, like a pile of cigarettes or a Facebook 'Like', taking something away can trigger an equally compelling evolved response. Just like opening the cookie jar to find only crumbs, sometimes the absence of something can be just as powerful when reinforcing the attractiveness and trustworthiness of an offer. It's little surprise that two of the most powerful words in marketing are "sold out" (or as Amazon sometimes more positively states, "So good its gone!").

Even the humble 'rip tag' flyer is a crafty piece of evolved psychology. Not only does it provide powerful social proof ("Someone's shown interest before me...") it also has an inbuilt scarcity driver ("There are only a few tags remaining!"). According to Sagarin, "The best adaptations solve multiple functions."[7] For the sea anemone, for instance, the evolution of its poisonous barbs didn't just enable it to stun or kill live prey, they also helped to protect from predators and even ward off competing anemones. The same can be true of evolved psychological solutions. For example, social proof can not only reinforce the safety and trustworthiness of a choice, it can also trigger our scarcity heuristic.

Now we're in the region of "Well, if it's that good, I better have some too!" It's the subtle difference between saying "sold out" and "until sold out." We move into *value creation*. For example, during the panic shopping that occurred in the early stages of the coronavirus pandemic, supermarket shelves across

Image 19 – What's been taken away?: (top) guitar lesson rip tag flyer normalises behaviour by illustrating the tags remaining; (middle) empty supermarket shelves in 2020 during toilet paper panic buying; (bottom) reinforcing product quality via stockouts in store – "So good it's gone!"

the planet were stripped bare of toilet paper and other essentials, creating the norm, "Others must know something I don't," then triggering hording through scarcity. ("If I don't get my loo roll too, I'll miss out!")

As a species, we are heavily influenced by the behaviour of others in guiding our own perception and action. If we do what other living people do, chances are we might continue not being dead too. It shows us what's safe and trusted. Through subtle environmental cues, the addition or creation of social evidence within an environment, or indeed the removal of elements illustrating the behaviour of others before us, we can help to engineer trust.

REINFORCING TRUST: INNOVATION CHECKLIST

1. What might be taken away to illustrate the behaviour of others previously?

2. What would people expect to see that, when removed, shows others have safely engaged?

3. What unexpected absence would increase trust that action is necessary?

We've now seen through the power of *signalling, operational transparency,* the *labour illusion* and *social proof* how psychological solutions have evolved to reinforce trust without changing the truth. By providing us with windows into otherwise unobservable information, they help us appreciate and trust the service, provider or product. Now all we need to do is decide which trusted options to go with.

It's time we explored **decision making**.

CONTRADICTION 2:
AIDING DECISIONS
Without
LIMITING CHOICE

CHAPTER 10
Spoilt for Choice

A HERD OF ZEBRA blissfully grazes just metres from a pride of stalking lions. With every step, the herd churns up the dry Serengeti plain, whipping it into a dusty fog. Shoulders sunken and chins buried, all that's visible of the lions are twitching ears amongst the dry grass.

It's time.

As one, the lionesses rise at a charge. High-pitched squeals ring throughout the herd of zebra as they scatter in every direction. Poised as they bound, the lions surround the patterned mass, isolating their target amid the dust. Left and right, twisting and turning, in a dazzling display the zebras avoid the swiping claws as the pride attempt to coordinate their efforts. The lions fixate on a smaller zebra making the least headway in the getaway. They sprint together as the lone zebra jots and zags across the open plain. The longer time passes, the further it gains. The lionesses' decision has been made too late. The advantages of surprise are now lost. The zebra is in the clear.

The hunt is over.

While powerful, near-200kg predators, this isn't an unfamiliar experience for the lions. On average they will only succeed with one hunt in every four.[1] On the other hand, with roughly 300 million years of evolution behind them, the elegant, slight and dainty dragonflies seem to have the knack of getting it right virtually every time. These ruthless killers intercept their prey with a 95% success rate.[2] They may well be the most efficient hunters in the animal kingdom. What's their secret?

By inserting a tiny probe into the dragonfly brain, researchers have pinpointed some of the traits that allow it to hunt so successfully.[3] Perhaps the most remarkable feature is that it possesses neurons that, once the dragonfly has locked onto a target, ensure that other nearby prey have virtually no influence. It's as if they're wearing blinkers and additional distractions are completely blocked out. The dragonfly has an amazing ability for selective attention, being able to focus on a single insect within a swarm.

Its brain is wired to choose.

MORE OF ANYTHING?

"More of everything!"

Choice is instinctively attractive. When rats are placed in a maze and given the choice between a direct path to food, or a branched path to the very same reward (which requires additional choices to be made), nearly every rat decides to take the option of a branching path.[4] In her book, *The Art of Choosing*, Columbia's Professor Sheena Iyengar shares that this inclination to value choice extends even further, to pigeons and monkeys trained to press buttons for food.[5] They also have a preference for conditions with multiple buttons. If all they valued was food, then there would be an easier way. It seems they also liked the choice.

In humans, choice is almost universally seen to be positive. No one wants to be choosing between vanilla or vanilla, and the response "I had no choice" is rarely positive. The more options we have, the greater the chance we feel we'll find what we want. The more choice we have, the freer we feel we are in making our decisions and the more confident we are that we've exhausted all options, removing the uncertainty that there's something better still out there. When it comes to choice, more *is* more.

Or so we're told.

The problem is, too many choices can also make people less satisfied with their decisions,[6] less confident that they have chosen the best option,[7] more likely to regret,[8] defer,[9] or reverse a choice.[10] Australian 'Behaviour Explainer' Bri Williams likens this to arriving at an empty parking lot. The turmoil we experience driving around to find the *perfect* space can be more painful than if there was only one spot remaining. In fact, Iyengar argues that the regret experienced over these lost options is often greater than the joy we feel from the choices that we ultimately make. When faced with (as some sources[11] suggest) a crippling 35,000 choices every day, it's not surprising that we're not always as happy with our decisions as we could be.

Difficulty in making decisions doesn't just influence trivial choices like where we park our car, or the shampoo we pick in a store, it can have significant impacts on our careers, long-term health and financial security. When researchers from Columbia University analysed more than three-quarters of a million individuals associated with a leading investment group, the team found that for every additional ten retirement savings funds available, participation declined by about two percentage points.[12] In essence, the more options available, the fewer people went on to save for their retirement. "The fact that some choice is good doesn't necessarily mean that more choice is better," reinforces psychologist Barry Schwartz.[13] He calls this the *paradox of choice*.

LESSER OF TWO EVILS

Counter-intuitively, particularly given our new found knowledge of the paradox of choice, one solution to aid decision making is actually *adding* options to the mix – even if these choices are rarely selected themselves.

Across several species it has been found that when we are choosing between two alternatives, the addition of a third inferior or less attractive option (a decoy) can influence and aid our decisions. When monkeys are trained to differentiate between the different orientation and size of shapes, their judgement is impacted by the presence of a decoy stimulus, such as one that's clearly smaller than the target shape, helping to reinforce their decision.[14] Similarly, when Canada jays are tasked with retrieving raisins from the end of a tunnel, when first presented with a single raisin 28 cm from one tunnel entrance, or two raisins placed 56 cm down another, the birds opt for the smaller yet closer reward in 80% of trials. However, when a third tunnel containing two raisins is introduced further away (84 cm), preference for the closest raisin fell to 64%, while the two raisins at 56 cm were now taken in 33% of trials.[15] Now, imagine that you're in the market for a mobile phone. One phone has a fantastic camera but poor battery life. The other has a good battery but a poor camera. It's a hard trade-off to make, right? In this instance, our preference may be shifted if the offer is accompanied by a third mobile phone that has a good camera but even *worse* battery life. It's like adding the same number of raisins further away. It's a decoy. While you might see this as just a technique to meddle with small birds or shift mobile phones, we can apply a similar evolved solution when encouraging the uptake of proactive health screening or retirement savings plans.[16]

The leading argument is that decisional short-cuts, like navigating via a decoy, were favoured by natural selection because of their computational efficiency.[17] Basically, over time, an evolutionary trade-off has been made between the speed of processing and the quality of the decision that's reached. It's another evolved solution. As for the monkeys, jays and mobile phone shoppers above, by having an additional frame of reference, an easy or sacrificial loser, we can help choosers feel less overwhelmed by the options available, shaping their decisions.

By appreciating the limitations of the evolved human brain in managing the complexity of the decisions we're faced with, recognising that we view the world relatively, not absolutely, we can begin to aid decision making, without removing or limiting choice itself.

We can become *choice architects*.

ARCHITECTING CHOICE

Initially coined by Richard Thaler and Cass Sunstein, choice architecture is a term used to describe how the decisions we make are influenced by the choice's layout, sequencing or framing. To quote the pair: "Decision makers don't make choices in a vacuum."[18] The environment a decision is made within can have an important impact on our final choice and, as the duo write, "Apparently insignificant details can have major impacts on people's behavior."[19] Just as we have explored with 'decoys', regularly, subtle features can have significant and, on occasion, counter-intuitive impacts. Today, instead of drowning in choice, we can recognise several evolved solutions that have emerged to help us architect it. With them, we can work to make the decisions of our customers, and ourselves, easier, while helping others to feel more comfortable with the decision they have made.

In the following pages we will explore a series of evolved psychological solutions to help frame, simplify and reinforce decisions. Just like the merciless dragonfly, we can create the conditions within which decisions can be made easier and faster. This can mean the difference between someone choosing your product, choosing someone else's, or choosing *nothing at all.* Because every moment of every day we are choosing, even when we choose to walk away.

In a nutshell:

- Despite the attractiveness of choice, more choice typically makes decision making harder and less enjoyable.

- Psychological solutions have evolved to help frame choices to enable easier and faster decision making.

- By applying these solutions within your own context, you can aid decision making without limiting choice.

CHAPTER 11
Go with the Flow

PSYCHOLOGICAL PRINCIPLE:
DEFAULTS

ONE OF THE most obvious traits that make us human is our big brain. Compared to other primates, our brain-to-body mass ratio is roughly three times larger than that of our closest cousins. It's so big, the human brain has literally evolved to fold in on itself to maximise the surface area within our skull. However, while universally appreciated for its size, the reason our brains grew so large remains one of the great questions in human evolution.

Although there is little consensus, there are several explanations as to why our brains mushroomed so dramatically over the course of our history. One hypothesis suggests the rapid growth of our brain was due to changes to our environment and our own migration from the equator.[1] This made it harder to find, hunt or remember sources of food, therefore we needed bigger brains in order to find sources of sustenance. Another theory is that the requirement for social cooperation and competition increased, which favoured those with brains big enough to anticipate the actions of others.[2] A third suggestion relates to the reproductive benefits of the accumulation of knowledge. In essence, those who were more likely to teach others or learn information were also more likely to reproduce.[3] Today, we can achieve amazing things with these hefty brains of ours. They help us write poetry, script code, solve algebra and compose music. But they also come at a cost. There are huge trade-offs involved in what is a fairly recent ballooning of our brain. Although only 2% of our body weight, our brains slurp up about 20% of our glucose-derived energy.[4] They're incredibly greedy organs.

Unsurprisingly (knowing the tendency of our large brains to guzzle energy), one of the most consistent takeaways from cognitive and psychological research is that sections of our brain believed to have evolved more recently (our System 2), are inherently lazy.[5] In most cases, our System 2 is happy to go with the flow of the decisions and recommendations made by our System 1 (our evolutionarily older brain) because constant interjection is simply too costly. As a result, solutions that work on low-effort mode – encouraging inertia or inciting the desired behaviour without the need for conscious engagement – are ultimately more likely to shape a decision. We've learnt that something as simple as creating a default choice (an option that is already pre-selected or assumed) can significantly shape decisional and behavioural outcomes.

DEFAULTED DECISIONS

In applied behavioural science, the use of defaults is one of the most robust and consistent solutions that has been assessed. In 2019, a meta-analysis of 58 studies (including over 70,000 participants) found that defaults consistently impact our decisions.[*6]

As an example, beginning in October 2006 the Walt Disney Company changed the default sides and beverage selection offered with all kids' meals at their restaurants. Prior to this, meals were routinely served with fries and a soft drink. With the change, the default became servings of fruit or baby carrots, while the default beverages changed to low-fat milk, water, or juice. An analysis of all 145 restaurants found that 48% and 66% of guests accepted healthy default sides and beverages respectively, reducing calories by 21%, fat by 44% and sodium by 43% for kids' meal sides and beverages – an impressive outcome from what could be considered a small shift to a menu's design.[7] From increasing organ donation rates to boosting retirement savings, defaults continue to be heralded for driving significant outcomes across multiple behavioural challenges.[8]

One reason defaults are believed to work is that they encourage the status quo and help us to avoid cognitive investment, a prospect that's attractive to our lazy (and expensive) human brain. It is also argued that defaults benefit from additional, more subtle, psychological factors – like implicit endorsement or social proof, conveying the expectations of what the decision maker *should* do.[9] For example, by only illustrating the temperature choice 38°C on the shower tap (in the following image), a natural default for the appropriate temperature to shower with is created, anchoring our decisions and guiding our actions ("What!? You want 40°C, you lunatic?"). Similarly, despite the smorgasbord of paid channels available to consumers today (and accessible by the click of a few buttons), by embedding Netflix and Amazon into their remote controls LG create an

---

* On average, defaults shifted decisions by 0.63 to 0.68 standard deviations.

Image 20 - Defaulted decisions: (top) by only referencing 38°C, this tap creates a default shower temperature (it also works to anchor our further decisions); (bottom) by championing Netflix and Amazon on the remote, LG defaults these providers over others (irrespective of their universal access).

implicit default, an endorsement, guiding our choices to these options first.

By enabling all options, but assuming a preference or default selection, we can once again aid decision making without actually limiting choice itself.

AIDING DECISIONS: INNOVATION CHECKLIST

1. How might we pre-select a beneficial outcome as default?*

2. How might we signal a desired or anticipated response?

3. How might we frame the decision in a way assuming a desired action?

DON'T GO CHANGING

Hosting a variety of tropical forest habitats, the Atlantic Forest of South America is one of the richest ecosystems on earth. Long ago it covered 1.3 million square kilometres, nearly one-tenth of the South American continent. Today, only 12% remains, surviving largely in small, degraded patches and protected areas.

In defence of this rainforest's steady decay, for over thirty years the non-profit foundation SOS Mata Atlantica has campaigned to raise awareness of the impacts of the pollution, deforestation and over-consumption of resources that affect the area. In 2009, they partnered with F/Nazca Saatchi & Saatchi to launch one of their most effective campaigns. To succeed, the team realised that the solution was not tasking people to do more, but to expect less.

"Our challenge was not to be another annoying eco campaign," copywriter Eduardo Lima told me. "We didn't want the idea to be too complex. We didn't want to give people work." Investigating

---

* We need to be particularly careful of unethical choice architecture or the use of 'sludges' here (depending on the outcome to an individual). While defaults have been illustrated to be effective in driving behavioural change, a significant limitation is the inaction of the decision maker. An alternative strategy to the opt-out/default has been found to require people to make an *active choice*.

the over-consumption of freshwater, the creative team identified that if a household avoids just one toilet flush a day, it can save up to 4,380 litres of water every year. "We then discovered that peeing in the shower was not unhygienic... Bingo!" So, rather than stopping what people were doing (there's evidence suggesting that most people do this on occasion anyway) or encouraging high-engagement water conservation activities, the campaign promoted a surprising water-saving solution: "Pee in the shower" (or "*Xixi no banho*" in Portuguese). The campaign itself features animated silhouettes happily peeing away behind a shower curtain. While the entire campaign was in Portuguese, the global attention it received illustrated the idea's universality. Without media spend, the campaign generated over $20 million of media coverage, with the team calculating that some 18.5 billion litres of water were saved in Brazil in one year alone.[10] Rather than breaking the status quo and seeking incremental activity, "Pee in the shower" gave permission for an existing behaviour. It encouraged people to go with the flow – quite literally.

In painful irony, contracting an infection is one of the most common adverse events to occur in hospital. In 2011 alone, over 700,000 people in the US contracted diseases while hospitalised, an alarming statistic that contributes to significant morbidity and mortality, while placing a heavy financial burden on healthcare systems across the globe.[11] To help busy hospital staff sanitise their hands between appointments, thus reducing the incidence of contamination, medical sanitiser company Altitude Medical has developed a clever technical and psychological innovation that 'bakes' the cleaning moment into daily routines. Their innovation, the PullClean, makes hand hygiene a default by embedding sanitiser dispensing units into door handles at critical points of contamination. Jon Horbaly, CEO of Altitude Medical, told me, "While the user may choose not to sanitise, that is now a conscious decision the user can make because they're touching the dispenser within the door handle every time they open the door." The approach appears to work, at least according to one trial published in the *American Journal of Infection Control*.[12] In this study, Johns Hopkins researchers tested the PullClean at a ward in Baltimore, finding that hand hygiene compliance increased from 25% to 77%. By making sanitation a defaulted and more automatic behaviour, instead of expecting people to go out of their way, their design builds the assumption – the default – that every time you open a door, you sanitise.

Inappropriate hand hygiene is clearly a challenge recognised beyond the walls of our hospitals. Even prior to the Covid-19 pandemic, poor handwashing has contributed heavily to illness- and infection-related death across the planet, particularly in areas where most people eat with their hands. Tragically, in India alone, more than 1,000 children die every day as a result of poor hand hygiene.[13] In 2017, seeking to help Indian children clean their hands more thoroughly at school, India's premier soap brand, Savlon India, partnered with Ogilvy Mumbai. Identifying that most of the country's rural schools still used chalk and slate to write, they developed *Healthy Hands Chalk Sticks*, an innovation which made the washing of hands less effortful by creating sticks of chalk infused with soap granules. When used to write, the chalk powder collected on kids' hands and turned into cleansing soap when in contact with water. With little deviation in the children's existing behaviour, the team helped make using soap their default.*

As we have explored in this chapter, the use of defaults is one of the strongest and most consistent solutions that has evolved to shape decision making and, ultimately, change behaviour. While presenting opt-in or opt-out choices is one way this psychological

---

* Of course, we must recognise that less choice was associated with this specific innovation, as when the children wrote with Healthy Hands Chalk Sticks the outcome was almost inevitable.

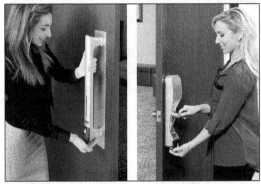

Image 21 – Don't go changing: (top) SOS Mata Atlantica encouraging Brazilians to "Pee in the shower" to save water; (middle) PullClean defaults the sanitation moment by embedding hand cleaner in door handles; (bottom) Savlon Chalk Sticks makes using soap the default for Indian school children.

principle presents itself, we can also learn from a plethora of other ideas that have convergently evolved to exploit the power of human indecision and the benefits of maintaining the status quo. From encouraging an existing behaviour to rewind the degradation of one of the world's most precious ecosystems (it can be as simple as peeing in the shower), to embedding hand hygiene within an existing system (be it a Boston hospital or an Indian schoolyard), by understanding the power of defaults we can work to guide decision making and change behaviour, one individual at a time.

AIDING DECISIONS: INNOVATION CHECKLIST

1. How might we embed our desired outcome into an existing decision?

2. What frequent choice could we bundle our desired decision with?

3. How might we bake a desired outcome into an existing behaviour?

CHAPTER 12
Easy Peasy, Lemon Squeezy

PSYCHOLOGICAL PRINCIPLES:
SALIENCE, CONCRETENESS, PROMPTS

A T 8 AM on 12 March 1938, Adolf Hitler's German Army crossed the border into Austria unopposed. Less than a month later, the annexation of Austria was retroactively sanctioned in a referendum decided by a single ballot. It simply asked the Austrian people, "Do you agree with the reunification of Austria with the German Reich that was enacted on 13 March 1938 and do you vote for the list of our leader Adolf Hitler?" This vote led to the Third Reich swallowing Austria with almost unanimous support. In fact, it is reported that more than 99.75% of Austrian voters supported a union with Germany.[1]

But there was a catch.

BIGGER IS BETTER

In biology, a flower's colour, contrast and size act as communication strategies to attract pollinators like bees and birds. It's been found that flowers displaying more saturated and high-contrasting colours are easily detected and more frequently visited by bees than less conspicuous flowers.[2] In fact, when investigating the trade-off between speed and accuracy when bumble bees arrive upon new foraging areas, one research team found that when the flowers were larger – therefore more easily detectable – the bees no longer considered the location of high-rewarding flowers (those rich with pollen) and simply flew between flowers more quickly (suggesting that rapid foraging might be a better choice than slower, more accurate foraging).[3,4]

Just like bees, we make decisions heavily influenced by what our attention is drawn to, as well as options that are most intuitive or accessible. Because of this, scale, contrast and luminance all help to guide a decision by attracting our attention. For humans, as it seems with bees, the clearer the cue, the lighter the cognitive load, the easier and faster it is for us to decide.

So what happened in Austria?

Well, while it must be said that there was some genuine enthusiasm for the country's loss of independence, among several elements of voter coercion (reportedly votes were cast under supervision of campaign workers, with no booths or envelopes to ensure privacy), one of the most striking features of the referendum was that the voting form made a clear signal to Hitler's appointment. Specifically, the selection circle for "*Ja*" (Yes) was roughly three times the size as that for "*Nein*" (No). Although it might be argued that people weren't forced to vote, the *size* of the options (rather than the creation of a default) 'helped' people to understand which choice was the expected or 'correct' one.

Eighty years following Hitler's annexation of Austria, in a very different European context, inadvertently or by design, similar ballot challenges hit the front pages in the UK. "Brexit Party logo 'subconsciously manipulates voters into backing Farage,'" wrote the *Metro UK* on Monday, 13 May 2019.[5] Okay, now what was the controversy this time?

In another speculated act of ballot manipulation, British anti-Brexit 'Remainer' audiences claimed that, when seen on the ballot, the Brexit logo worked to send people subliminal messages to sway their vote. It was argued that the Brexit logo, a giant arrow pointing to the right, literally prompted people where to mark *X*, giving an "unfair advantage to the Brexit Party."[6] Writing to the Metro, Richard Bentall, professor of clinical psychology at the University of Sheffield, claimed, "You should not require a psychologist with three decades of research experience to point out to you that this is an obvious cue to vote for the party." He continued, "You might as well put a bright red ring around the party's choice box." (That would not have been historically unprecedented, mind you…)

Selections that are prioritised, or that our attention is drawn to, are the ones we're more likely to follow through with. In the end – and not passing judgement on the intent or impact of this subtle cue on the vote itself – the Brexit Party became the largest single national party in the European Parliament.

While different shapes and sizes are often used to attract attention, this doesn't always mean that a message or 'ask' is comprehended. For this, we need to better understand additional factors impacting *processing fluency*.

Image 22 – Salient cues guide decisions: (top) Austrian Anschluss referendum ballot 'helping' people to vote; (middle) Brexit Party logo and ballot; (bottom) salient pay point 'hack' guiding our eyes and subsequently, our decisions.

AIDING DECISIONS: INNOVATION CHECKLIST

1. How might we use colour, contrast or size to direct attention?

2. What salient cues could we add to reinforce the 'expected' decision?

3. How might we otherwise guide attention to our desired outcome?

A THOUSAND WORDS

On Sunday 8 September 1940 a young apprentice mechanic named Marcel Ravidat took his dog for a walk in the Dordogne countryside, southwest France.

Climbing the hill that rises above Montignac, Ravidat's dog, Robot, bolted in pursuit of a fox. Hotfooting it behind him, Ravidat was luckily able to catch the dog just before it leapt into what looked like an exceedingly deep hole. Surprised by the discovery and thinking that Robot had found the legendary tunnel to the Montignac castle, with no rope or lantern Ravidat went home to prepare for his return.

Four days later, Ravidat went back to the hillside with three other teenagers. After dropping stones into the chasm to gauge its depth, the boys cleared the entrance. Guided by a dim light, Ravidat slipped into the darkness headfirst. Hoping for hidden treasure, he found himself in an unexpected yet instantly recognisable world.

Intuitively, we all know that our visual sense is powerful. Whether it's a ballot paper that subtly guides our eyes where to vote, or a bee that's drawn to the colour, size or contrast of a flower, salient signals capture our attention and aid decision making. We process visual stimulation at lightning speed, with images helping us to comprehend information efficiently. As we know from the cliché, a picture's worth a thousand words. Once again, evolutionary processes can begin to explain our natural affinity for imagery and visual cues.

The ability to encode and remember various aspects of our visual environment must have been beneficial for survival. In fact, the processing of imagery has been so vital that, throughout human existence, our visual system has evolved to process multiple images simultaneously. In contrast, text – comprehension of which developed more recently in human history – must still be scanned one character at a time.

Simply put, our early ancestors didn't sit around in caves writing sonnets; they drew pictures.

As Ravidat's eyes adjusted to the darkness, an ancient story revealed itself. Painted throughout the honeycombed walls of the limestone cave was a collection instantly recognisable as bulls, horses and stags: a series of ancient artworks dating back long before Stonehenge and the Pyramids of Giza. The boys had discovered the Lascaux caves. Although the caves had been painted by Palaeolithic inhabitants, Ravidat's instant comprehension helps us understand the transcendent power of imagery, not only enabling us to process information but aiding our decision making. Images make things *concrete*. Just as adding a decoy option can make it easier for us to compare relative choices, by increasing the concreteness of available options (particularly when faced with abstraction) we increase processing fluency, making comprehension and, ultimately, decision making, easier.

Concreteness increases processing fluency, making decisions quicker and easier.

The increased speed and ease of processing visual and concrete information has been explained by something known as *dual-coding theory*.[7] Imagine visiting the Louvre and seeing the phenomenon that is the *Mona Lisa*. Because both visual and verbal information is used to code pictures, we not only recognise a smiling woman looking back at us (visual coding), we also recognise it as the *Mona Lisa* (verbal coding). This same processing advantage also occurs with more concrete words. For example, concrete words (like *chair*) activate image-based codes to a greater degree than abstract words (like *equal*), resulting in a processing advantage.[8] Not only has providing concreteness helped to capture stories for many thousands of years, we'll soon see it's an adaptation that aids foreigners to safely select their sushi in Osaka. It can increase the effectiveness of modern-day safety communications, and can even help to guide appropriate decisions at recycling stations. When it comes to aiding decision making, the more *concrete*, the better.

At the end of World War II, five years after the discovery of the Lascaux caves, thousands of American servicemen were posted to Japan. Unfamiliar with both the language and local cuisine, deciding what to eat risked becoming a dangerous gamble for these naïve arrivals. Fortunately, instead of complex menus written in unintelligible Japanese, they were greeted with a powerful decision aid. All they had to do was point.

Known as *sampuru* (from the word *sample*), beautifully detailed hand-crafted wax or plastic replicas of food are commonly displayed in Japanese restaurants, helping people to see what they're ordering. Why not just print it, you ask? Surprisingly, *sampuru* didn't originate to help these American foreigners. It's actually an innovation that began nearly 100 years ago, a time before the reproduction of colour photography was common. Today, whether it's the topping on your ramen or the coloured sprinkles on your ice-cream sundae, *sampuru* are so wonderfully precise they remove almost every element of abstraction; you know exactly what you're going to get. They're *concrete*.

In safety communications, the use of imagery is also frequently recommended when looking to quickly deliver information and inform a safe decision. Here, once again, more often than not, it pays to be concrete with the use of clear imagery in communications. Taking this a step further, the Banana Cone is a good (and fun) example of how concreteness has evolved and adapted in the wild. A safety sign shaped like a slippery banana peel, through its concreteness and strong associations, it short-cuts the need for more complex information to land its message. Admittedly, there is cultural bias involved in the 'banana peel slip' (a history which dates back to the importation of bananas into New York during the 1800s) but even so, according to a 2015 study conducted by the brand, it seems to work.

Comparing the effectiveness of some of the most common caution signs and cones, the study of 246 people found that the Banana Cone significantly outperformed all other products examined (on elements like attention and comprehension).[9] On some measures, it's claimed to be more than 22 times as effective as standard safety A-Frames. Their innovative design draws more attention, intuitively and immediately notifying people of slippery conditions. It's both salient and concrete.

Just as Ravidat would have found it difficult to understand the walls of the Lascaux caves if they were decorated in ancient

Greek script (and not painted images), and American soldiers would have been left high, dry and hungry walking the streets of Japan without *sampuru*, modern-day airports are also valuable contexts to explore how communications have evolved under particular linguistic constraints. Because the shared familiarity of any one language is not guaranteed in airports, intuitive and concrete communication isn't just beneficial – it's imperative. In Singapore's Changi airport, for example, rather than just having bins with different signs labelled *Newspapers*, *Cans* and *Bottles* (as concrete as these words are, they're concretely English), they have bins shaped in the form of these key recyclates. By leading with a more familiar and easily accessible visual language, like seeing bulls on the walls of the Lascaux caves, they make it virtually impossible for us to get it wrong.

From bumble bees to ballots, through unconscious evolution or designed intent, we've explored how bigger, clearer and more concrete is better. By considering our attention and processing power, and designing the most intuitive response, we can, in essence, create latent choices within an environment.

Without limiting the options available, we can aid decision making.

AIDING DECISIONS: INNOVATION CHECKLIST

1. How might we use concrete words, images or other aids to simplify our choice set?

2. How might we help people to clearly see the outcome of their decisions (think *sampuru*)?

3. What is an associated concrete concept that would aid comprehension of something more abstract?

Image 23 – Concreteness & processing fluency: (top) plastic *sampuru* displayed in a Japanese restaurant window; (middle) the Banana Cone in action; (bottom) recyclate-shaped bins at Changi airport, Singapore.

FINDING THE RIGHT WORDS

Sadly, I recently needed to send flowers following the passing of a close friend's mother. I'm sure I'm not alone in finding these scenarios quite tough. Paralysed by indecision and the fear of coming across as contrived, I risked entering yet another scenario where, ashamedly, I've sent nothing at all. Thankfully, this time was different.

I was offered a lifeline.

> *"Yeah, I didn't write this, but whatever they wrote,*
> *I think the same thing."*
>
> —JERRY SEINFELD

In 2018, the market value of greetings cards in the UK was estimated at £1.57bn.[10] That's a lot of love. There's much evolved psychology underpinning this booming industry, including trust-reinforcing costly signalling.*

On another level it's a product built on making communication *easier*. While the pressure to be authentic assumes we should all look deep into ourselves, in reality, people look to others for help. Research has found that many people find it difficult to express themselves through the written word, looking to cards to help them find the right words.[11] "How do others express emotion?" or, "What seems to have worked in the past?" Seeing the value of providing this specific support, in 2007 Hallmark released an entirely new line of cards, helping people

---

* Interestingly, only 15–20% of cards are purchased by men, the figure rising to 45% for Valentine's Day. During this period, it's reported that producers create larger cards sold at higher price points, reasoning that because men feel anxious about what kind of card is expected, they gravitate towards more expensive-looking cards.

to communicate in situations that had previously been ignored. If someone has just been informed that they have cancer or are experiencing depression, "Get Well Soon" just doesn't cut it. Explaining Hallmark's research to NBC News, Theresa Steffens, an assistant product manager at the brand outlined, "They said, 'I don't know what to say during a difficult time, so I don't say anything at all.'"[12] (Sound familiar?)

In my situation, once I had decided on the flowers I wanted to send, predicting my need for an emotional crutch, a pop-up appeared on the screen. "Lost for Words?" it asked. You bet I was. In one click, just like having three different Hallmark cards magically appear in front of me, I was provided with a selection of pre-written messages that I could build from. By offering to start the process, pre-filling elements of my response, yet enabling co-creation, this helped me to quickly decide on something I was comfortable with. My condolences were on their way.

By providing prompts and pre-written examples, the "Lost for Words?" feature helped me to navigate a tricky social and emotional decision. Critically, a similar strategy has also evolved in scenarios where the constraints are not related to emotional indecision but are made harder by complexity or inconvenience. By doing some of the hard work upfront, it seems we can reduce the cognitive load, making decisions and completion easier.

A little while ago I noticed when playing with my young daughter that this is a shared strategy that's evolved to assist decisions when completing a children's puzzle. Whether it's a tractor or a giraffe, having the image of the appropriate picture embossed into the board makes it infinitely easier for her to decide which piece goes where. While an extreme example, it's a powerful illustration of how prompts can help to guide our decisions from a very early age.

With the acceleration of predictive technology, more sophisticated suggested decisions are now all around us. Word prediction is helping people enter text more quickly and accurately, with evidence that this technology is providing 'keystroke savings' of up to 45%.[13] Our mobile phones offer predictive text, social platforms like Facebook and LinkedIn aid responses by providing recommended phrases, email systems like Gmail can finish your sentences for you, and Apple even claim to be able to predict what you're likely to say next *no matter who you're saying it to.*[14] It's a little *1984*, isn't it?

If difficulty finding the right words can make it hard to observe our social commitments (like staying *Valentine's* compliant), it's certainly an issue when attempting to remain *tax* compliant. No one likes doing their tax (that's safe to say, right?) and for many of us, it's certainly not easy. Pre-filling responses appears to work here too. In 2009 McKinsey conducted a benchmarking study of tax administrations in 13 countries and reported that "Most high performers tend to prepopulate all the fields for individuals' tax forms."[15] Akin to providing pre-written copy on a condolence card, pre-filling complex tax information removes much of the mental effort associated with submitting a form.

Accessing financial assistance for college in the United States is equally tough, with individuals needing to complete a lengthy application with more than a hundred detailed questions. Because of its complexity and inconvenience, many are deterred from completing it, exacerbating the vast enrolment gap between high- and low-income students. Once again, with this scenario it's been found that removing some of the cognitive burden by pre-filling and providing streamlined support can also make a significant difference. Some universities, having introduced software that helps answer about two-thirds of the questions, in addition to a 10-minute interview and submission support, found that applicants were eight percentage points more likely to attend university the following year.[16]

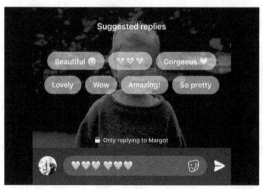

Image 24 – Decisional prompts: (top) "Lost for words?" prompt on florist website; (middle) puzzle prompts make piece selection easier; (bottom) Facebook's suggested replies helps to determine quick, appropriate responses.

Whether evolved from needing to send condolences, solve a puzzle or set up a bank account, by providing a prompt, pre-filling a suggested answer, or even removing a step from the process, we can help to reduce the cognitive load, guiding our decisions and facilitating our response. Although (in most cases) we remain empowered to intervene and interact, it seems some of the easiest decisions are the ones that are prompted or made for us.

AIDING DECISIONS: INNOVATION CHECKLIST

1. How might we pre-empt a likely response and complete this in advance?

2. How might we pre-complete elements of an answer or decision?

3. How might we recommend options to make it easier to choose?

CHAPTER 13
One Step at a Time

PSYCHOLOGICAL PRINCIPLE:
CHUNKING

WHEN YOU THINK about it, the fact a postcard can successfully navigate 510,000,000 km² of earth and find its way directly into your mailbox is a logistical phenomenon. But sending a postcard across the planet with near surgical precision isn't an accomplishment of logistics alone. We also need to remember and decide where to send it.

Astonishingly, according to a 2016 UK Royal Mail survey, nine in ten people find it easier to remember their postcode than their wedding anniversary, credit card pin, even their child's birthday![1] This isn't an accident or coincidence but a result of a carefully designed postcode system, with an appreciation of our evolved psychology at its core.

To support the mechanisation of mail in the 1950s, the UK needed a postal coding system that could not only divide the country into small areas but also be read by a computer and understood by a postman, all the while allowing a maximum number of permutations. As easy as that.

To help develop such a code, the Post Office turned to Cambridge University psychologists Reuben Conrad and Alan Baddeley. Two critical realisations paved the way. Firstly, the pair drew upon research discovering that short-term memory has a capacity of between five and seven pieces of information.[2] This is the reason why, by breaking down a long telephone number into smaller groups of units, or *chunks* (07-446-469-411), we make it easier to process and remember than a long string of un-chunked digits (07446469411). Secondly, they realised that number-only codes not only proved difficult to remember alone, but also have a smaller number of permutations (10 per digit, whereas letters have 26 permutations per letter). It was determined that a mixture of numbers and letters would not only aid memory, but also produce a significantly higher number of permutations.

In a 2010 interview, Baddeley recounts, "Conrad suggested that if you have a list of items, and you have an atypical one, by putting it in the middle, you boost performance."[3] Because digits are easier to recall than letters in a sequence, these were put in the middle of the code, and hard-to-recall consonants went at the easier far end. Sure enough, it worked. Baddeley continued with a chuckle, "The Canadians opted for alternating letters and digits, which we found was the worst possible solution. If you want to maximise the errors do what the Canadians did, and still do."

Today, as designed, the UK's postcodes generally consist of a combination of six or seven letters and numbers, separated, or chunked, by a space (for example, NW6 6AG). While the chunking of this information has made a lasting impact on the UK postal system, this is an evolved solution that we have deployed for centuries to intuitively and deliberatively help process complex information and make decisions.

In psychological literature, *chunking* typically refers to the process of taking individual pieces of information and grouping them or representing them as larger or smaller units (as we have seen through the development of the UK postcode, we have an upper threshold for the amount of information we can hold in our working memory). A file name like *Countries.txt* could be used to represent a file that includes the names of five countries instead of *EnglandAustraliaFranceJamaicaFiji.txt.* Here, we're chunking-up.

The concept of chunking isn't unique to human decision making, nor to the field of psychology alone. When copying the songs of adults, young zebra finches extract chunks of syllables from the song, add to them other chunks of syllables derived from one or more adults' songs, and then sing these chunks, strung together, as their own melody.[4]

Chunking also features in Altshuller's TRIZ methodology, within innovation principle no. 1: *segmentation.* In TRIZ, chunking and segmentation work to alter the value of a technical solution by dividing an object into independent parts (for example, the practice of fighting fire with mist – segmented water – to reduce water damage in houses) or making an object 'sectional' (turning couches into modular furniture or curtains into venetian blinds).

In the realm of psychological solutions, by enabling us to structure information, chunking allows us to process complex data more easily – supporting rapid decision making. Without limiting the choices available to us, the way information is chunked can make complex decisions that little bit easier – and, on occasion, decisions that appear deceptively easy, that little bit harder!

Image 25 – The SuperSchooner: to address the age-old problem of carrying four schooners at once (the standard Australian beer size), in 2020 Ogilvy Australia created the SuperSchooner. They chunked it up, making it one task, not four.

HOW TO EAT AN ELEPHANT

Think about the menu in your favourite restaurant.

It could list every item in a single alphabetised catalogue. It's a logical solution (to some degree). But approaching a menu like this also makes it near impossible for us to navigate it in a meaningful way. So instead, to help us decide, restaurants generally chunk the menu down into more meaningful categories, like starters or entrees, mains and desserts. If you're lucky, they may even chunk it down further by vegetarian, seafood, chicken or beef dishes.

Similarly, if you've ever bought something from IKEA, you'll have noticed that the flatpack shelving unit doesn't arrive with the singular instruction of "Step 1: make your FJÄLLBO." Instead, IKEA chunk it down into smaller steps to make each decision clear and the overall task more achievable.

By chunking information using colours, numbers, stages and spaces, we can create smaller, more manageable tasks and, as a result, easier choices that are far less daunting than big complex ones. Just as with the success of the UK postcode, from restaurants to online retailers, across industry we have adapted to chunk, making it cognitively easier for people to compute, process and recall information. We help people to eat the elephant, one leg at a time.

While we can chunk information down and break it into stages to make difficult decisions easier, this is a strategy that can also be deployed to reinforce the complexity of decisions at risk of appearing *too easy*. We can add friction. As we explored in the beginning of this book, people have a tendency to *magnitude match*. More units of something usually suggest a larger magnitude (because larger houses usually have more rooms, people use the number of rooms as a heuristic to judge the size of a house). For novices who may not appreciate the stark differences between two categorical decisions, chunking can again be used to frame the complexity or enormity behind what may at first appear to be a simple (or small) decision. In keeping with the theme of this section, it can be a valuable strategy when a novice thinks they're about to eat a mouse when it's really an elephant.

For instance, one of the most significant decisions we can ever make is determining the innocence or guilt of another. For some, the outcome of this decision might be a permanent criminal record. For others, it can literally mean life or death. Because of the enormity and complexity of this decision, during a trial it's imperative the jury understands the concept of *beyond a reasonable doubt* and the various burdens of proof that are required to make a criminal conviction. If there is any reasonable doubt, the jury must return a verdict of "not guilty."

To aid juror decision making, many legal firms have devised *burden of proof* charts, similar to that in Image 26. These charts offset the deceptively binary nature of the decision (guilty vs not guilty) by chunking down the multiple stages of reasonable doubt, for example: *proven not guilty, highly unlikely, less than likely, probably not, unlikely, perhaps, suspected, guilt likely* and *guilt highly likely*, all before reaching the stage of *guilt beyond reasonable doubt*. By chunking the decision and framing each stage in a way that forces consideration, decision making is aided and, hopefully, a more thorough assessment of guilt or innocence results. Akin to double-locking the front door or cross-checking the cabin on a flight (there are those checklists again), chunking is used here to create intentional friction in our decisions.

Although speculative (and certainly not the primary motivation to my understanding), I also expect that the common medical practice of chunking hypertension (blood pressure tests) results into *low-normal* and *high-normal* (rather than just *normal*) also works to ensure *high-normal* individuals don't become complacent and unknowingly cruise into *at-risk* status. Just as the *Mind the Gap* markings on the London Underground chunk a single platform into multiple zones of designated safety, chunks can be created and deployed to help frame decisions. They provide context around our options, helping us to choose without limiting our choices.

AIDING DECISIONS: INNOVATION CHECKLIST

1. How might we chunk *down* large tasks to aid decision making?

2. How might we use colour chunks or numbered steps to make choices easier?

3. How might we create additional steps to reinforce consideration and slow down deceptively simple or small decisions?

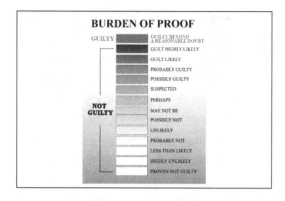

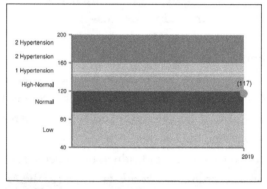

Image 26 – Chunking down to increase consideration: (top) chunked-down burden of proof; (middle) chunking-down hypertension chart; (bottom) *Mind the Gap* on London's underground network. Here, the platform is chunked into safe and unsafe zones.

ALL IN ONE

What do cinnamon, fennel seeds, star anise, Sichuan peppercorn and cloves have in common?

Although you'll likely never need to know it, these are the common ingredients of Chinese Five Spice. All are available to purchase individually, but by chunking the choices up into one decision, Five Spice, we make life that little bit easier. The opposite of chunking *down* is chunking *up*.

While chunking things down can help make complex decisions more manageable (breaking them into smaller tasks), we can also chunk up information to increase decision efficiency. For example, rather than making a series of individual decisions at McDonald's, we often opt for the meal deal (making one decision instead of three). Similarly, instead of planning every day of a summer holiday, many of us reduce the complexity of our decision by booking a packaged tour. This doesn't mean we can't spend weeks planning our own trip to Italy, we don't *have* to choose the *Nine Day Tastes of Tuscany* tour, but for many, chunking up this decision makes life that little bit easier.

By offering people one decision rather than ten, we can aid the decision-making process and, more often than not, work to maintain flexibility in choice, while offering a more attractive alternative.

AIDING DECISIONS: INNOVATION CHECKLIST

1. How might we chunk several steps *up* to ease decision making?

2. How might we repackage multiple decisions to create a single choice?

3. How might we anticipate future decisions and chunk these into one big one?

From applying *defaults*, to the use of *salience*, *prompts*, *concreteness* and *chunking*, a feast of psychological principles are available to help us aid decision making without reducing choice. These evolved solutions help us to frame our options, remove the cognitive load of our decisions and guide our choices.

Now all we need to do is **act**.

TRIGGERING ACTION

Without

FORCING A RESPONSE

CHAPTER 14
Invisible Strings

I N A TRAGIC series of events, within 36 days, physician Tobias Norton suffered two major strokes that damaged both his right and left visual cortices.* As he recovered, ordinary tests of his sight turned up nothing – he no longer reported seeing movement, colour or the presence of light. He was forced to navigate the world with a white cane.

Tobias was clinically blind.

However, despite his inability to consciously access the visual world, it was soon found that Tobias's brain still reacted to visual stimuli. When tasked with spotting differences in emotional expressions between angry or happy faces, for example, he responded correctly at a level higher than chance.

To investigate the boundaries of his perception even further, in 2008 a team of psychologists put Tobias through a particularly gruelling set of tests.[1] Researchers built an obstacle course in a long corridor. They filled the void with boxes and chairs, removed his cane and asked him to make his way to the other side. While again Tobias reported that he was unaware of seeing anything, to the psychologists' astonishment he negotiated the

---

* Name has been changed for this book. Tobias is known in the literature as TN.

corridor perfectly. Although he couldn't consciously see the world around him, it seemed Tobias had an uncanny ability to intuit his way through it. As if a puppet with invisible strings, he responded without even realising it.

Tobias had *blindsight.*

FEELING MACHINES

The phenomenon of blindsight provides a striking example of just how much occurs beneath the surface of our consciousness. Although rare, blindsight reveals the presence of less dominant perceptual pathways that have evolved in every healthy visual system, even if we're not consciously aware of them.

For example, threatening stimuli like angry faces capture our attention more readily than neutral faces.[2] Neuroimaging reveals that these kinds of images stimulate our amygdala (part of the brain believed to play a role in processing emotions) triggering a fear reaction before we even have time to realise what we're frightened of.

Our perceptual system appears hardwired to quickly perceive and respond to stimuli requiring urgent action, including changes in luminance, the arrival of new objects, or sudden movements.[3] We're even faster at detecting changes in a scene involving animals (an elephant, say) when compared with inanimate objects (like a mug).[4] In the interest of self-preservation, keeping a keen eye on our changing environment, particularly elements involving both predator and prey, was clearly important during our evolution.

The degree of influence these unconscious processes hold may surprise many. In part, this is because we often overestimate the impact of *thinking*. Being able to consciously access this part of our cognition, we tend to overestimate its power. But although it might be tempting to believe we are thinkers first – navigating the world weighing up all of the costs and benefits of an action, then making it – this simply isn't the case. As world-leading neuroscientist Antonio Damasio articulates, humans are "feeling machines that think."[5]

There are many instances where our conscious thoughts, beliefs and intentions are misaligned with our actions – sometimes referred to as the *intention-action gap*. While most of us are aware of (and deeply care about) climate change and the dangers of plastics in our oceans, we don't always act in ways that reflect this. Similarly, many of us wholeheartedly agree that it's important to wash our hands, yet still neglect to do so at critical moments. What's clear is that we can have good intentions, but if we don't trigger action, we still fail.

THE LAST MILE

When Google Glass was first announced, it offered the exciting integration of phenomenal technology and a compelling vision for the future. In the end, it just failed to be adopted.

Google had a last mile problem.

As we've recognised, the case of Glass is not without precedent or more recent comparison. This isn't an isolated example or outlier. In digital transformation programmes across the planet, where millions of dollars are often spent on upgrades to software and technology, organisational advantages (and the investments made) can be wasted if the new process or new technology is not adopted. It's too common for leaders to point to their vision and implementation strategies, roll out an awareness programme and consider it *job done*. As Dilip Soman argues in his book *The Last Mile*, this isn't a problem of technology or product and programme design, rather, the last mile problem is "one of understanding human psychology."[6]

When it comes to triggering action and focusing on the last mile, whether encouraging recycling or the adoption of a new Microsoft upgrade, it seems that once again our existing mental model is restricting us. Just as we've been brought up assuming innovation is the act of a lone genius, when it comes to triggering action, we also appear to search for solutions aligned with a particular mental model. Soman argues that we prioritise and spend a disproportionate amount on the early stages of the value creation process – creating strategy and developing the product – but less time on the choice and final behaviour. The last mile is about opening the envelope that's delivered. It's about using the tool and closing the sale – it's about triggering action. Since its initial failed launch, for example, Google Glass has received far more success being deployed in mechanical and production roles – a subtle shift positioning it as a specialised *tool*, not just an exciting piece of tech for our everyday lives. While these tactics may sometimes seem less sexy than a new corporate vision or advertising campaign, without them it's all for nought.

But triggering action isn't just about recognising the investment in an existing product or technology; it's also about appreciating the role of small actions in achieving large cumulative impacts. For example, it's been estimated that if everyone could simply sort paper, plastic, glass and aluminium, and recycle accordingly, we could reduce the waste in landfills by 75%.[7] When flying, if we all packed our bags 4 kg lighter we could save 1.3 billion litres of fuel every year (that's enough for a 747 to fly non-stop for 10 years).[8] Without switching off the lights or, indeed, switching our energy providers, we'll never reduce our emissions.

Without triggering action, we'll never achieve impact.

While there are multiple evolved psychological solutions to help trigger action without forcing a response, we will now explore just a few in greater detail, including examples of their evolved adaptations across multiple industries and categories.

The main points here are:

- A myriad of processes occur beneath conscious awareness. The strength of these unconscious drivers surprises many because we often overestimate conscious and deliberative thought.

- Our conscious intentions are often misaligned with our ultimate actions (this is sometimes known as the intention-action gap).

- By understanding evolved solutions that trigger action, we can unlock significant opportunities for impact, while realising the investments made further upstream.

CHAPTER 15
Fits like a Glove

PSYCHOLOGICAL PRINCIPLES:
PATTERN DEVIANCE & COMPLETENESS

FOLLOWING QUEEN ELIZABETH II's ascension to the throne in 1952, the Bank of Canada set wheels in motion to produce a series of notes bearing her image. But rather than attempt to summon the monarch to sit for a photograph, an image was selected from her previous sitting with celebrated Canadian portrait photographer Yousuf Karsh, just a year earlier.

While striking portraits, in each of these pictures the Queen sported a royal tiara that, for its reproduction, needed to be removed. Without the benefits of photoshop, the selected image was sent to a local Toronto graphics and engraving firm where skilled artists worked to retouch the image, removing the tiara and reproducing the Queen's hair that had been covered. Mass production of the notes began in 1954.

Just two years later, they were brought back into the spotlight.

TOAST AND TEALEAVES

*"I went to take a bite out of it, and then I saw this
lady looking back at me."*
—DIANE DUYSER

If you've ever seen an elephant floating amongst the clouds, a face in your soup, or even the buttons of your washing machine longingly watching your every move, you've likely experienced *pareidolia*: the phenomenon of seeing recognisable features in unrelated objects.

For some of us, this may have forced a second look at the front of our cars, with an irk of disbelief as it appears to smile back at us. For others, it could be the look on an intimidating 'drunken octopus' looking to start a fight from the back of a door. For Florida resident Diane Duyser, this marvel of human perception led to a major windfall when her decade-old toasted cheese sandwich, believed to bear the likeness of the Virgin Mary, sold on eBay for a whopping $28,000.

While admittedly a strange experience, there's no need to panic. Pareidolia isn't a flaw in our cognition or perception. Rather, it's a condition that's come about through years of need. Our brains have evolved as pattern-recognising machines, constantly working to create meaning from the information available, connecting the dots we see in nature. Our ancestors who were better able to identify and react quickly to faces, whether needing someone's help or to detect their ill-intent, clearly experienced some sort of survival advantage. And if they occasionally did make the mistake of seeing a face in a shadow (or a piece of toast for that matter), this was ultimately less serious than failing to spot something altogether. Fearing the rustle in the grass is a predator when it's only the wind doesn't cost us

Image 27 – Pareidolia: (top) The Queen's curls on the infamous 1954 Devil's Face Canadian note – can you see it?; (middle) Diane Duyser with her $28,000 slice of toast; (bottom) a 'drunken octopus' looking for a fight... careful.

much. But happily assuming a sabre-toothed tiger is *only* the wind is an efficient way to exit the gene pool. As a result, when believing something is real costs less than presuming it's not, we usually favour this *patternicity*, or tendency to draw conclusions. Over time, it's paid to assume the car really is smiling back at us.

On 27 March 1956, this inclination to jump to conclusions led the *Toronto Daily Star* to alert its readers to the devil's face leering from the Queen's retouched curls on the freshly pressed Canadian currency. This announcement resulted in the discontinuation of the note (with the Devil's Face Series later becoming one of the most collectable banknotes in Canadian currency). Importantly, this wasn't due to human error on the part of the Toronto engraving firm. They didn't intentionally carve an eery looking face staring out from the Queen's curls. Rather, it was the result of this evolved (and mostly helpful) element of our psychological make-up. Our ability to identify, connect and respond to patterns like this is ultimately why we're still around today. By understanding the importance of pattern recognition for the human brain, we can begin to see how evolved psychological solutions in the world around us have worked to make and break patterns, to engage us and trigger us into action.

A LITTLE TO THE LEFT

In a world where we seek patterns and crave order, it's understandable that we also find repetition and symmetry oddly satisfying. "The brain doesn't like things that are accidental," says Mary Peterson, director of the Visual Perception Laboratory at the University of Arizona.[1] Dancers in motion, a flawlessly mechanised production line, even the symmetrical wings of a butterfly. Our brain loves symmetry.

Experiments have found that symmetrical stimuli are consistently detected quicker, discriminated more accurately and remembered more frequently than asymmetrical ones.[2] We prefer symmetric art and sculpture, and we even seek symmetrical faces in potential mates.[3] Balanced and symmetrical objects appear to play by the rules that our brains are programmed to appreciate and recognise most easily. They represent order. They're economical.

> *"If we see a picture that's not straight,*
> *we go and make it level again."*
> —LOOVE BROMS, DESIGNER

It's understandable then, when things aren't quite right, a repeated pattern is disrupted or a sense of symmetry is broken, that we tend to find it all a bit uncomfortable. It's times like these that the picture straightener in us wants to jump in and correct it. Many, for example, will find the following image of a pizza strangely painful. It makes our skin crawl – even if only a little. Known as *pattern deviancy*, psychological studies show that many of us experience an aversion to broken patterns or deviations from design expectations.[4] When we see these awkward images, our inner obsessive-compulsive starts screaming.

When exploring solutions to reduce energy use in homes, Swedish interaction designer Loove Broms stumbled across a fascinating solution benefitting from this aversion to pattern deviancy. "As a designer, you can deliberately or accidentally inform people," Broms tells me. "Design is always shaping us." Broms recalls that when visiting homes for his research "We didn't just talk about electricity, we talked about lots of things. What do they value in their home? What do they think is beautiful?"

During one site visit, the connection between energy use and our evolved pattern-seeking brain struck Broms and his research partner, designer Karin Ehrnberger. The lightbulb moment, as it were. One resident identified the symbolic power of turning off the lights as creating a sense of closure and completeness. "Switching off the lights was like cleaning up after yourself." This simple insight inspired the Aware Puzzle Switch, a genius example of behavioural design. When turned off, the puzzle switch forms a seamless zebra pattern. When the lights are switched back on, the pattern is broken, and with it, we feel the very same uneasiness as when witnessing the denigrated pizza. At some level, it's like scratching nails down a chalkboard. In Broms's puzzle switch, we can see the work of tangible design: creating pattern deviancy to summon action. We *need* to set it straight.

The implication of this sort of awkwardness removal has been shown in other aspects of consumer preference, including a product's pricing. Research shows, for instance, that simply making a product's pricing appear round, clean and simple ($200 vs. $198.76) can make it just *feel* right, particularly when shopping for more emotive and less cognitive purchases.[5] By understanding our evolved pattern-recognising brain, an element of our adapted psychology that's helped us to connect the dots in nature in order to survive (as well as occasionally leading us to see religious icons in our breakfast), we can work to harness this patternicity to our advantage.

Without forcing a response, we can trigger action.

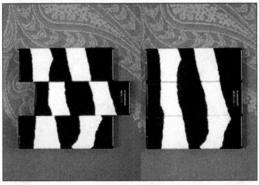

Image 28 – Pattern deviance and completeness: (top) Pizza pattern 'deviancy' makes us feel awkward; (middle) the Puzzle Switch designed by Loove Broms and Karin Ehrnberger encourages us to switch off the lights; (bottom) making a product's pricing appear round, clean and simple can help it just feel *right*.

TRIGGERING ACTIONS: INNOVATION CHECKLIST

1. How might we make our desired action *feel* familiar, symmetrical, ordered?

2. How might our solution complete an otherwise desirable pattern?

3. What pattern might we break to encourage people to react in response?

CHAPTER 16
"Marco..."

PSYCHOLOGICAL PRINCIPLE:
SALIENT FEEDBACK

I T'S COLD. FREEZING in fact. Unknowingly, your body has begun to redistribute blood to your torso, safeguarding the warmth of your vital organs. You look at your arms. Goosebumps. Vasoconstriction is slowly cutting off your capillaries, decreasing the flow of heat to your skin. Your teeth chatter. You begin to shiver.

While this all may seem like a waste of energy, you're actually experiencing an adaptive response increasing the production of heat, breaking down more and more nutrients to fuel your body's internal oven. Without knowing it, and without your control, your body is regulating its temperature using an adaptive feedback loop.

Feedback loops are critical for human survival. They not only help in important biological functions, like keeping us warm or clotting our blood, they're also the primary way our brains learn. Whether it's acquiring a new language, improving our social skills or sticking to the speed limit, we constantly rely on feedback to guide us in making connections between our actions and the outside world. We even get a little chemical kick when we receive it.

But when we don't – or can't – receive feedback, initiating learning or triggering action can be difficult. In a perfect world, we would immediately feel better the moment we begin our new diet or start exercising. Alas, this simply isn't the case. As we drive along a vast and empty highway, the absence of relative feedback from the environment whizzing past us (that we may otherwise receive when driving down a tight alley or tree-lined country road) means that it can be hard to know if we're driving at the speed limit or have slowly crept over it.

To address challenges like these, many categories have evolved to embed a sense of tangibility and responsiveness into their experiences, products and services. They have adapted to provide feedback that otherwise would have been absent. By closing this perceptual loop, these evolved solutions help trigger us into action.

FASHIONING FEEDBACK

Shockingly, it's estimated that one in four women in the United States will be raped in their lifetime.[1] Almost 75% of rapes are classified as 'date' or 'acquaintance' rapes.[2] It's a horrifying statistic.

In many of these instances, date-rape drugs are used by perpetrators to sedate their victims, the most notorious being Rohypnol. Colourless, odourless and tasteless, Rohypnol is placed into the drink of an unsuspecting victim. With no cue or visual feedback to alert that a drink's been tampered with, it's near impossible for a target to detect. That is, until it's too late.

To address some of the hidden challenges posed by drugs like Rohypnol, in August 2014 four science and engineering undergraduates from North Carolina State launched an inventive nail polish, *Undercover Colors*. Comparable to mood-changing polishes, their innovation changed colour – from pink to black – upon contact with drugs like Rohypnol. Through this clever innovation, by simply stirring her drink with her finger, a potential rape victim can now detect the presence of this otherwise invisible danger. She can be alerted to the fact that her drink has been spiked and be empowered to act.

Just as salient feedback can alert people to what they shouldn't drink, creating a sense of feedback can also work when encouraging people to drink even more.

A 2019 study published in *JAMA Pediatrics* found that a staggering 20% of children in the US didn't drink a drop of water on any given day.[3] While some didn't like how it tasted (opting for high-calorie juices and sugary drinks), others simply didn't realise how much their bodies actually need it.

Without the sugary hit or immediate buzz of a soda, convincing kids of the benefits of a humble glass of water is an uphill battle. When working with Nestlé's United for Healthier Kids initiative, Ogilvy, in partnership with MediaMonks, recognised this lack of feedback and reward when looking to encourage children in the Middle East and North Africa to drink more water (and less soda!). Their creative solution? Growing fish in children's bellies.

"What if we could persuade kids that there was a fish in their tummy, and it needs water?" recounts former Ogilvy executive creative director Will Rust. Their answer was Tummyfish.

Tummyfish is a Tamagotchi-like mobile app that helps kids to directly see the impact of drinking water, or soda, through virtual fish living inside their bellies. Activated when the phone is placed on a child's stomach, Tummyfish provides kids with an immediate portal inside their belly, seeing their Tummyfish as it swims around. When kids drink more water, the Tummyfish grows, becomes happier and more active. With every soda, the fish becomes sad and slow, and the water becomes murky.

"We found almost immediately that kids began to drink more water," reports Rust. Tummyfish functions to close the loop between an action and its impact. Rather than warning unsuspected victims of a spiked drink, this innovation helps children to see, and value, the immediate benefits of water in their bodies (as well as some of the less obvious impacts of drinking too much soda). It created a salient feedback loop to trigger kids into action.

While of lesser social significance than preventing date rape or reducing childhood obesity, comparable innovations have evolved in many parallel industries facing similar feedback challenges. For example, the clever people from Dulux paint recognised that an absence of visual feedback also wreaks havoc for exhausted DIYers looking to decorate white ceilings with white paint (it's near impossible to know where you have already painted!).

Addressing this issue, Dulux created *NeverMiss*, a ceiling paint that goes on pink (providing clear feedback against white ceilings) and dries white, helping painters create a uniform finish. Likewise, to prevent 'creepers' edging over the speed limit, radar-enabled speed displays providing real-time feedback now reduce speeding by up to 10%.[4] There are nappies that signal when they're soiled, tissues that change colour when you're nearing the end of the box, razorblades that turn green when it's time to change the blades, and even tyres that wear away to reveal the message "change tyre" when your tread becomes dangerously thin.

By creating salient feedback where there otherwise wouldn't be any, we can innovate to close this perceptual loop, cuing a desired reaction and reinforcing learning. By understanding the necessity for this feedback and identifying the patterns of psychological solutions that have evolved to generate it, we too can trigger action without needing to force it.

Image 29 – Salient feedback: (top) the Tummyfish provides salient feedback to encourage water consumption; (middle) Dulux *NeverMiss* makes it easy to paint white ceilings by going on pink, then drying white; (bottom) radar-enabled speed displays have been found to reduce speeding by up to 10%.

TRIGGERING ACTION: INNOVATION CHECKLIST

1. How might we create an obvious trigger for when action is necessary?

2. How might we turn the invisible benefits of a behaviour into tangible experiences?

3. How might we help people to realise unseen challenges ahead of time?

CHAPTER 17
Dig Your Heels In

PSYCHOLOGICAL PRINCIPLE:
REACTANCE

FOR OVER 18,000 years, the coastline of California has been devoured by the sea. With rising sea levels exacerbating the erosion, and with significant infrastructure facing ruin, understanding the nature of this phenomenon is critical for the people of the Golden State. To support their protective efforts, in 2002 the California Coastal Records Project was founded, providing researchers with free and readily accessible aerial images of the eroding coast. Of more than 12,000 images taken, one (image 3850) sparked a $50 million lawsuit.

The plaintiff was Barbra Streisand.

In 2003, singer Barbra Streisand sued Kenneth Adelman, photographer and creator of the project, for distributing aerial pictures of her mansion in Malibu. Her lawsuit claimed it was an invasion of her privacy, with the image showing access to her private residence. According to documents filed in a California court, before Streisand commenced her legal action the image of her property had been downloaded a total of six times (including twice by her own lawyers).[1]

Following her demands, interest exploded.

As news outlets around the world reported on Streisand's outrage and attempts to suppress this information, the photo quickly received more than a million views online. Coined the *Streisand effect*, this public response is a prime example of a psychological principle classified as *reactance*: a phenomenon triggered when people feel their independence is being restricted or restrained.[2] In essence, by trying to suppress information, you can actually make it more widespread.

Limit our choice, or impede our freedom, and we naturally react against it. We just can't help ourselves. Try *not* to think of a white bear, for instance.[3] It's not so easy, is it?

"SAY 'NO' DADDY!"

Having a sense of control is a fundamental human need. It's critical to our psychological wellbeing and ultimately, our survival. But because of this, when asked to do something by others, particularly those we see as different to ourselves, it's easy to feel this control is being taken away. And we *react*.

Following the tragic US school shootings of 2012, it would be reasonable to assume that gun sales dropped. Sadly, this assumption would be wrong. After demands for stricter gun control, sales went up.[4] The war on drugs is another often-cited example of reactance in society. Again, in response to reduced drug availability and heightened penalties from authorities, rather than slowing down, drug use increased.[5] As a personal favourite, inflamed by objections from the Bank of Canada, for years Canadians have joyously disfigured certain editions of their five-dollar note, altering the face of their seventh prime minister

Image 30 – Image 3850, the photograph of Barbra Streisand's Malibu mansion that triggered a $50m lawsuit.

(Sir Wilfrid Laurier) to resemble Spock from Star Trek (an act lovingly known as *Spocking*). Whether being heavily persuaded to buy a product, scolded not to walk on the grass, or subjected to overly strict rules preventing the use of your mobile in a restaurant, reactance can be triggered by stimuli all around us.

While the clear downside of this phenomenon is risk to our compliance, the reverse can also be true. Just this evening, as I tried to fill our two-year-old daughter with a healthy serving of peas and carrots, the only strategy that seemed to work was to instruct her *not* to eat them. "Say 'no', Daddy!" she begged as she defiantly guzzled them down. On occasion, it seems, we can use reactance to our advantage.

Just as parents have adapted their dinner time routines to exploit this innate desire for control, marketers, communicators and product designers have similarly evolved to implement psychological reactance to trigger a desired response. Whether communicating that a brand or product is wrong for potential customers (like why you *shouldn't* become a Monzo customer), or even challenging an audience not to read our advertising, as the *Guardian* did back in 2019, reactance-fuelling advertising is all around us.

Akin to the way we react against restrictions from authority, when information is purposefully withheld from us, it also naturally boosts curiosity and increases the information's attractiveness. This is often referred to as *information-gap theory*.[6] These knowledge gaps are painful, so we seek a similar resolution. For example, Pringles' brilliantly named WTF (What's the Flavour?) removed critical product and flavour information from their audience, creating a frustrating and intriguing itch that needed to be scratched ("What could it possibly be!?"). In 2020, in a similar fashion, Matel launched *Colour Reveal* Barbie, where "Each doll's look remains a mystery until revealed."[7] Arriving in a futuristic tube (resembling a cryogenic deep-freeze!) each Barbie starts bubblegum pink until she's re-submerged into the same tube (now filled with water), where the skin-colour, make-up and dress of the Barbie is unveiled. By better understanding our natural inclination to react against limitations, knowledge gaps and threats to our freedom, we can begin to explore solutions that trigger action in response.

TRIGGERING ACTION: INNOVATION CHECKLIST

1. What restriction might encourage people to react in a desired way?

2. What information might we withhold to create intrigue?

3. What can we ask people not to do (knowing they may be tempted to...)?

Image 31 – Reactance and information gaps: (top) Spocked Sir Wilfred Laurier; (middle) reactance triggering advertising "Don't read this poster" by the *Guardian*; (bottom) Pringles WTF creates a information gap and an itch we feel the need to scratch.

BUT YOU ARE FREE

Imagine yourself walking down the street when someone steps in front of you asking you to sign a petition. It's uncomfortable, isn't it? These unwelcome interceptions threaten our personal freedom, once again causing the itch of reactance. But they don't have to.

To better understand human responses to these sorts of reactance-inducing scenarios, in the spring of 2000 a team of social psychologists conducted a fascinating study in an urban French shopping mall.[8] Donning the inconspicuous local uniform of jeans, sneakers and a t-shirt, researchers approached a random selection of individuals and made a simple request: "Sorry, Madam, would you have some coins to take the bus, please?" (I think we can all feel the unease.)

For half of those intercepted, the researchers added a simple tweak to the request: "but you are free to accept or to refuse." Surprisingly, with this simple addition, passers-by were markedly more likely to comply. In fact, those whose freedom was reinforced gave twice as much. Several studies have since shown that this effect, classified and commonly known as the *But You Are Free* effect, is a successful means of increasing compliance in most contexts.[9] By reinforcing personal freedom and empowering our audience, it seems we can trigger people into action.

During the coronavirus pandemic, for example, when seeking to encourage social distancing on public transport, rather than signage instructing people where not to sit ("Don't sit here"), many governments adopted a more positive, freedom-affirming position of "*Please sit here.*" Similarly, as opposed to saying, "Checkout Closed" my local supermarket in Australia empowers its customers by cleverly redirecting us, "Let us serve you at another checkout."

While it may feel like brand suicide to encourage people

to shop at your competitors, by understanding the positive repercussions of the *But You Are Free* effect, it's easier for us to justify this sort of activity. Many brands have already realised the opportunities here.

In 2020, following the announcement of a second nationwide lockdown which threatened the hospitality industry in the UK, Burger King issued what was publicised as an unthinkable statement: "Order from McDonald's."[10] Not only a costly signal from the brand (illustrating its confidence and fitness – see Chapter 7), this declaration likely also benefitted from reinforcing our freedom *not* to visit the home of flame grilled beef. "Getting a Whopper is always best, but ordering a Big Mac is not such a bad thing." Australian spring water brand Cool Ridge took a similarly courageous decision by actively promoting alternative water in their advertising. Here, rather than heavy-handed persuasion, the brand acknowledged themselves as a suitable alternative for occasions "when you can't" access your reusable bottles.

Stemming from our evolved need for control, by allowing people the opportunity to refuse a choice we can increase acceptance. When it comes to closing a deal, initiating an ask, or triggering an action, it can be as simple as reminding people that they actually don't have to do it that makes all the difference. While using language like *you should*, *you ought* or *you need* risks threatening our freedom, by reminding people they are free to *consider*, or that your solution *could* be used, you can achieve a similar outcome without the same risks.

However, while one-off action is valuable, for many challenges in business and delivering societal impact today, it's the frequency of that behaviour that really counts. Our job doesn't stop when we trigger a single behaviour or encourage a one-off sale. Whether it's increasing the frequency of consuming nutritious products, committing to a long-term subscription programme

Image 32 – Reactance avoidance: (top) reactance avoiding checkout and (bottom) Cool Ridge benefiting from the *But You Are Free* effect by recommending suitable alternatives.

or remaining faithful to the local café for your daily vanilla latte, the holy grail is loyalty. Here, just as psychological principles like *pattern deviance, completeness, salient feedback* and *reactance* can help make the first move, there are a suite of evolved solutions we can learn from to **reinforce loyalty** – to *put a ring on it,* so to speak.

TRIGGERING ACTION: INNOVATION CHECKLIST

1. How might we reinforce individual control, particularly when close to acting?

2. How might we endorse an unexpected competing behaviour, reinforcing a desired one?

3. How might we illustrate that the choice is *theirs?*

CONTRADICTION 4:
BOOSTING LOYALTY
Without
INCREASING
REWARDS

CHAPTER 18
Together for the Kids

MONOGAMY, GENERALLY SPEAKING, is a losing strategy for virtually every animal on the planet. Whilst these romantic and long-term relationships may be sacred for many humans, in the animal kingdom, promiscuity prevails: only an estimated 3–5% of mammals on earth form long-term pair bonds* (we're not so good at it ourselves, just ask Jerry Springer).

When we consider an organism's goal to pass on its genes, from an evolutionary perspective the near-universal rejection of monogamy makes a lot of sense. Here, genetic variation is actually a very good thing, while bunkering down with a single lifelong partner is a costly reproductive strategy (it's putting all your eggs in one basket).

Because the genetic case against monogamy is so strong, understanding the adaptive processes of this select group of animals has long been of interest for evolutionary and behavioural ecologists. One of the most common beliefs is that monogamy evolved where offspring had a better chance of surviving if both parents participated in rearing.[1] Emperor penguin chicks, for

---

* An exclusive list including beavers, otters, wolves, a few monkeys and a selection of birds.

example, must be sheltered from predators by one parent, while another travels back and forth to the sea to gather food.

An additional view is that the difficulty of guarding or finding solitary females, particularly when widely dispersed, further shapes male sexual loyalty.[2] For the *Schistosoma mansoni*, a waterborne intestinal parasite, the relative size and the scale of the human gut means that if one is ever lucky enough to encounter a mate, it's more than happy to settle down for the long term, right there and then!

Predictably, when seeking to better understand loyalty in humans (even in forms beyond romantic relationships) there are parallels to be found in the animal kingdom. Given the abundance of choice and the vast selection of temptations that modern-day humans are surrounded with, it's maybe unsurprising that most of our behaviour also tends to be a little more promiscuous than that of an isolated parasite.

When considering loyalty in consumer behaviour, marketing science has established that high volumes of infrequent buyers remain a reality for many (there are lots of one night stands going on), even for some of the world's most famous brands. For instance, almost a quarter of Coca-Cola's yearly sales volume is driven by roughly 4% of Coca-Cola's buyers.[3] As we might expect, any opportunity to enhance this loyalty, to put a ring on it and be a little more *emperor penguin*, means big business.

SKIN IN THE GAME

One of the most common techniques to encourage consumer loyalty is to offer up a reward or exclusive bonus. In essence, to incentivise our fidelity and pay for our devotion. According to Accenture, more than 90% of companies in the US have a commercial loyalty programme, resulting in over 3.3bn loyalty memberships (that's a whopping 29 for each household!).[4]

The effectiveness and return-on-investment of many of these programmes are weak. Professor Byron Sharp of the Ehrenberg-Bass Institute in South Australia argues that in some instances expensive loyalty programmes can actually have negative impacts, as they tend to appeal to existing customers by offering them something for nothing, rather than attracting new buyers.[5] They give away rewards and incentives with little change of behaviour in return.

Thankfully, there are several evolved psychological principles where the opposite is true. One example is classified as the *sunk cost* bias. Here, instead of paying for loyalty or commitment, patterns in behaviour illustrate that someone's investment of time, money or energy towards an outcome can actually increase their tendency to pursue it.

Despite being credited with an assortment of catastrophic human failures (from disastrous investments in Concorde to the refusal to withdraw US troops from the Vietnam War), this sunk cost bias looks to be a beneficial adaptation, at least on some level. The painstaking labours of love often required from a male bird prior to copulation, like extravagant nest building, have been proposed as a crafty adaptation of sunk cost.[6] By increasing a male's investment before mating, his temptation to desert afterwards may be reduced. We could almost consider this as an evolutionary prenup.

Moving underwater, research further shows that some female fish (cichlids, for those playing at home) are easier to scare from their young when their brood is experimentally reduced, with the reverse occurring when numbers of fry are increased with foreign young.[7] With more to lose, she puts more on the line.*

---

* Female digger wasps have been found to behave in a similar manner. Those who find themselves nesting in the same burrow as another, defend it for a period proportional to her investment (the number of grasshoppers she's personally caught) rather than the 'true value' of the burrow (the total number in the shared burrow).

Building from our propensity to pursue a sunk cost, in the following chapters we will look at a series of additional evolved psychological solutions that work to boost commitment, stickability and loyalty, helping us to innovate in ways beyond costly rational incentives. We will explore adapted initiatives beyond commercial programmes, offering a more holistic perspective of how psychology and behavioural science can help us stay true to ourselves, and others, in the face of temptation. We will see how innovations have evolved to help us stick to our diets and exercise regimes, complete a course of vaccination, keep our environment clean, and keep us coming back for more.

Just as monogamy has evolved in certain circumstances beneficial for survival and reproduction, when looking to understand loyal behaviours across industry and category, we can see evolved patterns in psychological solutions and adapted ideas. Through these, we can better understand the conditions for loyalty.

Thankfully, there's more to it than just paying for it.

In short:

- Surrounded by an abundance of temptations, disloyalty reigns supreme (and putting your eggs in one basket can be a risky strategy).

- Although one strategy is to incentivise or pay for loyalty, evidence suggests the effectiveness of many 'classic' or 'rational' loyalty programmes is weak.

- Thankfully, there is a smorgasbord of evolved psychological principles that we can draw upon to help boost commitment, stickability and loyalty without increasing compensation.

CHAPTER 19
I Am My Word

PSYCHOLOGICAL PRINCIPLE:
COMMITMENT

WHEN LAURA CLARKE'S husband told her that he was being posted to the archipelago of Palau in 2015, she thought he was making some sort of a cruel joke. "When I Googled it, I thought it was a made-up place – it looked too beautiful to be real!" Clarke tells me. Run ragged by her high-pressure role in Sydney, the marketing and PR executive soon embraced this opportunity for a sea change in the heavenly cluster of Pacific Islands.

Although the world's seventh smallest nation in GDP, Palau is a heavyweight when it comes to conservation. In 1979, it was the first country to vote for a nuclear-free constitution, banning the testing of nuclear weapons, and in 2009, it turned its waters into the world's first shark sanctuary. But it was in October 2015, the year of Clarke's arrival, that Palau's leaders established one of its most historic policies: the National Marine Sanctuary Act.

This legislation banned the drilling of oil and fishing by

foreign trawlers, turning its 500,000 km² area into a fully protected marine reserve. While a monumental step for Palauan conservation, it coincided with an unfortunate influx of a new demographic of visitors who didn't share Palau's conservation culture.

"Palau has always been a high-value dive destination but in 2015, large, packaged tours started arriving on charter flights," recalls Clarke, and the collective impact of these visitors, who were not eco-aware, put pressure on Palau's pristine reef and local culture. Cumulatively, this posed a huge problem for Palau and, left unchecked, could have led to devastating erosion of environment and culture. "These package tour visitors had very little environmental awareness. They wanted to take everything and had little respect for local culture… they just didn't understand or know better."

The islands of Palau were in trouble.

> *"We've got a whole country, we've got no money, but we need to preserve this pristine environment and set a precedent."*
> —LAURA CLARKE, CO-FOUNDER, PALAU PLEDGE

"We just didn't know what to do!" recounts Clarke, following a chance conversation with Palau's first lady at a diplomatic party. Despite having some of the strictest environmental laws on the planet, with limited resources to enforce the rules across its islands, the nation felt powerless to stop the destruction of its precious ecosystem.

Believing that a marketing mindset could help address the issue, Clarke soon gathered a group of likeminded Palauan and expat women to found the Palau Legacy Project. Next they turned to their black book of contacts for help. With the

Image 33 – The Palau Pledge, asking arriving visitors to pledge to preserve the beautiful islands of Palau, created a valuable commitment device.

support of Sydney-based agency Host/Havas, the team set to work communicating Palauan customs in a way that would make the islands' visitors take notice and change their ways.

"The biggest part of the brief," recalls Seamus Higgins, executive creative director at Host/Havas, was that "We don't want to stop these tourists coming… but we need to educate them on the collective impact that they have placed on the environment of Palau."[1] The agency developed 47 ideas aimed at instilling a sense of environmental responsibility, so central to traditional Palauan culture, in its visitors. The top three of these were then taken to the president of Palau. The idea he chose was *Pledge*.

A disarmingly simple intervention, the Palau Pledge is a passport stamp with a difference. Instead of a coat of arms or departmental logo, it consists of 59 words and an empty box. The words ask travellers to commit to the preservation and protection of Palau for the land's natural inheritors: its children. The box is for the traveller's signature.

For Palau, a previously mindless security process is now a powerful commitment device.

I HEREBY SWEAR

Whether it's a presidential inauguration or an eyewitness testimony in court, swearing-in typically involves the act of raising the right hand and placing the left hand on a text. The origins and implications of this gesture are fascinating in themselves, and can tell us a lot about how ideas have evolved to generate commitment and consistency.

The practice of raising the *right* hand is believed to have originated in the central criminal court of London during the seventeenth century.[2] At the time, while judges took great pleasure doling out a range of creative punishments, they lacked the ability to maintain long-term criminal records. To help keep track of their sentencing, judges occasionally chose to punish offenders by branding letters into their right hand (T for *theft*, for example). If a convict appeared before the court again, they would first be required to raise their right hand to reveal whether they had committed any crimes or received leniency in the past. Despite significant changes to record taking (and indeed punishment), this symbolic pledge remains.

Historically, swearing with your *left* hand upon a sacred text forms a verbal contract between the oath-taker and God. Today, to respect the traditional beliefs of Canada's indigenous communities, blessed eagle feathers are also now an option for swearing oaths in all Alberta courts. In reality, *Alice in Wonderland* or *The Gruffalo* are legally just as acceptable. What remains central is that the document reflects our personal values. In 2014 US ambassador Suzi LeVine took the oath of office on an e-reader. "As cool as a copy of the Constitution from the eighteenth century would have been," LeVine said, "I wanted to use a copy that is from the twenty-first century, and that reflects my passion for technology and my hope for the future."[3]

Psychologists support this view that the most significant element of an individual's commitment is that it's aligned with their self-identity or self-concept. When we comply with our internal values, we feel good, whereas acting against our stated beliefs, evidence shows, can lead to a painful sense of regret and discomfort. It's even been found that simply drawing our attention to existing standards, like signing a university honour code before completing a test (not so different to the Palau Pledge), can be effective in curbing dishonesty.[4] Making this sort of pledge with a handwritten signature internalises this commitment even further. Our handwriting, so it seems, is worth more than the ink it's written in.

When technical glitches marred their Manchester concert in June 2009, mega-band Oasis turned to the symbolic power of a signature to rescue them. Recognising the gig's disruptions, the band sent out an eye watering £1m worth of cheques in reimbursement. "People can obviously cash them in," a spokesperson told the *Manchester Evening News* after the band offered the crowd a refund.[5] Their genius? Anticipating that fans would never take them to the bank, every cheque was hand signed by Oasis frontmen Liam and Noel Gallagher. With pen and ink alone, the band saved themselves a fortune.

Our signatures act as symbolic extensions of ourselves, explains Eileen Chou, an associate professor from the University of Virginia.[6] This isn't only valuable for fans seeking a greater connection with their heroes (as it was for Oasis), it also helps to reinforce our loyalty, commitment and compliance. We sign marriage certificates to pledge our faithfulness, and credit card receipts accepting our commitment to pay. It's even been found that patients who personally sign for their follow-up

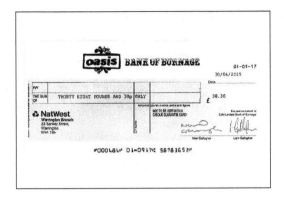

Image 34 – Oasis signed cheques: anticipating that people would never redeem them, Liam and Noel Gallagher personally signed £1m in reparations cheques for technical disruptions.

appointments are less likely to default than when receptionists act on a patient's behalf.[7]

As a representation of self, the more personal or close a commitment is to our identity, the more powerful it becomes. Just as a hand-signed baseball is worth far more than one mass-produced in a factory, research shows we're more likely to cheat when typing our names (an act that's distanced from our selves), than when handwriting a signature.[8] The symbolic value of our personal signature, a tangible extension of our identity, mustn't be underestimated.

Be it a pledge to keep the archipelago of Palau pristine for its children or a promise to our spouse or bank, patterns of evolved solutions reinforcing our commitment and loyalty are all around us. Even without the prospect of reward, by employing simple signatures and pledges we can cultivate honesty and encourage actions consistent with our values. We've found that we can help people remain loyal to others, and to themselves.

BOOSTING LOYALTY: INNOVATION CHECKLIST

1. How might we enable personal interaction (like a signature) to increase commitment to an outcome?

2. How might we encourage people to vocalise or externalise their future intentions?

3. How might a request for loyalty align with existing personal values?

YÜCEL'S CONTRACT

After his father tragically died from lung cancer, Ibrahim Yücel knew something needed to change.

In 2013, following a series of failed attempts, the heavy-smoking 42 year old from Kütahya in Turkey devised a radical solution to kick his 26-year habit. It wasn't using nicotine replacements or even a patch. It was with the help of 130 feet of copper wire.

Inspired by the helmets worn by motorbike riders, Yücel's innovative solution was to build a cage for his head, making it impossible for him to put a cigarette in his mouth ("Oh, of course!" you say). Every morning the father of three would lock his head in the cage, leaving the keys with his wife and kids as he set off for work. Although this drastic solution didn't prevent him from experiencing cravings, it did stop him from acting on them at work.

While radical, Yücel's approach isn't without parallel or comparison when it comes to commitment. The pact that Yücel made to himself and his family is often classified as a *Ulysses contract*. This refers to Homer's *Odyssey*, in which its hero Ulysses (the Romanised form of Odysseus), makes a pact with his men as they approach the deadly Sirens: creatures that used their irresistible song to lure sailors to their deaths. Wanting to experience their enchanting song without suffering the consequences, Ulysses instructs his men to put beeswax in their ears and tie him to the ship's mast. Unable to jump into the sea, Ulysses could hear their beautiful sounds and live to tell the tale.

Yücel's intervention and the mythical idea of Ulysses are both psychological solutions enabling preventative action (like locking your head in a cage) while in a cold emotional state. Conscious decisions like these limit our future choices, helping us stay true to our intentions when we're tempted or in a warm state (we see someone else smoking, for example).

If Yücel's behaviour still sounds extreme, from a psychological perspective it's comparable to evolved solutions we might all identify with when surrounded by an abundance of vices. Cutting up your credit card to prevent yourself from overspending. Deleting your Ex's phone number so you're not tempted to call them ever again. Research has even found that we tend to constrain our own purchases to slow consumption, like a regular smoker buying their cigarettes by the packet, even though they could afford a ten-pack carton (sure, it's no cage, but it's close).[9,10] Over time, a pattern of psychological solutions like these has evolved to help us stay true to our intentions.

Implementing voluntary and self-imposed commitments has been proven successful across a variety of contexts, with several commercial brands also thriving by promoting self-imposed commitments as their central proposition. The pharmaceutical Antabuse is commonly used to treat alcoholism by producing an acute sensitivity. For those who agree to take it, if they then have a drink, it induces a hangover with almost immediate effect. Similarly, for those looking to kick the habit of biting their nails, Stop'n Grow (marketed as *Willpower in a bottle*) is an invisible, odourless nail polish that's self-administered by the user. The catch? It tastes horrible.

As self-imposed commitments, consciously or unconsciously, these evolved psychological solutions bind us to our intentions. They make it easier to remain loyal to ourselves, even when conditions around us change. They tie us to the mast.

BOOSTING LOYALTY: INNOVATION CHECKLIST

1. How might we help people commit to a desired action while in a 'cold' emotional state?

2. How might we enable people to limit alternative (undesirable) future choices, now?

3. How might we help people impose an unattractive ultimatum for themselves?

HALF NOW, HALF LATER

In 2019 an estimated 5.2 million children under five years died mostly from preventable and treatable causes.[11] One of the most cost-effective approaches to prevent this tragedy is vaccination.

In 2017, to help close the immunisation gap in India, UNICEF partnered with the Indian government to develop a creative solution that would help parents to follow through with their children's vaccinations. "We created a unique range of toys so that they would keep people coming back," says Sambit Mohanty, former national creative director at advertising agency JWT in India. But this is only half the story.

While citizens of western countries may quarrel over the dangers of vaccination, incomplete and incorrect immunisation remains a significant public health problem across the planet. Although India's programme is now one of the world's largest, in 2016 38% of children still failed to receive all basic vaccines in the first year of life.[12] Reported Mohanty, "Even if they do take their child for one shot, parents don't understand that one shot isn't enough and that the child needs to complete a full vaccination." While it might feel beneficial to have one shot, as is now all too familiar from the Covid-19 pandemic, it's far from *job done*.

They were facing a problem of half measures.

Cleverly mirroring the challenge of incomplete immunisation, the team from JWT created a novel series of gifts, including small wooden elephants, sparrows and rocking horses. The brilliance was that these were only given to children one half at a time.

They were gifts of half-measures.

"Half-toys were symbolic of incomplete immunisation," says Mohanty. "The other half became an incentive to come to the camp again and complete the circle." The team found this incentivisation model to be an effective commitment, particularly in a region where education, social economic status, literacy and religious bias were limiting complete immunisation. For a country as heterogeneous as it gets, explains Mohanty, "this was a solution that crossed borders."

But this insightful approach to driving commitment through a *half now, half later* technique isn't reserved for UNICEF, nor the challenge of pharmaceutical adherence alone. While waiting for my morning coffee before work in Sydney, I experienced a similar loyalty-inducing commitment device.

During the morning rush hour, when the length of the line risked customers leaving to go elsewhere, the staff had adapted to walk up the queue with takeaway coffee cup lids, taking orders and then handing the lid to each waiting customer. Although

Image 35 – Half now, half later: (top) UNICEF half-toys (JWT India); (bottom) coffee lids handed out at Sydney's QVB, keeping long-waiting customers committed.

I can't recall my order ever being placed in advance (I always seemed to order again at the counter!), the fact I had a coffee cup lid in my hand committed me to the transaction.

By giving customers a tangible yet insignificant element of the product in advance, with negligible costs, they had sealed the deal and kept us loyal.

BOOSTING LOYALTY: INNOVATION CHECKLIST

1. What could we give to our audience that encourages them to follow through?

2. How might we create a *partial* incentive that's fully realised upon completion?

3. What can we give our audience in advance, committing their future action?

CHAPTER 20
So Close I Can Smell It

PSYCHOLOGICAL PRINCIPLES:
GOAL GRADIENT & ENDOWED PROGRESS

IMAGINE FOR A moment you're asked to play a quick game with your friend. The rules are simple: if you're able to flip a coin and both have it land on either heads or tails, there's a $1,000 reward. If the two coins don't come up the same, neither of you win. You decide to flip first. It's heads. Now, it's your friend's turn to step up to the plate. All they need to do is flip another head and the prize money is yours. They flip the coin. It goes high into the air. You both hold your breath... it's tails.

Who's to blame?

Despite the independence of each coin toss, when posed with similar scenarios under experimental conditions, studies have found that people tend to attribute more responsibility and therefore more blame to the person who tossed the coin last (i.e., your friend), rather than the person who tossed first (you).[1]

Our imagination plays a crucial role here, with thoughts of *what if* swaying our perception of responsibility, fairness and deservedness of blame. As a result, the ordering of events influences our perception of different alternatives. Early events tend to be seen as harder to influence than later events, even when both contributors have an equal impact on an outcome.

It would seem odd, for example, for Usain Bolt to be positioned on the second leg of the Jamaican Olympic 4×100m relay team and not the home stretch, even though the impact on overall race time may be negligible. To most of us, it makes intuitive sense that the fastest man to ever walk the planet assumes the greatest responsibility because, psychologically, later events simply count more. As the relay makes its way to the final bend, we feel we have more to lose.

A WHISKER AWAY

First recognised in a now-classic 1930s experiment, American psychologist Clark Hull noticed that rats show a similar pattern of response to that which we just experienced in the coin toss game, working harder during the later stages of a maze task.[2] To investigate his initial observations, Hull built a runway for his rats with electrical contacts to accurately measure the time taken for the rats to pass through each of the six-foot sections. His analysis found that the closer the rats got to the reward, the faster they ran.

Classified in behavioural science as the *goal gradient hypothesis*, similar patterns of behaviour have been witnessed in humans. Rather than invasive electrical probes, here the extent of human motivation can be measured through the time taken between purchasing items, and even increased purchase volumes. It's an evolved solution encouraging us to see it through to the end – to stay loyal.

In one study, Kivetz, Urminsky and Zheng discovered that members of a classic *buy ten, get one free* coffee rewards programme purchased more frequently as they got closer to earning a free one (on average, the time between coffee purchases decreased by about 20% throughout the programme).[3] By seeing ourselves on a journey, particularly getting closer to the outcome, we increase our motivation to continue. The closer we get, the more it counts, and the more committed we are to following through.

Now here's where it gets interesting. While a logical argument can be made that the closer we are to a goal the more valuable each progressive step, it's been found that when people are provided with artificial advancement, we also continue to show a greater persistence in achieving it. In essence, by making us *feel* closer to a reward, even if the reality has not changed, our motivation to continue is enhanced.

An innovative 2006 study illustrated this motivational 'glitch' when a group of market researchers collaborated with a local carwash.[4] The team distributed 300 loyalty cards to the carwash customers, half of which required eight washes before earning a free one while the others required ten. The key difference between these groups was that the cards requiring ten purchases were pre-stamped with two stamps (i.e., they were artificially gifted 20% progress).

Although both conditions now required eight purchases to unlock the reward (the same level of investment), the experimenters found that the redemption rate was significantly higher for those perceiving their progress to have been boosted, with 34% redeemed vs. just 19%. By creating the illusion of progress the team established that we can increase motivation to complete. They classified their discovery as the *endowed progress effect*.

Through a mixture of natural adaptation and deliberate engineering, many organisations reliant on our loyalty (or patience!) have evolved to implement what we now identify as endowed progress. My local GAIL's café in London certainly had a great grasp of this. Every loyalty card from GAIL's is printed with the first purchase pre-stamped, artificially boosting me on my journey to reward (it's the café equivalent of placing the rat in the middle of the maze).

Even modest design cues can create a sense of progress and thus enhance our motivation to continue. When landing at Heathrow airport, the wayfinding signs subtly reinforce a sense of progress for arriving passengers. Despite what we might like to think, passengers haven't actually played a role in landing the plane. However, by signalling landing as an objective that's already been achieved (tick), we feel closer to immigration and our subsequent exit (and hopefully less likely to throw up our arms in despair).

Extending this thinking, it's easy to imagine a future where airports recognise travel time that's already completed when framing the last steps remaining – "Flight BA011 from Singapore to London: 17 hours and 42 minutes travelled, only 18 minutes remaining to exit." These cues can be even subtler still. For people tracking their packages from Canada Post, even the minimalism of a progress update signifying "more than halfway" can indicate that progress is being made (irrespective of specific dates or times). Customers are thus kept committed and loyal to the cause.

While achieving predictable steps on a journey can enhance our motivation to continue – when we add a degree of variability to this mix, we can light our brains on fire.

BOOSTING LOYALTY: INNOVATION CHECKLIST

1. How might we help people to see that progress has been made?

2. What invisible steps have already been taken? How might we make these more evident for others?

3. How might we provide an artificial boost to encourage follow-through?

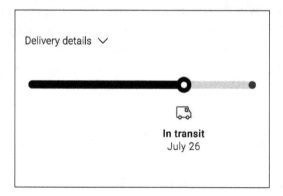

Image 36 – Goal gradient and endowed progress: (top) by pre-stamping their loyalty cards, my local GAIL's in London creates a sense of endowed progress. Similarly, Heathrow Arrivals (middle) and Canada Post (bottom) also signify advanced progress with subtle design cues.

CHAPTER 21
You Win Some,
You Lose Some

PSYCHOLOGICAL PRINCIPLE:
VARIABLE REINFORCEMENT

IT'S 1949 IN a small Harvard Laboratory.

A hungry two-year-old white Carneau pigeon enters B.F. Skinner's experimental chamber, a small space fashioned from a picnic icebox. To mask outside distractions, white noise plays into the chamber while, mounted to its side, a blower collects feathers and dust. The pigeon stands patiently on a wire mesh floor. At the end of the cage, a light snaps on, prompting the bird to peck through a one-inch hole.

Rewarding this response, grain is fed into a shallow tray below as a pen scratches across a polygraph, tracking every action. The faster the bird pecks, the steeper the line. This was the setup for B.F. Skinner's study of conditioning, a body of research that covered over 70,000 recorded hours and measured almost one-quarter of a billion responses.[1] Time and time again, Skinner's subjects learnt the cause-and-effect relationship between the cue (the light), its action (the peck) and the reward (the grain).

Then he made an unexpected discovery.

One day, after conducting a series of tests (reportedly on rats), Skinner ran out of food pellets.[2] Unwilling to interrupt his research, he abandoned his standard practice of giving food for every response, instead giving his subjects a pellet only once a minute. To his surprise, not only did they continue to respond, Skinner found that varying the rewards often resulted in *more* instances of the behaviour, even after the rewards stopped completely. It was a monumental finding, one that has shaped our understanding of reward, learning and loyalty forever.

To help us understand why variability is so rewarding, it's time for another quick thought experiment. Which would you prefer: a last-minute trip to a faraway location or to have a month's notice for the very same holiday?

Most people, it seems, would choose the second option not only because it allows them to make suitable work and childcare arrangements, it also seems our brains enjoy the *anticipation*.[3] In 2008, seeking to better understand the role of anticipation in risk taking, Stanford's Professor Brian Knutson and colleagues ran a study investigating the human brain as people gambled.[4] Rather than peak when a reward was given, as we might have expected, his team found that activity in the *nucleus accumbens*, part of our brain central to processing reward, actually increased in anticipation of a win.

It seems our brains are wired to search endlessly for the next reward, to continue to crack the code and solve the pattern, rather than sit back in satisfaction when we've achieved it. We really have evolved for the *pursuit* of happiness, and virtually nothing fuels this journey like the mystery and uncertainty of variability. From dating apps like Tinder and Bumble to slot machines, we can see the potency (sometimes dangerously so) of variable reinforcement that has evolved in products and services all around us. However, Variable Reinforcement is a psychological principle that extends beyond gamification alone. It's one that can be adapted into products and guaranteed through innovative organisational policy. Even here, sometimes you win and sometimes you don't.

VARIABILITY BAKED IN

"I thought I was going to die," reported one girl who landed one of the chips.[5]

Unless you have a serious allergy, eating a bag of Doritos isn't normally a high-risk operation. This was until June 2014, when PepsiCo launched Doritos Roulette, a creation allowing merciless friends everywhere to enjoy an entirely different corn-chip experience. "So spicy it may bring you to tears" explained the description on their website.

So what was different?

While each bag of Doritos Roulette contained mostly standard chips, in every handful there was an identical-looking super-spicy one. By applying a formula that's worked wonderfully for numerous hot-wing restaurants in the past, injecting a little anticipation and uncertainty into their experience, the humble Doritos corn chip quickly became an online sensation. Hundreds of people recorded themselves playing Doritos roulette, with the resulting content featured on everything from Buzzfeed to Good Morning America. By considering every chip as an opportunity for engagement, Doritos supercharged the anticipation of each bite. They baked variability into their experience – and people couldn't get enough of it.

Adding variability into a product isn't just a novel solution adapted by Doritos. Entire brands have also thrived through the convergent evolution of embedding anticipation and uncertainty into a product experience. Inspired by the Italian Easter tradition of giving children chocolate eggs with toys inside, in 1968 Michele Ferrero set the ambition to mass-produce a product providing a similar surprise every day. With the help of variability embedded in every egg, Kinder Surprise has earned its role as a year-round favourite, selling over 30 billion eggs since 1974.[6]

Let's be honest, it's not the chocolate, it's not even the toy. It's the anticipation produced by the uncertainty and variability of the surprise.

Staying just a little bit longer in the confectionary aisle, while best known for their work in producing 100% slave-free chocolate, Tony's has created a variable experience not by embedding uncertainty *within* their Chocolonely product, but by changing the way their product is shaped. Compared to the structured regularity of a Cadbury's block (the Manhattan of chocolate), Chocolonely has a haphazard layout whereby sometimes you break off a small piece and other times an excessively large one (it's a roadmap more closely resembling Venice). Because of this, when sharing a slab of Tony's Chocolonely in front of the telly, reaching over to your partner's lap for a piece, sometimes you win and sometimes you *really* win.

Image 37 – Variability baked in: (top) Doritos Roulette created a sense of variability and anticipation by making one in six chips super spicy; (middle) Kinder Surprise embeds anticipation in every egg; (bottom) Tony's bake variability into their Chocolonely product through its disordered structure and different sized pieces.

BOOSTING LOYALTY: INNOVATION CHECKLIST

1. How might we include an element of variability in our product experience?

2. How might we 'bake-in' an element of novelty so our product is always fresh?

3. How might we experiment with infrequent negative outcomes (think Doritos Roulette)?

PLANNED SERENDIPITY

Predictability is a strategic imperative for fast-food restaurants across the globe. From their products to their service, giants like McDonald's have thrived off their ability to offer virtually identical experiences when visited in New York or Nagasaki. Consistency brings comfort. But even in quick-service categories like this, there are moments when unexpectedness can be a good thing.

For international coffee and sandwich franchise Pret a Manger, the directive to be different comes straight from the top, particularly when it comes to customer loyalty. Rather than employing a predictable and consistent *buy ten, get one free* loyalty scheme like you might find at Starbucks or Costa, Pret's staff are encouraged to hand out a certain quota of hot drinks to customers of their choice each week, free of charge.

Michael, a barista from Pret's York Way branch in the UK told the *Guardian*, "There's no rule, it's just a nice thing to do."[7] The discretionary nature of this system means that roughly 28% of their customers have been gifted a free drink or item of food at some point.[8] Although there has been critique regarding lost data and even discrimination (oddly, a large amount of free coffees appear to be given to attractive customers), it's a compelling example of variability created at an organisational level. An unpredictable loyalty incentive generated through staff empowerment, not an algorithm.

Authorising staff to reward customers at their own discretion has meant that, for Pret, variability has become an outcome and not a formula. It's no longer about buying a certain quota for a free coffee in the future, it's about popping in every day for the chance of one at any time. While providing unexpected moments of reward and variability help to reinforce commitment (sparking our anticipation machine and setting us off to find the pattern) these evolved solutions can also work to shape our enjoyment and memory of experiences.

We've just seen how the power of *commitments, goal gradient, endowed progress* and *variable reinforcement* can help to boost loyalty. As we'll see in the next section, not all **experiences** are memorable – but just like Doritos Roulettes, some certainly are.

BOOSTING LOYALTY: INNOVATION CHECKLIST

1. How might we create a system that is variable *by design?*

2. How might we empower individual discretion to create unpredictable experiences for others?

3. How might we remove an element of unnecessary consistency or predictability?

CONTRADICTION 5:
IMPROVING EXPERIENCES
Without
CHANGING THEIR DURATION

CHAPTER 22
Brain Time

"**I**T'S IN THE corner!"

A black housefly zips across the room, narrowly escaping the clap of your hands, just after taking a bath in your gravy. It seems to have an uncanny ability to move at just the right moment.

Unphased, it strides across the kitchen bench in defiance. *Slap!* Down comes your swat. Again, it moves just in time, shifting its attention to your fruit bowl. As if it has all the time in the world, the fly moves like it's navigating a parallel universe. It's like it's in the Matrix.

Amazingly, there is some truth to this.

In 2013, a study conducted by Trinity College and the University of St Andrews revealed that a species' perception of time is related to its size.[1] From chickens to leatherback turtles, the researchers measured the neural activity of more than 30 species while showing them a series of rapid flashing lights. When flashed quickly enough, the light is perceived as a solid stream (just like our experience of watching television). However, if an animal's physiology can detect the blinking of light at higher frequencies, this illustrates their ability to see time at finer resolutions (as with the flickering of a TV). Ultimately, the more units of information that can be processed within a given time (the number of individual flashes), the slower this time feels.

To put it another way, imagine watching the second hand of a ticking clock. While humans may see this moving at a particular speed, this would appear twice as fast for a turtle (they process fewer temporal units). For a fly, each tick would feel four times slower. While *clock time* may be constant, the *perception* of time is by no means universal.

Differences in the perception of time are believed to be yet another outcome of thousands of years of evolution. Fast-moving perception is helpful for a species needing to engage in more rapid pursuits, like a hawk. At the same time, having eyes that update the brain faster than the body can react is of no advantage to survival. It would be a waste of a whale's precious energy to see the world as fast as a fly, for instance.

Critical for our story is that the experienced duration of time can also differ within our own species. That is, our experience of *clock time* and *brain time* – the difference between the minutes that pass and the time we feel has passed – can be two very different things.

THE BRAIN CLOCK

The experience of time is so essential for our survival that it is arguably one of our most finely tuned functions.

While there's still no absolute agreement on where and how time is processed in the brain, theoretical models assume that an internal clock produces subjective time units. When we turn our resources on by directing attention, through high arousal or stress, this can increase the number of pulses in an assumed unit. When this happens, we expand the duration of the time that's felt. Alternatively, when everything is as expected, or we are calmly distracted in safe and familiar surroundings, time shrinks.

Experimental methods are helping us to better understand

how different factors alter our experienced duration of an event. For example, when a random picture is added to a sequence of blinking images (an unexpected image of a cow amongst a repeated series of apples, say) it is consistently reported as being displayed for longer, despite being shown for the exact same time.[2]

Known as the *oddball effect*, this phenomenon illustrates how the introduction of novel stimuli increases perceived duration. It's as if your brain becomes bored of the repeated image and, when a novel stimulus pops up, it switches back on again. A similar effect can also be achieved with emotionally charged images. We perceive angry faces as lasting longer than neutral ones and spiders as lasting longer than butterflies.[3] Threatening signals, like objects coming towards us, are also associated with longer durations.[4] These studies reinforce anecdotal feedback that when we're exploring new things, taking risks or facing threats, time feels longer. At these moments our brain kicks into overdrive, recording every last detail of the experience. We *stretch* it.

Alternatively, the more familiar the world becomes, the less information your brain needs to register and the more quickly it all seems to pass. As we age, it makes sense that time also seems to speed up (there's less information to take in to slow us down). The details of most of life's moments are just like this. The thousands of times we've brushed our teeth, taken the bins out or commuted to work. In most instances, they simply enter the brain and then disappear.

But, as we know, life isn't just filled with nothingness. What then determines the moments that impact us and stay with us, compared with the moments that are lost forever? To truly understand how we might improve experiences without changing their duration, the last piece of our puzzle is understanding the role of memory.

When it comes to our memories, it seems stories matter and time doesn't.

HAPPILY, EVER AFTER

Consider this analogy:

A music lover is listening intently to a long symphony when the record is scratched just near the end, producing a ghastly sound. It's common for unfortunate moments like these to be described as "ruining the entire experience." But there's an important distinction to be made. The majority of the experience, in fact, wasn't ruined; only our memory of it. The minutes of orchestral glory that were enjoyed meant little because of the ugly memory we were left with. It's the memory, psychologist Daniel Kahneman argues, that is all we get to keep.

Kahneman's musical analogy exposes an important distinction between a memory-based and a moment-based approach to understanding experience.[5] A difference, he describes, as one between our *experiencing self*, who knows the present, and our *remembering self*, who tells the stories from our memory. Although we might assume that a measure of the total experience is the sum of both, research suggests that it isn't.[6]

It's the remembering self, Kahneman argues, that maintains the story of our life. This is the self that encourages us to participate a second time. To truly understand how we improve experiences without changing their duration, it's critical we consider our remembering self. And in stories, it seems again that the absolute duration, or clock time, doesn't matter (who knows how long "happily ever after" really lasts?). Rather than their absolute duration, we will see these stories are defined by changes, significant moments and, importantly, their endings.

By mistakenly prioritising clock time over brain time – our moment-by-moment experience versus the memory that remains – it seems we're missing the main event. Instead of counting minutes, we need emotional metrics.

EMOTIONAL METRICS

In Rory Sutherland's 2009 TED talk "Life lessons from an ad man," he opens with an engineering conundrum: the challenge of increasing the speed of the Eurostar between London and Paris.[7] At the time, Sutherland recalls, the rational engineering solution was to spend roughly £6 billion to build new tracks from London to the coast, reducing the time of the trip by about 40 minutes. "A slightly unimaginative way of improving a train journey merely to make it shorter," remarked Sutherland. As an alternative, rather than innovate to make these trains go quantifiably faster, his creative *perceptual* solution was to employ top supermodels and encourage them to walk up and down the aisle handing out free champagne. With this, he provoked, "you'll still have about £3 billion in change, and people would ask for the trains to be slowed down."

Sutherland's Eurostar analogy exposes a far greater challenge within business today. Despite the growing and long-standing evidence of our flexible perception and experience of time, we continue to use a highly rational mindset when it comes to optimising our experiences. Although we use some of the same names to describe them, the precise measures of time and distance measured by physicists can vary considerably at an emotional level and according to context. Transport planners have found, for example, that commuters can perceive a minute of delay when waiting for a bus as costing two to three times that of a minute riding it.[8] Similarly, the time we experience waiting for the bill in a café can feel considerably longer than the time taken to receive our coffee. Both are particularly worrisome when research shows perceived waiting time is a more accurate predictor of customer satisfaction than *actual* waiting time.[9]

Over and over again, it seems, we're being distracted by the wrong objective. As Sutherland argues, we're missing *emotional metrics.*

If you're in business today, you are in the business of experience. Whether it's tourism or travel, banking or dentistry, the way we develop and deliver our products and services can significantly impact our moment-by-moment experience and, importantly, our longer-lasting memory of it.

In the following section we'll see that, by expanding our scope of solutions from those addressing quantifiable or objective metrics (miles per hour, time spent, time to service) to those that truly impact our memory of events (attention, arousal, emotion and time felt), we can create experiences that boost enjoyment, without changing the duration itself. We'll see that by reducing painful uncertainty, idleness and boredom, *brain time* isn't the same as *clock time.*

Just like an accordion, we can expand it and contract it.

Very quickly...(well, you be the judge).

- The experience of time isn't universal. There's a difference between clock time and brain time.

- Psychological factors – like familiarity, novelty, threat and stress can stretch or compress our experience of time.

- To improve experiences without changing their duration, we need to look beyond optimising in-moment experience and also innovate for our memory of it.

CHAPTER 23
Better the Devil You Know

PSYCHOLOGICAL PRINCIPLES:
EXPECTATION & AGENCY

"IN 50 YEARS, I have never told a joke in a sermon," Pastor
John Piper recounts, ten years after one of his most bizarre on-
stage experiences.[1]

It was in 2009 at a gathering of the American Association
of Christian Counsellors in Nashville. With thousands in
attendance, and seeking not to present himself as arrogant, the
pastor began by openly sharing some of his own imperfections.
"I feel honoured and humbled and vulnerable and exposed,"
he started.[2] "I don't think I could think of any other audience
more likely to see straight through a speaker than you would."
To his surprise, the audience began to laugh. Visibly thrown, the
pastor continued. "I thought I would spare you the analysis and
tell you upfront that I'm a sinner." At this, the crowd erupted.
"You're a very strange audience, I totally didn't expect laughter,"
continued Piper. It's leg-slapping now. "This is a serious talk,
in case you wondered," pleaded the pastor as he continued

to struggle through spurts of laughter. To this, a raucous and long-held applause.

Despite the reactions of his audience, Pastor John Piper was entirely sincere. It wasn't until much later that he appreciated the predicament he was in.

ESCALATORS AND LIME JUICE

If you've ever stepped onto a stationary escalator and felt like you were about to topple over, you're not alone. Despite being aware that it isn't going to move, the discrepancy between our conscious awareness and our learned physical response leads to an experience known as the *broken escalator phenomenon*.[3] Our body anticipates movement. Over time it's simply grown to expect it. Because of this, although knowing full well that it's not going to move, this expectation-led motor response still unsettles us.

It's a jarring reminder of the power of expectation.

Our brain is built to anticipate. It's evolved to continually make judgements about our environment to determine how best to respond, and drawing upon experience is a valuable strategy to increase the odds of getting it right. Before we know it, these expectations can begin to shape our reality. We see what we expect to see, and hear what we expect to hear, with unrelated factors – like the visual cue of an escalator – influencing expectations and significantly impacting our experience.

By actively shaping expectations, we can meaningfully change experiences. When a lime-flavoured drink is coloured orange (a powerful cue setting expectations), people can be convinced it's orange juice.[4] Subtle cues can also work to reinforce the enjoyment of an experience by aligning with expectations. Cheddar cheese is tastier when yellow, tomato sauce tastes more like tomato sauce when it's red, even Coke tastes better from a branded cup.[5] When a sommelier invites us to appreciate the asparagus notes on a freshly opened Sauvignon Blanc, we find it hard to notice anything else. Expectations prime the brain for what comes next. If only someone had warned the pastor sooner.

"It took me totally off guard," Pastor John reports many years later. "I suspect that I walked into a set of expectations at that conference." Over the course of the event, after listening to a series of comical presenters, it was as if the attendees had been trained to expect humour from all of the speakers. As a result, what was spoken by Piper wasn't what was heard by the crowd. Despite his sincerity, his audience was simply incapable of seeing him as being serious.

The audience was expecting stand-up. They received a sermon.

When we fail to set expectations, or otherwise leave people in a position of uncertainty, not only do we miss the opportunity to shape and improve their experience, we risk leaving them in distress. In fact, there are times when uncertainty can feel even more distressing than facing physical pain itself.

THE PAIN OF UNCERTAINTY

Which would you prefer: knowing that you will definitely receive a painful shock or that you probably will? In 2016, a group of researchers from University College London explored this very question and discovered an intriguing paradox.[6] Playing a computer simulation that challenged volunteers to overturn rocks with the potential of having snakes hidden under them, these participants received a shock if a snake appeared. Through this paradigm, they found that people who knew they were guaranteed a painful electric shock actually felt calmer and were measurably less agitated than those who were told they only had a chance of one. Although we all know that uncertainty is stressful, this study illustrated that it can actually be more stressful than a predictable negative consequence.*

The UCL study also illustrated that, just as our reward system has evolved to anticipate the possibility of positive or negative outcomes, it seems it can also compute the *length* of these odds. The researchers found that the closer participants came to a 50% probability of a shock (the point of least predictability and maximum uncertainty), the higher their stress response. From an evolutionary perspective, once again, this makes a lot of sense. When consequences are least predictable, or most uncertain, harder work is required to ensure success (we work harder to score a goal from an oblique angle than from directly in front). When we find ourselves in a scenario where the right response is unclear, our brain needs to work double time to improve those odds and take back control. The result of this requirement is high arousal and stress which, as we know, stretches time.

To help manage this uncomfortable experience, reduce stress and thus shrink time, two evolved solutions are: to *set* our expectations and to *update* them appropriately. By helping people to better predict what comes next, thus arming us with a sense of control over our future, we can boost experiences without changing their duration.

THE DOCTOR WILL SEE YOU SOON

It was an early Sunday morning when the Taylor family set off for their home in Brooklyn after a wet week in Maine. Although it

---

* As if the threat of execution isn't enough – in an act condemned by many in the international community, Japan does not tell death row prisoners that they are to be executed until the last possible minute. Never knowing which day will be their last, the condemned prisoner is informed on the morning of their execution.

had promised to be the trip of their year, it was a vacation that tested them on every front.

The cabin they had booked was far smaller than the advert made out, and the unyielding rain meant the four of them spent their week locked away, solving old puzzles and looking solemnly out of the fogged-up windows. The trip didn't even start well. They were barely clear of Connecticut before the first "Are we nearly there yet?" rang out from the back seat – and it was downhill from there. With a collective deep breath, as the sun began to poke through the clouds, the Taylors's car crawled out of the vacation home's wet gravel drive onto the main road.

Thankfully, this was going to be a very different journey.

When people buy a product or sign up for a service, they enter with a particular set of expectations. When we order food in a café, our experience tells us it should be on the table in about 15 minutes. Longer than this, there will likely be objections – any shorter, we may grow suspicious. Similarly, we wait more calmly when we're told "The doctor will see you in five minutes," than when we're left in the lurch with "The doctor will see you soon." Because we simply don't know how long it will take, the high arousal associated with uncertainty makes this wait feel longer.[7]

When the Taylors finally pulled into Brooklyn, this time they arrived without the fighting and seat kicking they had become accustomed to on the way out. Their trip just seemed shorter. Although exhausted after a tough week away, they weren't losing their grip on reality. They were experiencing a phenomenon that's been widely researched.[8] It's called the *return trip effect*.

Several studies have confirmed the existence of the return trip effect, whereby outbound journeys tend to feel longer than similar inbound trips (with the return trip feeling up to 22%

shorter).[9] While there are elements of the outbound trip (like novelty) that have been associated with stretching time, a large reason for the effect is argued to be expectation management. Because we simply don't know how long it will take on the way out, it's very difficult to truly manage expectations. The high arousal associated with this uncertainty makes it feel longer. It stretches brain time.

By setting expectations in advance, we can not only focus our audience's attention on the positives, and what we want people to experience (just like our crafty sommelier or this example from Sharp's on every pint glass in Image 38 (top)), we can also reduce the degree of stress-inducing uncertainty, shrinking the time that's *felt*.

A colleague of mine recently returned from a trip to the US. In this instance, United Airlines didn't only manage her expectations by informing the cabin of time to arrival (as is now expected on all flights), they provided passengers with a detailed overview of what was expected on the trip – even to the degree of when the lights would be switched on or off (it was obviously destined to feel shorter than her *outbound* trip anyway).

I came across a similar adapted solution when working with an Australian car insurer some time ago. My client told me about one of the single biggest shifts they had made to their customer service. Their simple innovation was to say that the service technician would arrive in 45 minutes instead of a more accurate 30 minutes wait. This helped them in two ways – they had wriggle-room just in case there was a traffic jam and, if not, they were always welcomely received early. According to touringplans.com, signs listing wait times at the beginning of ride queues at theme parks also tend to be inflated when compared to the actual wait time.[10] It turns out that the time you're likely to wait can be as little as two-thirds (65%) of the time posted. When seeking to better understand the *return trip effect* in more detail, researchers developed an experimental manipulation which

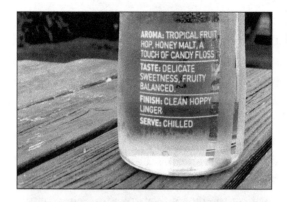

Image 38 – Expectation management: (top) Sharp's guide consumer attention and shape expectations by communicating the desired experience on every pint; (bottom) beyond take-off and arrival times, United Airlines sets expectations of meals and cabin lighting, removing painful uncertainty, shrinking the time that's felt.

made participants expect a longer outbound trip (just like our car insurer and theme park).[11] When expectations were set in this way, people experienced the trip as taking *less* time.

To address the time-extending experience of painful uncertainty, across industry there is an array of convergently evolved solutions that works to set expectations – even if it's setting them below (i.e., longer than) what we might initially want to hear. By providing easily accessible, realistic estimates we can improve the accuracy of the customers' own guesses at how long they waited, having a positive effect on their ultimate experience. While honesty is always the best policy, when in doubt, underestimating clock time seems to be a dangerous strategy.

IMPROVING EXPERIENCES: INNOVATION CHECKLIST

1. How might we set expectations to shape experiences?

2. How might we show or tell people what's coming next to remove painful uncertainty?

3. If expectation-setting information is unavailable, how might we tell people what to do instead? (For example, some airports communicate "relax" rather than just "delayed" on their departure communications.)

I SEE WHERE THE HOLD-UP IS

Worldwide, Uber is famous for expectation management. The brand was launched on the comfort and certainty of seeing an animated black car crusing through the streets on its way to pick you up, a reassuring signal helping you time your exit and know that you'll be on your way soon. However, in early 2018, when Uber launched Express POOL, the product team noticed that the cancellation rate on rides was higher than expected.

Hit with an extra and unexpected wait, people weren't hanging around.

Uber's Express POOL allows people to share with other travellers headed in the same direction. By creating a more efficient ride for the network, it naturally costs less. While many of us will be familiar with waiting for our Uber, Express POOL takes this one step further. The algorithm first finds people who can travel together, then it matches them with a suitable driver. "It can be faster, it will be less expensive, but you will be waiting," former lead at Uber Labs, Candice Hogan tells me. "Psychologically, it's a different experience from simply waiting to get into the car," she continues. "A bit like the difference between a very long flight and a short flight that's been delayed." So, while Uber couldn't change the wait itself, it was clear there was room for improvement. Hogan's lab was set to work.

As we've explored previously, providing a sense of transparency can increase our trust in a product, reinforcing its value. This transparency can also work to justify unexpected waits – shaping expectation and removing painful uncertainty.

In the restaurant industry, it's not uncommon for people to complain about the wait for their food. Teppanyaki restaurants offer us an interesting, and often contrasting, specimen to observe here. They don't seem to suffer from this problem. Mesmerised, we watch the chef juggling salt and pepper, see the flames dance up from the hot oil and hear the crackle of our food as it's cooked right in front of us. This theatre doesn't only distract us, it helps to manage expectations through *operational transparency* (as we explored in Chapter 8).

By showing people *why* things are taking so long, providing a window into the operations beneath, we can illustrate that progress is still being made (and reinforce the effort put into its production). We can't complain that our Teppanyaki shrimp is taking too long because we can see the effort that's going into preparing it. Domino's famous Pizza Tracker is another fabulous digitised example of how operational transparency has evolved to manage our expectations, improving a wait experience. Developed to reduce uncertainty, the tracker's ability to visualise every stage of the process in real time, from placing an order through to quality check, enables hungry pizza lovers to see every step of the journey.

But this transparency doesn't always require algorithms or expensive design. Via a simple series of lights, the elevators at London's Borough Underground station provide waiting passengers with a sense of where their elevator is on its journey – shaping expectations of our ascent. Maybe unsurprisingly then, when customers were cancelling their Uber Express POOL because of an unexpected wait, the team at Uber approached their customer experience with a similar, transparent mindset.

"We were able to leverage expectation setting a lot," says Hogan. The team from Uber Labs tested a series of interventions providing Express POOL customers with a sense of progress and transparency. At a more granular level, they explained what was going on behind the scenes of this new and uncharacteristic wait. They informed riders with messages like "Finding other riders going your way..." and put them into testing. "We experienced a significant reduction in cancellations," reports Hogan. In fact, with only small tweaks to the user experience, the team observed an 11% reduction in the post-request cancellation rate.[12] No small feat.

When people can see work being done for them, whether it's waiting for a meal or a lift to the next train platform, it appears they enjoy the service more and are willing to wait longer for it. Through observing patterns of evolved psychological solutions we can see that 'showing the work' and justifying the time spent can improve experiences without changing the duration itself. In fact, on some occasions, we can even improve the overall experience when the duration of the wait is *increased.*

Image 39 – Operational transparency managing expectations: by providing progress updates, the elevators at London's Borough Underground station arm waiting passengers with a clear idea of where the lift is, shaping expectations of their ascent.

IMPROVING EXPERIENCES: INNOVATION CHECKLIST

1. How might we transparently tell people what's taking so long?

2. How might we expose the process so people can see what's happening and where they stand?

3. How might we illustrate a sense of progress and set clear expectations?

KNOCK ON WOOD

In the early part of the twentieth century, anthropologist Bronislaw Malinowski spent months studying the tribes of the Trobriand islands off the coast of Papua New Guinea.

Amongst his many findings, Malinowski's fieldwork revealed a fascinating relationship between the tribe's experience of uncertainty and their practices of ritualistic magic. Specifically, for tribes who fished in the deep sea where results were uncertain and varied, he reported higher degrees of ritualism, yet far fewer for those who fished in shallow waters and lagoons where men could rely more on knowledge and skill.[13,14]

When their activities were almost entirely controllable, like boat building, the islanders didn't engage in magic at all.

Now while you may not identify with practising ritualistic magic yourself, through unintended accident or design we are surrounded by evolved innovations providing us with a similar sense of control. Just as the Trobriand tribes sought comfort in ritualism as they prepared for the unknown perils of the sea, a sense of control is important for us as we shuffle into tiny steel elevators suspended in mid-air, or wait nervously for an important file to download.

In these scenarios, we'll not only see a plethora of examples in the world around us but also that a sense of control can indeed be manufactured. This can help to improve our experience of painfully uncertain waits, without changing the duration itself.

Malinowski's work represents a fascinating aspect of our evolved psychology. When outcomes are uncertain, we have a tendency to act in ways that restore our feelings of control. Ritualistic magic exists in modern society too (beyond spilling the salt and tossing it over our left shoulder). Sports professionals create rituals matching the unpredictability of their position.[15] When times are financially uncertain, we see superstitions increase (for example, interest in astrology increased during the Great Depression.)[16] A study conducted during the Gulf War also found that Israeli citizens living in areas of greater risk of missile attacks were more likely to engage in magical thinking than those who lived in safer areas.[17]

By enhancing our perceptions of personal agency, superstition and ritual help to lessen the painful feeling of being out of control. Instead of completely withdrawing from the world (falling into helplessness and depression), with this illusion of control we can engage with our environment, instilling confidence and a belief in our ability. They appease our inherently panicky brain and help us to move forwards.

While we may not recognise it, evolved examples are all around us.

In 1975, about 750,000 cars entered Manhattan daily. By 2004, this number had jumped to more than 1.1 million. To manage the increase in traffic, without advertising the fact, computer-controlled traffic signals were introduced disabling most of the control buttons that once operated pedestrian crossings throughout the city. Initially, the buttons themselves survived because of the cost of removing them, but it turned out that even inoperative buttons served a purpose.

Just as magic increased the perceived control for Trobriand fishermen, the presence of these buttons maintained a sense of control for New Yorkers waiting patiently to cross. "Perceived control is very important," Harvard psychologist Ellen J. Langer told the *New York Times*.[18] "It diminishes stress and promotes well-being." In fact, having studied behaviour at crossings, Tal Oron-Gilad of Ben-Gurion University of the Negev in Israel reports that pedestrians who press a button are also less likely to cross before the green man appears.[19] "When you press the button, you're getting a sense that you are being noticed," Tal tells me. "You feel you have been acknowledged, removing the need for you to compensate with an unsafe crossing." By removing their functionality, yet leaving their mechanics, they had created a placebo for psychological control.

In a similar stroke of unintended psychological innovation, following the Americans with Disabilities Act in 1990 (a civil rights law prohibiting discrimination against people with disabilities), elevator lifts needed to remain open for at least three seconds to provide safe entry for those with a disability. In this instance, it was the speed of legislation that outpaced the physical removal of *close door* buttons. Just like the gradual deletion of active pedestrian buttons in New York, close door buttons were rendered inoperative in elevators across the United States. Once again, without us realising, these buttons were converted from a technical innovation to a psychological one. While waiting for an elevator to close, they now worked to provide a greater sense of control (one that is much appreciated as we enter a tiny box that hangs by a thread). The reality is, writes Nick Paumgarten for the *New Yorker*, "It is there mainly to make you think it works."[20] The fact that the door eventually does close just reinforces our belief.

Through accident or conscious design, Netherlands-based file-sharing platform WeTransfer also provides their users with an enhanced sense of control while waiting (reducing inevitable download anxiety). Via an advertising partnership with Shutterstock, in 2020 the platform shifted the power balance of its audience, from disempowered 'hostages' to active participants. To do this, WeTransfer offered users the opportunity to "find the right image" by which to upload or download files to (with image selections like *bliss, calm, fresh, intense, alone, agony*). While the ability to inform and control our digital environment serves no real benefit from a rational *clock time* perspective, it didn't speed up the download itself. It's an interesting example reinforcing our sense of control, removing painful uncertainty and time felt. A solution shrinking *brain time*.

When we're out of control or left uncertain, time feels longer. It's painful. By providing a sense of agency, even just the prospect of it, we can help to focus attention, reduce uncertainty and increase our enjoyment without changing duration. The pattern of evolved solutions we have just explored is not just a collection of tricks. It's wise for us not to feel fooled by the system when this does occur. These buttons have evolved to do a job, it's just not the one you may have been expecting.

These buttons have evolved to do a job, it's just not the one you may have been expecting.

IMPROVING EXPERIENCES: INNOVATION CHECKLIST

1. How might we provide a sense of control in scenarios that feel ambiguous, unclear or stressful?

2. What decisions can we enable people to make for themselves (even if these might be tertiary to the ultimate goal)?

3. What could we give people to increase their sense of agency during times of uncertainty?

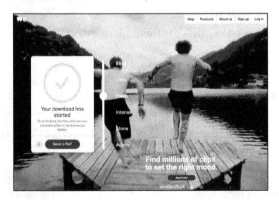

Image 40 – Providing a sense of control and agency: (top) placebo control at pedestrian crossings; (middle) inoperable elevator buttons following the Americans with Disabilities Act; (bottom) WeTransfer and Shutterstock partnership enabling user control while downloading.

CHAPTER 24
Time Flies When You're Having Fun

PSYCHOLOGICAL PRINCIPLE:
OCCUPIED TIME

SEVERAL YEARS AGO, Houston had a problem.

It wasn't at NASA and it had nothing to do with landing on the moon. It was a problem with the experience of incoming passengers at their international airport.

Houston airport was receiving an unexpectedly large number of complaints, specifically regarding delays at the luggage carousel. To address the issue, airport executives increased the number of baggage handlers, speeding up the process and reducing the waiting time by eight minutes.[1] An impressive reduction in clock time.

However, to their dismay, the complaints continued to roll in. Despite all the engineering and process improvement, getting bags in the hands of travellers faster had not begun to solve the problem. Airport executives had to look deeper into what was making its travellers tetchy at the carousel.

A WATCHED POT

Although we may feel sluggish when we're bored, at a physiological level we are in a state of high arousal. As we sit there twiddling our thumbs, we're actually quite stressed. Despite the discomfort we feel, the common experience of boredom across cultures indicates it's actually a valuable adaptation.[2] It tells our brain that its current situation is unfulfilling, motivating us to do something else. The downside is that this increase in arousal and stress also works to slow down our brain clock. Time *expands*. Now not only do we feel physiologically stressed, we also feel more time has passed than actually has. There's little wonder that people overestimate how long they've waited in a line by about a third.[3]

It's a double ouch.

Back in Houston, on even closer inspection, the team unearthed a critical finding. When breaking down the arrival experience in detail, they discovered that it took their passengers only a minute to walk from the gate to the luggage carousel, meaning that roughly 88% of their arrival time was spent standing waiting for their bags. A vast majority of their time was spent standing idly. In a genius stroke of psychological innovation, instead of reducing waiting time through further marginal engineering improvements, the team decided to move the arrival gates away from the main terminal, re-routing bags to the outermost carousel.

While this didn't change the time between stepping off the plane and receiving their luggage, it forced passengers to walk six times longer to get their bags. Idle time was drastically reduced, and passenger complaints virtually disappeared.

Mercifully, our experience of boredom can be altered by redirecting our attention. If we can convince our brains that we've already moved on to richer and more exciting social or emotional stimulation, it all appears to move more quickly (it seems we're more likely to find the love of our life walking to the carousel than staring blankly at the conveyor belt). Just as Sutherland quips that free-champagne-serving supermodels would urge people to ask for the Eurostar to be slowed down, since the 1950s organisational theorist Russel Ackoff has emphasised the importance of boredom-reduction activities during key moments of unoccupied time. It was Ackoff who introduced the now folklore floor-to-ceiling mirrors around elevators, giving passengers the means to comb their hair or fix their ties as they wait. Analogous to the innovation in Houston and Sutherland's perceptual hack, it doesn't make the elevator any faster, it simply gives us something to distract ourselves with: ourselves.

If we can create a reason for people to get busy, or even create conditions persuading our impatient brains that we've already moved on to richer social, cognitive or emotional opportunities, we can avoid periods of painful boredom and shrink idle time. Unsurprisingly, there is a plethora of evolved psychological solutions across categories that have adapted to do just this. Together, they help us to do something else while the kettle boils – not just sit there watching it.

In three bullets:

- When we're bored, we're stressed.

- When we're stressed, our experience of time slows down.

- By tricking our brains into thinking we're actually not bored, we can speed time up again.

THE IMAGINEERS

When Disneyland first opened its doors on 17 July 1955, it was chaos.

Scheduled as a soft launch for press and local dignitaries, forged invitations meant that the small group that was expected turned into an uninvited mob of thousands. Restaurants ran out of food and drink, there were reports of children being passed over the crowd's shoulders and even water lapping the deck of the Mark Twain Steamboat as it struggled with so many on board.

While a huge 160-acre property, with only 13 attractions when it first opened, Disneyland soon became victim to its own success. Within a year, over five million people had flocked to the park and snaking queues became a mainstay of its most popular rides. 60 years later, Disneyland hosted more than 18 million visitors in one year alone, with the wait for some rides across the global franchise being over 100 minutes long. How can Disney continue to claim its park is "the happiest place on Earth" if much of the day is spent waiting in a queue?

They became the experts of *occupied time*.

Even though its opening day was complete pandemonium, Disneyland's creators learnt immeasurably from the experience. They were able to see how people moved through the park and began to innovate the best ways to accommodate large crowds in the future. Today, a significant part of the park's success boils down to the fruits of this work: a series of clever psychological solutions that have adapted and evolved over time, all brought to life by a team of *Imagineers*.

When you apply for a position at Disneyland, one of the first things you're told is that the park is a *stage*. Disney employees aren't just staff, they're cast members. This same mentality extends to their queues. At Disneyland, the story begins as soon as you enter the line. When waiting for a ride, you're welcomed by characters and invited to interact with the story itself. By designing fast-moving, long-snaking, yet visually short lines, and applying the same level of production found on the rides themselves, Disney's Imagineers make waiting in line an experience with an entertainment value of its own. They have discovered that the best solution to make time spent in lines more enjoyable is to avoid it feeling like a line at all. They've proved that waiting can become part of the experience.

But you might be thinking that with a smartphone in virtually every pocket, most of us are already walking around with millions of hours of music and years of content to entertain our every moment. This is true. However, with a little creativity, this technology is now being integrated *into* experiences, removing idle time while improving a brand or service's core offer.

In fact, it seems that Wifi can even be an enabler of time-accelerating experiences in another environment altogether: underwater.

For decades, British and French children have been asking staff aboard the Eurostar one question. "Will we see fish through the windows?" On 12 July 2017, Eurostar announced *Eurostar Odyssey*, a virtual reality experience creating an adventure through specially designed headsets. As travellers take their seats, the roof transforms into a glass ceiling revealing the underwater world around them. Instead of disappearing into darkness, as the train speeds into the channel tunnel, passengers are joined by a host of whales, pirates and mermaids. There's even a guide showing you what to collect. While it's not quite scantily-clad supermodels handing out free champagne, it gets us some of the way there. By simply logging onto the WiFi and opening the app, Eurostar travellers are transported under the sea. And, as they say when you come up for air (in what feels like record time) in Paris, *voilà*.

Despite a constant source of distraction in our pockets, there is still ample space for Lower-fi creative solutions to pass idle time. For example, as opposed to Ackoff-esque floor-to-ceiling mirrors, in Seattle's quirky Maxwell Hotel, they fix puzzles to the wall of the lifts, challenging passengers to solve them as they travel. To help weary passengers pass the time at train stations and airports, Short Édition is also addressing painful unoccupied time by breathing new life into the art of storytelling. At the push of a button these free story dispensers produce one-minute, three-minute or five-minute reads covering everything from sci-fi to romance, helping waiting passengers immerse in a story and forget about their wait. As a final example, during the Covid-19 pandemic, in an act encouraging social distancing while also seeking to occupy shoppers during longer queues, Australian wine merchant BWS created a clever innovation. Providing their customers not only with a cue for where to stand, BWS also gave people something to pass the time: hum happy birthday to themselves.

At some stage of your product or service experience, boredom-inducing unoccupied time is a risk. For many industries, like with travel, it's nearly impossible to avoid. By appreciating the power of stimulation and distraction, learning from evolved psychological solutions across industries, we can now more easily deploy them ourselves. By converting idle moments into occupied time (with a note of caution not to be *so* flamboyant they reinforce our recollection of the wait!) we can improve experiences without changing their duration.

Image 41 - Convincing our bored brain it's actually active: (top) Eurostar Odyssey; (middle) short story dispenser, used to improve waiting experiences at airports and train stations; (bottom) social distancing with distractions in BWS, Australia.

IMPROVING EXPERIENCES: INNOVATION CHECKLIST

1. How might we embed activities or create distractions during unoccupied time?

2. How might we make unavoidable waiting times an opportunity for alternative experiences?

3. How might we make existing boredom busters (like playing on the phone) more relevant to the overall service experience (just like the Eurostar)?

CHAPTER 25
All's Well That Ends Well

PSYCHOLOGICAL PRINCIPLE:
THE PEAK-END EFFECT

WE ALL HAVE one: a food or drink, the thought of which alone makes us feel a bit queasy. The chicken enchilada that made you ill. That warm California sushi roll that turned you pale and gave you the sweats.

Let's not mention the Irish cream liqueur that, despite your best intentions, left you hugging a toilet bowl on a Sunday.

Although we might curse the fact that these foods are now excluded from our repertoire forever, the ease with which we gain this aversion is worth some attention.

It's an important survival response.

Species that readily form memories and associations between a food and illness are more likely to avoid those foods again in the future, bettering their chances of survival and reproduction. For our ancient ancestors, recalling a particular fruit that made them violently ill was worth remembering more than a berry that was just like the rest.

Being able to recall positive or negative experiences can help guide us to seek out these situations again, or, alternatively, avoid them like the plague. However, because of how these instances are coded in our ancient brain, believe it or not, there can even be times when people want to endure longer and more painful experiences, not less.

ICE BATH CHALLENGE

In 1993, Nobel laureate Daniel Kahneman and his team exposed a group of students to two particularly uncomfortable experiments, both involving bone-chillingly cold water.[1]

In the first trial, students were asked to hold their hands in an ice bath (14°C) for a total of 60 seconds. In a second, they were instructed to plunge their other hand in the very same water for the same duration, but this time, to keep their hand submerged for an additional 30 seconds while the temperature was raised ever so slightly to 15°C. Following these first two trials, students were given a choice of which condition to do again. From the comfort of our armchairs, the answer may seem obvious (every bit of the discomfort felt in trial one was also felt in trial two, and then some). Surprisingly, when offered to repeat this cold water experiment again, most students opted for the longer 'clock time' condition with a less uncomfortable finish. Kahneman concluded that "Subjects chose the long trial simply because they liked the memory of it better than the alternative."[2] This experiment uncovered a fascinating element of our evolved psychology, now classified as the *peak-end effect*.

The peak-end effect explains that when people form evaluations of an experience, they tend to neglect its duration and instead be influenced by their memory of it. This recollection is shaped by two key moments: how it felt during the most intense moment (the peak) and how the experience ended. "Our brains don't have the capacity to remember everything," writes habit expert Nir Eyal.[3] "It makes sense for us to only keep the memories that most aided our survival." Evidence of the peak-end effect has since been recognised across medical procedures, watching horror films and even providing student feedback (yes, it seems you probably should give the good news last).[4,5]

What's clear from these studies is that when we assess an experience, we don't average out our minute-by-minute enjoyment (like evaluating all the elements of a weekend away to formulate an *average* score: 6/10, say). Instead, the memory and story we get to keep, our ultimate enjoyment, is influenced by a few critical moments (creating more 9s and 10s as peaks and ensuring positive endings). This is mostly a good thing (the positive memory of a baby being born can outweigh the average impact of the pain endured during childbirth), hence its adaptive qualities. But it also means that a bad return flight can take away from an otherwise pleasurable holiday and, if you fall apart on the 18th hole on a Sunday, you may as well have stayed in bed.

By recognising the moments that matter most, the peak-end effect tells us that you really don't need to put a lot of weight on the duration, or even the total average of an experience, just on how bad or good it was at its peak, and whether it ended well. Needless to say, there are few positive reviews celebrating the initial nights aboard the Titanic.

WARM COOKIES AND POPSICLES:
CREATING PEAKS

At midday on 19 September 2019, we arrived in Athens, Greece. This being our first European holiday with a now walking toddler, we were bursting to get out of our small London flat and into the sun and water of the Greek Isles. But to arrive in Athens for midday, this means an early start in London. A very early start. We set our alarm for 4 am, bundled ourselves (and what seemed a lifetime's supply of clothes) into a taxi to Luton airport. After an hour of toddler distraction and three-and-a-half hours of knees-to-ear travel on the flight, we walked out of the plane to begin our holiday. Despite the regimented nature of our morning, I don't really recall much from this trip. I can't remember the flight attendants or the decor upon arrival, and I may as well never have visited the luggage carousel. I also don't recall how tired I must have felt or even the sting of my arms from the weight I was carrying. But I do remember one moment – an element of the experience that stands out in my mind, distinct from the otherwise exhausted blur of travel.

In life, we often think of peak moments as being unforeseen or up to chance. Meeting our spouse, winning that match, escaping unscathed from the tropical storm… These can indeed be defining and memorable events, but it's also important we recognise that moments like this, these peak moments, can be constructed and created. In epic storytelling, these are decisive elements requiring an author's special attention. They're instances of conflict, elevation and significance. They are highly scripted yet unexpected twists and turns ("Then one day, he is visited by a wizard called Gandalf…"). And the same can be true in real life. By carefully designing peaks, we can create distinctive and powerful moments that shape our enjoyment and leave a positive lasting memory, without changing an experience's duration.

"I want to come back to LA just to come here."

—AJAY G., TRIP ADVISOR

In their exploration of the peak-end effect, captured in their wonderful book *The Power of Moments*, Chip and Dan Heath introduce us to the Magic Castle Hotel in LA, just a block from Grauman's Chinese Theatre in Hollywood.[6] In August 2021, the Magic Castle Hotel was ranked seventh best hotel in LA (out of 407 on Trip Advisor). This is an astounding achievement for a family hotel up against the InterContinental, the Sheraton Grand and the Hollywood Roosevelt. Even more impressively, it does this while not resembling anything close to a castle at all (it's really just an old converted apartment block with a small pool, lots of stairs and no elevator).

It certainly *is* magical, though.

Amongst a generous free snack bar and laundry service, arguably the hotel's most magical moment is delivered by their *Popsicle Hotline*. The Magic Castle Hotel website explains: "Just lift the red phone, and we'll answer, 'Popsicle Hotline'. In a couple of minutes, your free popsicles magically appear."[7] And, as if popsicles on demand wasn't enough, as you relax in the sun the waiter will even carry them out on a silver tray, white gloves, the works. In the words of Chip and Dan Heath, this surprising and generous act works to "break the script."[*]

Like the Magic Castle, equivalent psychological solutions have convergently evolved in other hotels and restaurants across the globe. In fact, 8,000 kilometres away in a dark and quirky

---

[*] There's a natural overlap here with elements of variability from our exploration of loyalty (the outcome of a good experience is, of course, to come back). For example, Chip and Dan Heath report that when loyal customers on Southwest Airlines were on a flight with a humourous safety announcement they flew one half-flight more over the next year (compared to similar customers who hadn't).

restaurant on the other side of the Atlantic, it's not a red phone but a tiny gold button that sits on every table. At Bob Bob Ricard's flamboyant restaurant in London's Soho, instead of popsicles on demand, it's champagne. Earning them the reputation of serving more champagne than anywhere else in the UK, their *Press for Champagne* button acts as a mayday signal for bubbles, setting the tone for the Gatsby-esque experience to follow. Once again, rather than seeking to remove painful uncertainty by setting expectations (as we've explored previously), these solutions set out to disrupt them with novelty. They focus our brains and stretch our perception of time. And, as a result, they help to form longer-lasting positive memories.

Rory Sutherland has a lovely term for solutions like these – they're all examples of *emotional efficiency*. Rather than playing defensively, improving the breakfast service or the thread count of the linen in a hotel, they create intangible and emotional value through unexpectedness and distinctiveness. Once again, instead of looking across the board to bring the average score of every touchpoint up from 6 to 7, they sprinkle the experience with unexpected 10s.

Instead of striving to be better on average, it pays to be distinct and memorable.

So, what was it that created such a defining positive memory upon our arrival in Greece? Well, after a long morning of travel to reach Athens, we were also met by an unexpected, sensorial experience. In fact, before we had left the airport, we already found ourselves at the beach. As we walked through the terminal, the stark white walls magically turned to sand and sea as a large overhead projector transported us to the calming, lapping waters and peaceful sounds of the shoreline. After a tough morning of travel, our prayers had been answered. Transfixed, our young daughter clambered to the wall to experience it for herself. We watched her explore, we breathed it all in and then, rejuvenated, we continued on our way.

Despite the temptation to make every element as good as it possibly can be (boosting the average), the peak-end effect shows us that increasing long-term enjoyment (and creating lasting positive memories) isn't about making *everything* better. This simply isn't how we encode or store information. Unless it's particularly bad, you're unlikely to remember the softener on your towels. But you will recall the convergently evolved 'peak' solutions like a warm DoubleTree Hotel cookie on arrival or the unexpected coloured rubber duckie with your bathroom amenities, and you'll certainly remember the outlandish Popsicle Hotline. By breaking the category norm, these generous and unexpected multisensory interactions seize and focus our brain. They manufacture the oddball amongst a familiar pattern, slowing down time while capturing a snapshot for our remembering self (the one that encourages us to participate a second time). While many expensive performance vehicles have a sports mode, only Tesla has *Ludicrous Mode*. While all great restaurants serve champagne, only Bob Bob Ricard's serves it at the press of a button. As the Heath brothers acknowledge, if you find people wanting to take out their phones and capture the memory themselves, consider it *job done.*

IMPROVING EXPERIENCES: INNOVATION CHECKLIST

1. How might we disrupt expectations to create a memorable experience?

2. What multi-sensory element will heighten specific moments?

3. How might we break category norms with a big-hearted or fun gesture?

Image 42 – Peak moments: (top) The *Popsicle Hotline* at LA's Magic Castle Hotel; (middle) *Press For Champagne* at London Soho's Bob Bob Ricard's; (bottom) a virtual beach at Athens airport, 2019.

SAVE THE BEST TILL LAST:
OPTIMISING ENDINGS

Several years ago, I was invited to Singapore to present to a group of consultants from Changi Airport. On my whistle-stop tour, I had the opportunity to speak with one of the lead consultants charged with improving customer experience. During our discussion (and after showering him with deserved praise), I mentioned an observation that I had made during a previous trip through the airport (one that, if mentioned in any other circle, would probably have seemed innocuous).

If you haven't had the pleasure of visiting Changi, it's like no airport on earth. While it's one of the busiest and highest-volume thoroughfares on the planet, it's also home to an orchid garden, Singapore's tallest slide and the world's first butterfly garden within an airport. At the time of writing, Changi holds the title of the world's best airport (the first to have achieved this for eight consecutive years). It's a destination in itself.

When I mentioned my observation, the consultant's face beamed. Clearly, this wasn't by accident or chance, it was a conscious and carefully considered element of the Changi experience. Amongst the extravagance, it was a subtle, yet purposeful, inclusion.

Repeat purchase is essential for any industry (even international airports). But it's particularly critical for local restaurants more limited by geographic reach and a finite customer base. Because of this, unlike high-volume tourist venues that may be more concerned with maximising the profit from a single visit, the creation of a positive memory is paramount for local eateries. In many restaurants, it's common practice to be gifted a generous token (chocolate mints, for example) at the conclusion of a meal or when receiving your bill. While this has been found to increase tips,[8] it also leaves us with a more positive reflection on the evening than we may have otherwise had. As a very subtle peak-end, some time ago, while paying at a McDonald's in Australia, I noticed a shrewd social reinforcement cue (a smile on the payment device). Again, regardless of intention and scale, this subtle reinforcement offers a small splash of dopamine softening the sting of payment, helping to leave a more positive memory than a cold and purely transactional end alone. We rarely leave a restaurant saying that it was a *long* meal or a *quick* meal; instead we leave with a view on whether it was a good or bad one. To help sway this judgement – and encourage people to come again – the ending of an experience really does matter.

While Changi is famous for world firsts and extravagant statements, it is also masterful at carefully designed detail, optimising its customer experience at every stage. Amongst the spectacle at Changi, knowing that airport immigration and customs are typically cold and transactional experiences (they need to be in many respects), I mentioned to the Changi consultant that I had noticed they were giving away free branded sweets on every immigration counter. Instead of recalling the length of the queue, or even Singaporean efficiency and discipline, passengers left with an ever-important sweet taste in their mouth thanks to this small gesture. Sure, it's not a farewell Mariachi band or light show on exit, but by fitting each immigration desk with a box of free sweets Changi had created the departures equivalent of a slightly warmer ice bath. And, as we know, when it comes to our experience, even 1°C can make a difference in the end.

Image 43 – Warm endings: (top) free Mastiha following a meal in Milos, Greece; (middle) McDonald's Eftpos machine smiles when we pay; (bottom) sweets at Changi's immigration desks.

TO THE LAST BITE:
PEAK-ENDED PRODUCTS

Splash Mountain doesn't start with a splash.

It's a carefully engineered experience that withholds, then thoughtfully delivers, its most distinctive and memorable product benefit: a thrilling saturation. In theme parks and movie theatres, we expect this sort of thoughtful composition. We don't question the importance of emotional peaks and troughs to determine whether the experience will be well received and enjoyed. So why is it that we often don't approach the development of *physical* products in this same way?

As the story goes, the lump of chocolate at the bottom of a Cornetto ice cream was initially an unintentional by-product of its production. The cone's chocolate coating would drip down and pool at the base, creating a solid block of deliciousness. This glitch (or *mutation* in standard evolutionary theory) not only helped Cornetto plug unwanted drips, but for many, it soon became the most enjoyable part. In fact, it was so widely enjoyed that when manufacturing changed and the lump could be avoided, it's believed to have been retained due to its popularity.[*] When investigating peak-end effects in higher-order mammals, researchers have discovered that capuchin monkeys share a similar preference for food rewards with the most delicious part at the end rather than the beginning.[9] Are you *still* wondering why most assorted chocolates and toffees have evolved to store the exciting bit in the middle (where we end up), and not the outside (where we start)?

While it was an accidental production error that improved the experience of the Cornetto, the implication for psychologically

---

[*]   Wall's even launched Cornetto Tips in March 2021, a product containing no ice cream, just the tip of a wafer cone filled with solid chocolate.

designed products in the future, especially for those that may otherwise be less attractive, like healthier or nutritious snacks, is particularly exciting. When encouraging healthier eating, one of the biggest challenges we face is the instinctive appeal of sugars and fats. Because of millions of years of evolution, where the risks of starvation were ever present, consumption of these energy-intense ingredients is now closely linked to the pleasure centres of our brains. This pull is so strong that simply telling people what to eat makes little difference. However, by understanding how our memories prioritise peaks and endings, we can help ourselves to spend longer consuming healthier products, failing to notice how long we've been chewing away at them. We can use *duration neglect* to our advantage.

In his *Atlantic* article 'How junk food can end obesity,' David Freedman reports that by loading nutritious ingredients into the middle, leaving most of the fat and sugar at the ends, companies can work to slip healthier ingredients into candy bars without anyone noticing.[10] Citing University of Oxford's Professor Charles Spence, "We tend to make up our minds about how something tastes from the first and last bites, and don't care as much what happens in between." This understanding of our evolved psychology, coupled with advances in food processing, arms the food industry with a potent tool for ensuring the consumption of undesirable ingredients – boosting enjoyment while maintaining the benefits they deliver.

Just as an epic story has a start, a middle and an end, we can consider the same tried-and-tested story arc within physical products. We can optimise experiences even if we retain what was a previously aversive element of it.

IMPROVING EXPERIENCES: INNOVATION CHECKLIST

1. How might we consider a product's consumption over time?

2. What would ensure that the most positive elements are enjoyed at the end?

3. What valuable (yet less attractive) components could we include in the middle of an experience?

WHEN LIFE GIVES YOU LEMONS:
TURNING TROUGHS INTO PEAKS

On 16 July 2018, Seattle-based giant Amazon kicked off their 36-hour sales extravaganza. Shoppers were projected to spend as much as $3.4 billion.[11] It was Prime Day. This was, until it all came to a grinding halt.

Within minutes, the retailer's website crashed with an issue that impacted customers for hours. The widespread frustration not only jeopardised millions in sales (estimated at about $1m a minute), it also risked a mass exodus of customers ditching their Prime accounts in annoyance. Before long, unsatisfied shoppers took to Twitter to complain about the blackout. Fortunately for Amazon, a significant proportion of their disgruntled customers were soon completely absorbed with something else.

> *"Bad news: Amazon seems to be crashing from demand for Prime Day sales. Good news: Amazon's error page is amazing."*
> —TWITTER USER, 16 JULY 2018

At some point in the lifetime of a product or service, it's inevitable things won't go as planned. Thankfully, particularly for online experiences, most of these bugs can be covered up by a smooth relinking to other webpages; that is, an error can occur without us even knowing it. On the occasions where an obvious outage is unavoidable, rather than panic, close shop or shift to expensive damage control, some companies have learnt to embrace this chance to build rapport with their customers. They do their best to ensure that people leave more positively, despite a time-wasting event. For example, while we may not think that Error 404 messages are at the top of the list when designing a website, over time these pages have become a creative battlefield for brands and services. When you run into a problem on Airbnb you're met with a cartoon girl who drops her ice cream, while the 404 page for animation goliath Pixar features Sadness, the character from their 2015 film *Inside Out*. To help remove some of the sting from Amazon's Prime Day outage, it was their dogs, not their deals, that came to the rescue.

> "NEVER APOLOGIZE WAFFLES!
> I KNOW IT'S NOT YOUR FAULT!!"
> —TWITTER USER, 16 JULY 2018

To soften the blow of the outages, frustrated Amazon customers were met by a pack of dogs (outrageously cute company dogs, to be precise). On any given day at Amazon's Seattle headquarters, they report that their employees share their workspace with as many as 7,000 dogs.[12] On Prime Day 2018, each time someone failed to log in they were presented with a different dog (thankfully no one met all 7,000). Whether it was Waffles, Muffin, Hunter or Ranger – an Amazon dog came to the rescue, helping to lessen the sting of rejection and,

Image 44 – Making lemonade with lemons: Amazon dog provides a warm error message for Amazon (UK), softening the blow of the disruption and helping to create a more positive memory.

through their presence, turn what otherwise would have been a particularly cold ice bath into a slightly warmer one.

In the end, despite these significant glitches, Amazon still managed to break records for their 2018 Prime Day sales. While the brand didn't disclose its sales figures, Amazon was adamant that the technical anomalies didn't severely impact the promotion's overall results. One perspective, shared by the *Retail Gazette,* is that the outage may have actually *improved* sales thanks to the increased media coverage.[13]

Whether ice baths, handshakes or the salutations on an email signature, across industry, category and challenge, the evolved power of the peak-end effect illustrates that experiences are best left warm. And, when life unexpectedly gives you lemons, hold the lemonade; having puppies on standby is a far sounder strategy. Through trial, error, success and failure, even when things don't go as planned, we've found that how it ends really does matter.

IMPROVING EXPERIENCES: INNOVATION CHECKLIST

1. How might we turn an unexpected negative event into a positive one?

2. How might we share bad news in a more enjoyable or memorable way?

3. What positive association could we create to remove the sting of an error?

Part 3
CONCLUSION

CHAPTER 26
New Eyes

TWENTY-THOUSAND DOLLARS JUST fell into your lap.
It's a particularly good day.

Of all the things you could spend it on, you've decided you're now in the market for a classic 1960s VW – the sort of car you've always dreamed of. Iconic for its time, these days part of the attraction is the car's rarity and obscurity. It's a statement car. You look online and browse some dealers; you even make a few calls. The strange thing is, now that you've started looking, suddenly you're seeing them everywhere. It's uncanny.

Once again, there's a name for this feeling. You're experiencing the *Baader-Meinhof* phenomenon, another upshot of our evolved psychology.*

Bombarded with thousands of pieces of information every day, we're rewarded for detecting patterns (but you already know this). As a result, our brain promotes the occasions when what you're unconsciously thinking about is spotted in your

---

* The term itself was coined in 1994 by a commentator on the St. Paul Pioneer Press online discussion board, who came up with it after hearing the name of the ultra-left-wing German Baader-Meinhof terrorist group, that had been around since 1970, twice in 24 hours.

environment. These two instances make up the beginnings of a sequence.

It's the start of a pattern.

At the beginning of the book, we cross-examined some of our natural revolutionary tendencies. That is, we sought to better understand why, when faced with significant or novel challenges, we have a propensity to look for big or new solutions by which to solve them. We explored the myth of the lone genius, our perceived relationship between scale and status, and our inbuilt optimism (whispering in our ear) "You can do it ... ."

But as we've seen, the truth is that revolutions are rare.

Extremely rare.

1% rare.

So, rather than start from a blank slate, hoping for the best, or convincing ourselves that "this time it's different," by identifying successful patterns of evolved solutions in nature, our psychological principles, behavioural science has handed us a new set of keys to systematically breed new ideas from the old.

Through human intuition, trial and error, social learning or intelligent design, today we're surrounded by a rich array of these psychological solutions. Just as evolutionary processes have helped to craft the wing and dorsal fin over millions of years, thousands of human problem solvers, engineers, designers, marketers and advertisers have already toiled to solve the problems you're facing right now – just in slightly different ways. By recognising these patterns of solutions, we can also see that many of our most pressing challenges have been solved before.

As our journey through *Evolutionary Ideas* comes to an end, my hope is that, in the same way that you're now seeing 1960s

VWs on every corner, you'll also be noticing these patterns of solutions all around you. You'll see costly signals and defaults. You will appreciate variable rewards and forever be on the lookout for that subtle peak-end effect at your local restaurant or Black Friday website crash. There's a chance you'll never see the world in the same way ever again.

This was certainly the case for me.

Fortunately, unlike the slightly unnerving experience of *Baader-Meinhof*, seeing these patterns is actually a good thing. It should fuel your curiosity and feed your excitement. Why? Because identifying these patterns brings competitive advantage. It's an advantage that's unlocked via the better questions these psychological principles (and their adaptations) help us ask.

QUESTIONS TRANSLATE

In their contribution to *Behavioural Science in the Wild*, "Prescriptions for Successfully Scaling Behavioral Interventions" Laura Goodyear, Tanjim Hossain and Dilip Soman share their concerns regarding the field of applied behavioural science.[1] They highlight the risk of approaching behaviour change like shopping in a nudge-store. Here, the risk is that we come in looking for off-the-shelf solutions expecting them to work in all contexts, only to be disappointed. In *Evolutionary Ideas*, rather than assume the direct transferability of solutions (like buying them off the shelf), we celebrate and seek to transfer an existing solution's creative or innovative *potential*.

Let's imagine for a moment that rather than being in the business of psychological innovation, we are now manufacturing and transporting electrical goods. We're in the fridge business! From one perspective it makes sense to centralise production of our fridges. We benefit from huge factories and economies of scale before shipping to every corner of the globe. The problem is this strategy assumes that when the product arrives, there are trucks big enough to transport it, we have customers ready to pay for it and, when all is signed and delivered, the electricity plug fits the local socket.

An alternative approach is to centralise the sourcing of the raw ingredients and to distribute these to local markets, empowering them to build the fridge themselves. I believe this same analogy works for distributing behavioural and psychological innovations. Rather than transporting the final product (like shipping a fridge), we can distribute a solution's potential via its raw ingredients. To create *Evolutionary Ideas*, these ingredients are, ideally, more powerful *questions*.

Unlike evolution in the natural world, with innovation the generation of new solutions is not spontaneous. It must be initiated by people looking to solve problems in new ways. At the end of the book, you'll find a collection of innovation questions generated on this journey. Each question is designed to help you more easily access the underlying evolved psychological principle and, through them, be better able to interrogate your challenge. They will help you translate the value of existing solutions into novel contexts and, because of their abstraction, connect categories and industries typically never discussed in the same sentence. They will help you to convergently adapt on purpose. Over time, you may even begin to internalise these questions in the form of your own checklists.

Despite our best efforts to ensure the transferability of these solutions, it's also important to acknowledge that, unlike our fridge business, in *Evolutionary Ideas* we're not transporting cast iron, copper and steel. Instead, we're working with the most complex organ in the universe: the human brain. With the brain, it's never so simple.

A LENS, NOT A SILVER BULLET

As we end our exploration of *Evolutionary Ideas*, it's important to recognise that behavioural science isn't a perfect or exact science. Throughout the book we have explored a vast array of evolved solutions, sometimes with an overly casual assumption of universality. This isn't always the case. We can't always assume that a solution will work in every context (even if distributed through its raw ingredients), or that people are universally wired to respond in the way an existing theory might anticipate. Context is king.

In his book *When More Is Not Better*, Roger Martin shares a compelling example of the power of context through his examination of the killer whales of Argentina's Valdes peninsula.[2] These splendid creatures have developed an extraordinary way of hunting seals, propelling themselves up onto the beach (essentially beaching themselves) to capture their unsuspecting prey. Because of the smooth pebbles of the Valdes peninsula, the whales are able to work their way back into deeper water. While successful in this particular context, it would be suicidal to transfer the same approach to other environments. Although in *Evolutionary Ideas* we have sought to find similarities across solutions, like the convergent evolution of a dorsal fin, we can't blindly assume transferability. Just sharing this fin doesn't guarantee success in all contexts or environments; place a freshwater fish in salt water and it still dies.

For example, despite strong and wide-reaching evidence on the impact of defaults on decision making and behaviour (as we explored in Chapter 11), when a new default was introduced to encourage organ donation in the Netherlands, the number of residents who registered as non-donors spiked to roughly 40 times the previous month's.[3] Rather than defaulting or subtly endorsing a choice, it was seen as a signal of governmental coercion – threatening the freedoms so highly valued in that society, triggering reactance (as we explored in Chapter 17). Without realising, it became a freshwater fish in salt water.

Just as we cannot dismiss the power of context, it's also important to recognise that behavioural science's classifications are not undisputed laws either. They're broad tendencies.[4] While we have predominantly explored the evolutionarily older, more universal, drivers of human decision making, cultural and individual differences play a significant role when generating and piloting our solutions. By better understanding the hypothesis to be tested, the context or cultural differences to be explored, we can continue to enrich our learning. As Michael Hallsworth, managing director of the Behavioural Insights Team in North America stressed to me, "Behavioural insights is a lens, not an alternative." Sadly, nothing in what you have read so far offers a silver bullet. It can, however, help us to both expand and focus our search for the best solutions.

THE FREEDOM OF A TIGHT BRIEF

A final word on creativity.

The traditional view is that the creative process is unstructured. We assume great ideas are a result of an unpredictable mix of chaos and genius, certainly not a process unlocked via a systematic or replicable approach (heaven forbid, a checklist). In reality, creativity and innovation need both discipline *and* structure. They require processes to broaden our thinking (exploring multiple categories and industries) and focusing (through the single-mindedness of a question or provocation). Throughout this book I have made a similar case for systematic creativity and the structure required for psychological innovation. My ambition has been to share an approach that can be learned, yet still applied with a magical touch.

This book has demonstrated how the classification of evolved psychological solutions (our *psychological principles*) enables us to escape our classic domain and category – transversing industry. Just like the field of biomimicry and TRIZ methodology, these principles help us find new frames to solve the problems we face; our *psychological contradictions*. By identifying similarities in solutions across categories, not only can we broaden our sources of inspiration, avoiding the traps of our category, this also brings us focus and constraint to accelerate our innovation.

While checklists can be valuable when looking to avoid catastrophe on a Boeing 747, when used to innovate they also ensure we don't commence our ideation at random or without hypothesis. We can now more systematically approach our innovation by focusing on the most relevant patterns of psychological solutions, converting these into powerful questions. Limits like these promote focus, which, in turn, stimulates creativity. Just as there may be only seven basic story plots yet thousands of stories, by limiting the number of variables to consider we can accelerate our innovation. Constraints actually fuel it.

As my mentor and former boss, Mark Sareff, reminds us all, "Don't be distressed, even the violin has only four strings!"

EXTINCTION IS EVOLUTION

In innovation, just as in nature, survival is never guaranteed. Sometimes ideas fail. Sometimes (as we've just seen in Dutch defaults), they even backfire. This is true of many creative pursuits. When innovating we also often stumble across ideas that just work, then get excited and ask ourselves how we might generate them again. Jason Hill, chief strategy officer of Ogilvy in Singapore, has a lovely way of putting it: he calls these "happy accidents."

When Jason and I were working to embed behavioural science at Ogilvy in Australia, he reflected, "Now we can have fewer 'happy accidents' and more planned ones." Jason was right. *Evolutionary Ideas* is not about perfection or certainty. It's about making fewer blind assumptions in our innovation, providing a new lens as we continue to ideate, apply, learn and adapt. Rather than luck and chaotic "shots-on-goal," failures help us see how we can consciously adapt moving forwards. When we understand *why* something may have worked or failed, we can increase the likelihood of success in the future.

When it comes to evolutionary ideas, the trick is to apply the right selection pressures early and often, testing our hypotheses within the desired context – only then can we see if it's a fish out of water or not. Knowing this, we can refine our hypothesis or quickly decide to end the breeding programme.

THE CONDITIONS FOR LIFE

As we close, it's important I also square the argument against revolutionary or radical innovation. In truth, we need both.

While following its public launch, Google Glass failed spectacularly, it also unquestionably accelerated the field of wearable technology – paving the way for many others to follow. Just as asteroids colliding with the Earth can create shockwaves and atmospheric changes destroying entire groups of organisms, they also bring new life. Inland tsunamis flood the earth with rich nutrients, forming entirely new habitats with these new constraints then spawning the evolution of novel species. In a similar way, revolutionary, radical and moon-shot innovation can also change the conditions for life. As defined by Altshuller and his colleagues, these moon-shots (the 1%), are capable of changing industries and creating entirely new systems. The invention of the laser enabled surveyors to measure distances with greater accuracy, for example; while the digital camera drove Kodak to extinction. What's inescapable is that between these exceptionally rare impact events, the forces of evolution take over. Good ideas, stable businesses and powerful campaigns survive; the bad ones die out. In this unforgiving and competitive context, *Evolutionary Ideas* offers an alternative route for survival and competitive advantage.

Next time you're faced with a novel challenge, although you might feel you need a revolution or be tempted to start from scratch, close your eyes and swing for the bleachers, now you know that revolutionary ideas are expensive and rare. They take years to develop and have a terrible reputation for failure. Alternatively, every day, someone, somewhere, is facing the very same challenge as you. They may just be looking to solve it in an entirely different category or industry to your own.

Now, next time you need to reinforce trust, aid decision making, trigger action, boost loyalty or improve experience, rather than think you need to conjure something the world has never seen, produce lightning from your pencil or summon that earth-shattering meteor by staring at a blank sheet of paper, you can seek comfort knowing that your solution already exists. More importantly, now you have the tools to find and apply it.

With *Evolutionary Ideas* you can breed from the best. You can accelerate natural processes and systematically – and successfully – out-innovate your competition.

Stop rolling the dice and start birdwatching.

Vive la évolution.

A SUMMARY OF
EVOLUTIONARY IDEAS

- While it's tempting to feel the need to start from scratch when faced with a new challenge, thousands of people have already toiled to address the same problems you're facing right now.

- By classifying patterns of evolved psychological solutions, behavioural science has handed us a new set of keys to systematically innovate – our *psychological principles.*

- These psychological principles can be called upon to address many of the innovation challenges (or *psychological contradictions*) we face, just like the challenge of 'Aiding Decision making without Limiting Choice'.

- By identifying nuanced examples of these principles in the wild, then converting them into powerful questions, we're able to translate these ideas across categories and industries – accelerating innovation.

- Although not a perfect or exact science, this is a process enabling fewer blind assumptions. It's a methodology that can be learned yet still applied *magically.*

- While it's true that revolutionary moon-shots and impact events do happen, in between, the forces of evolution take over.

INNOVATION CHECKLIST

CONTRADICTION 1:
REINFORCING TRUST *WITHOUT* ALTERING THE TRUTH

1. What expense or cost would demonstrate our trustworthiness?

2. How might we illustrate the sacrifice we're willing to make for others?

3. What investment or waste would show our confidence in our product or service?

4. How might we create a clear signal of otherwise unseen trust-affirming activities?

5. What detail is hard to fake yet telling of the honesty of the offer?

6. How might we focus on one specific feature to increase confidence in the whole?

7. What cues would illustrate that there is reputation at stake?

8. How might we ensure broad viewership to enhance reputational costs?

9. How might we communicate promises publicly to reinforce message trustworthiness?

10. How might we open the doors to help people see behind the scenes?

11. How might we cue elements of our production in the product itself?

12. What is an unseen element of our offer which would reinforce trust if noticeable?

13. How might we visualise how complex technology works?

14. How might we deconstruct our product to highlight its hardest-working elements?

15. What unique name might we provide to the hardworking components?

16. What would illustrate that others have conducted the behaviour before?

17. What might we leave behind to show it's a normal or safe response?

18. How might we enable others to rate the trustworthiness of an actor or offer?

19. What might be taken away to illustrate the behaviour of others previously?

20. What would people expect to see that, when removed, shows others have safely engaged?

21. What unexpected absence would increase trust that an action is necessary?

CONTRADICTION 2:
AIDING DECISIONS *WITHOUT* LIMITING CHOICE

1. How might we pre-select a beneficial outcome as *default?*

2. How might we signal a desired or anticipated response?

3. How might we frame the decision in a way *assuming* a desired action?

4. How might we embed our desired outcome into an existing decision?

5. What frequent choice could we bundle our desired decision with?

6. How might we bake a desired outcome into an existing behaviour?

7. How might we use colour, contrast or size to direct attention?

8. What salient cues could we add to reinforce the 'expected' decision?

9. How might we otherwise guide attention to our desired outcome?

10. How might we use concrete words, images or other aids to simplify our choice set?

11. How might we help people to clearly see the outcome of their decisions?

12. What is an associated concrete concept that would aid comprehension of something more abstract?

13. How might we pre-empt a likely response and complete this in advance?

14. How might we pre-complete elements of an answer or decision?

15. How might we recommend options to make it easier to choose?

16. How might we chunk down large tasks to aid decision making?

17. How might we use colour chunks or numbered steps to make choices easier?

18. How might we create additional steps to reinforce consideration and slow down deceptively simple or small decisions?

19. How might we chunk several steps up to ease decision making?

20. How might we repackage multiple decisions to create a single choice?

21. How might we anticipate future decisions and chunk these into one big one?

CONTRADICTION 3:
TRIGGERING ACTION *WITHOUT* FORCING A RESPONSE

1. How might we make our desired action feel familiar, symmetrical, ordered?

2. How might our solution complete an otherwise desirable pattern?

3. What pattern might we break to encourage people to react in response?

4. How might we create an obvious trigger for when action is necessary?

5. How might we turn the invisible benefits of a behaviour into tangible experiences?

6. How might we help people to realise unseen challenges ahead of time?

7. What restriction might encourage people to react in a desired way?

8. What information might we withhold to create intrigue?

9. What can we ask people not to do (knowing they may be tempted to...)?

10. How might we reinforce individual control, particularly when close to acting?

11. How might we endorse an unexpected competing behaviour, reinforcing a desired one?

12. How might we illustrate that the choice is *theirs*?

CONTRADICTION 4:
BOOSTING LOYALTY *WITHOUT* INCREASING REWARDS

1. How might we enable personal interaction (like a signature) to increase commitment to an outcome?

2. How might we encourage people to vocalise or externalise their future intentions?

3. How might a request for loyalty align with existing personal values?

4. How might we help people commit to a desired action while in a 'cold' emotional state?

5. How might we enable people to limit alternative (undesirable) future choices, now?

6. How might we help people impose an unattractive ultimatum for themselves?

7. What could we give to our audience that encourages them to follow through?

8. How might we create a *partial* incentive that's fully realised upon completion?

9. What can we give our audience in advance, committing their future action?

10. How might we help people to see that progress has been made?

11. What invisible steps have already been taken? How might we make these more evident for others?

12. How might we provide an artificial boost to encourage follow-through?

13. How might we include an element of variability in our product experience?

14. How might we bake-in an element of novelty so our product is always fresh?

15. How might we experiment with infrequent negative outcomes (think Doritos Roulette)?

16. How might we create a system that is variable by design?

17. How might we empower individual discretion to create unpredictable experiences for others?

18. How might we remove an element of unnecessary consistency or predictability?

CONTRADICTION 5:
IMPROVING EXPERIENCE *WITHOUT* CHANGING DURATION

1. How might we set expectations to shape experiences?

2. How might we show or tell people what's coming next to remove painful uncertainty?

3. If expectation-setting information is unavailable, how might we tell people what to do instead? (For example, some airports communicate "relax" rather than just "delayed" on their departure communications.)

4. How might we transparently tell people what's taking so long?

5. How might we expose the process so people can see what's happening and where they stand?

6. How might we illustrate a sense of progress and set clear expectations?

7. How might we provide a sense of control in scenarios that feel ambiguous, unclear or stressful?

8. What decisions can we enable people to make for themselves (even if these might be tertiary to the ultimate goal)?

9. What could we give people to increase their sense of agency during times of uncertainty?

10. How might we embed activities or create distractions during unoccupied time?

11. How might we make unavoidable waiting times an opportunity for alternative experiences?

12. How might we make existing boredom busters (like playing on the phone) more relevant to the overall service experience (just like the Eurostar)?

13. How might we disrupt expectations to create a memorable experience?

14. What multi-sensory element will heighten specific moments?

15. How might we break category norms with a big-hearted or fun gesture?

16. How might we consider a product's consumption over time?

17. What would ensure that the most positive elements are enjoyed at the end?

18. What valuable (yet less attractive) components could we include in the middle of an experience to benefit from duration neglect?

19. How might we turn an unexpected negative event into a positive one?

20. How might we share bad news in a more enjoyable or memorable way?

21. What positive association could we create to remove the sting of an error?

ACKNOWLEDGEMENTS

TRUE TO ITS philosophy, this book isn't a result of the lone pursuit of any one individual in isolation.

Firstly, I'd like to thank my wonderful and ever-supportive family, particularly my amazing mum who has been my 'editor at large' for decades and continues to this day. My dad, whose cunning passion for ideas I have been fortunate to have inherited, and my wonderful, ever-supportive sister, Hannah. To my beautiful Michelle, Mila and Riley who have so generously lent me out over years of weekends and evenings for the creation of this book.

To the wonderful team at Ogilvy who continue to inspire and challenge me – I couldn't ask for a group of smarter, kinder and more creative people to spend my days with. I hope this book does justice to the quality of thinking and creative standards you have set.

I thank Gerry Cyron, David Fox, Adam Ferrier and Mark Sareff for their ongoing mentorship and support throughout my career. This book wouldn't be here if it wasn't for your critical input over several years.

I thank Tim Philips for his thoughtful guidance and belief

that this book could be possible, and, of course, Christopher Parker, Nick Fletcher and the team from Harriman House.

I would also like to thank Richard Shotton, Dilip Soman, Michael Hallsworth, Nina Mazar, Ryan Buell, Koen Smets, Eaon Pritchard, Laura Clarke, Loove Broms, Nir Eyal, Jon Horbaly, Eduardo Lima, Dane Smith, Mike Hughes, Dan Bennett, Tal Oron-Gilad, Jordan Buck, Phil Barrington, Sambit Mohanty, Michael Pawyln, Bri Williams, Will Rust, Vinod Kumar, Tom Hussey, Declan Grindrod, Nic Stone and my very talented cousin, Phil Murrills, all of whom have touched this book and informed its development in some way.

Finally, this book has undoubtedly been influenced by my opportunity to work alongside the great Rory Sutherland. Rory has shaped my interpretation of our industry and the creative application of behavioural science. I consider myself extremely fortunate to have worked so closely with Rory for many years. It's a relationship I cherish and one which has inspired many elements of this book. I am forever grateful for this.

IMAGE ATTRIBUTIONS

The author has made every effort to credit the copyright owners of any material that appears within and will correct any omissions in subsequent editions if notified. All images not attributed are photographs by the author.

Image 10 (middle): Johan Swanepoel. Shutterstock ID: 145307344.

Image 10 (bottom): Pexels (CC0).

Image 11 (top): Sardaka. CC BY 3.0.

Image 11 (bottom): Permission granted by Octopus Energy.

Image 12 (top): Jeff Morgan; Alamy Stock Photo Image ID:B7M5E7.

Image 12 (middle): Evan-Amos, Public Domain.

Image 12 (bottom): Michele Salvatore. Shutterstock ID: 1555620848.

Image 13 (bottom): Source: Adil Ray OBE @adilray.

Image 14 (top): Permission granted by Colenso BBDO.

Image 14 (bottom): Permission granted by Agency: MARCEL; Chief creative director: Anne de Maupeou; Executive creative director: Dimitri Guerassimov & Fabien Teichner; Creative director: Julien Benmoussa; Copywriters: Damien Lebreuilly, Jonathan Wawer; Art directors: Pierre Delort, Ally Qamari, Guillaume Delattre.

Image 15 (bottom): Permission granted by Beatrice; Image Credit: Vi Huu Wood.

Image 16 (top): Blanchi Costela, Getty Images. Image 641194872.

Image 16 (middle): Permission granted by Nestle Australia.

Image 16 (bottom): Asadykov. Shutterstock ID: 581979928.

Image 18 (top): Public domain.

Image 18 (bottom): Wee dezign Shutterstock ID: 382183615.

Image 21 (top): Permission granted by F/Nazca.

Image 21 (middle): Permission granted by Jon Horbaly, CEO Altitude Medical.

Image 21 (bottom): Permission granted by Savlon India and Savlon Swasth India Mission.

Image 22 (top): Public Domain.

Image 23 (top): By Lombroso, Public Domain.

Image 25: Permission granted by Ogilvy Australia.

Image 26 (top): Source: www.bhwlawfirm.com/reasonable-doubt-burden-of-proof.

Image 26 (bottom): Mind the gap sign by Vladislav Gajic. Shutterstock ID: 225810664.

Image 27 (top): Permission granted by the Bank of Canada.

Image 27 (middle): Ramin Talaie, Getty Images. Image no. 526086332.

Image 28 (middle): Permission granted by Loove Broms & Karin Ehrnberger.

Image 29 (middle): GagoDesign, Shutterstock ID: 1575044092.

Image 29 (bottom): Dwernertl at the English Wikipedia (creative commons).

Image 30: Copyright (C) 2002–2021 Kenneth & Gabrielle Adelman,

California Coastal Records Project, www.Californiacoastline.org.

Image 31 (top): Creative Commons.

Image 31 (middle): Permission granted by Kate Davies; Image Credit - Oliver Agency; Creative Director Sam Jacobs; *The Guardian.*

Image 31 (bottom): © Kellogg Europe Trading Limited used with permission.

Image 32 (bottom): Permission granted by TBWA\Melbourne.

Image 33: Public Domain (Media Kit).

Image 34: *The Guardian,* Public Domain.

Image 35 (top): Permission granted by Madhusudhan Rao.

Image 36 (bottom): Source - Canada Post.

Image 37 (top): Permission granted by Erika Erwin.

Image 37 (middle): A. Kniesel; GNU Free Documentation License.

Image 37 (bottom): Permission granted by Dan Bennett.

Image 38 (bottom): Permission granted by Kimberly Richter.

Image 40 (top): KungCrayfish. Shutterstock ID: 1838245186.

Image 40 (middle): Siam.pukkato. Shutterstock ID: 1151311997.

Image 40 (bottom): Source - WeTransfer.

Image 41 (top): Permission granted by AKQA.

Image 41 (middle): Copyright © Anna van Kooij.

Image 42 (top): Permission granted by @danishadventurer.

Image 42 (middle): Permission granted by @stadtkanzler.

Image 44: Source - Amazon.co.uk.

ENDNOTES

INTRODUCTION

1   Christensen, C. M., Dillon, K., Hall, T., & Duncan, D. S. (2016). *Competing Against Luck: The Story of Innovation and Customer Choice* (1st ed.). New York, USA: Harper Business.

2   Emmer, M. (2021, January 5). 95 Percent of New Products Fail: Here Are 6 Steps to Make Sure Yours Don't. Retrieved 26 October 2021, from www.inc.com/marc-emmer/95-percent-of-new-products-fail-here-are-6-steps-to-make-sure-yours-dont.html.

3   Gage, D. (2012, September 20). The Venture Capital Secret: 3 Out of 4 Start-Ups Fail. WSJ. Retrieved from www.wsj.com.

4   Gleeson, B. (2017, July 25). 1 Reason Why Most Change Management Efforts Fail. Forbes. Retrieved from www.forbes.com.

5   Afeyan, N., & Pisano, G. P. (2021). What Evolution Can Teach Us About Innovation Lessons from the life sciences. From the Magazine (September–October 2021), *Harvard Business Review*.

6   Ridley, M. (2015). *The Evolution of Everything* (1st ed.). New York, USA: Harper.

7   Leman, P.J., & Cinnirella, M. (2007). A major event has a major cause: Evidence for the role of heuristics in reasoning about conspiracy theories. *Social Psychological Review*, 9(2) 18–28.

8   Gilovich, T., & Savitsky, K. (2002). Like goes with like: The role of representativeness in erroneous and pseudo-scientific beliefs. *Heuristics and Biases*, 617–624. doi.org/10.1017/cbo9780511808098.036.

9 Henslin, J. M. (1967). Craps and magic. *American Journal of Sociology*, 73(3), 316–330. doi.org/10.1086/224479.

10 Sharot, T. (2011). The optimism bias. *Current Biology*, 21(23), R941–R945. doi.org/10.1016/j.cub.2011.10.030.

11 Terninko, J., Zusman, A., & Zlotin, B. (1998). Systematic Innovation: An Introduction to TRIZ (Theory of Inventive Problem Solving). *APICS Series on Resource Management* (1st ed.). Boca Raton, USA: CRC Press.

12 Ridley, M. (2020). *How Innovation Works: And Why It Flourishes in Freedom* (1st ed.). New York, USA: Harper.

13 Ridley, M. (2015). *The Evolution of Everything* (1st ed.). New York, USA: Harper.

14 Propos d'un Normand (1908); as quoted in Ridley, M. (2015). *The Evolution of Everything* (1st ed.). New York, USA: Harper.

15 Fogg, B. J. (2020). *Tiny Habits: The Small Changes That Change Everything*. Boston, USA: Mariner Books.

16 Sagarin, R. (2012). *Learning From the Octopus: How Secrets from Nature Can Help Us Fight Terrorist Attacks, Natural Disasters, and Disease* (1st ed.). New York, USA: Basic Books.

Additional Sources & Further Reading

Bilton, N. (2021, September 9). Why Google Glass Broke. *The New York Times*. Retrieved from www.nytimes.com.

Gogatz, A., & Mondejar, R. (2004). *Business Creativity: Breaking the Invisible Barriers*. London, UK: Palgrave Macmillan.

Loh, H. T., He, C., & Shen, L. (2006). Automatic classification of patent documents for TRIZ users. *World Patent Information*, 28(1), 6–13. doi.org/10.1016/j.wpi.2005.07.007.

Norman, D. A. (2013). *The Design of Everyday Things* (Revised and Expanded Edition.). Cambridge, Massachusetts, The MIT Press.

Orloff, M. A. (2006). *Inventive Thinking through TRIZ: A Practical Guide* (2nd ed.). New York, USA: Springer.

Spina, R. R., Ji, L. J., Tieyuan Guo, Zhiyong Zhang, Ye Li, & Fabrigar, L. (2010). Cultural differences in the representativeness heuristic: Expecting a correspondence in magnitude between cause and effect. *Personality and Social Psychology Bulletin*, 36(5), 583–597. doi.org/10.1177/0146167210368278.

Yusof, S. M., & Awad, A. A. (2014). A brief review of theory of inventive problem solving (TRIZ) methodology. *Jurnal Teknik Industri Universitas Bung Hatta.* Retrieved from ejurnal.bunghatta.ac.id/index.php/JTI-UBH/article/view/3399.

CHAPTER 1: SWAPPING SPIDERS FOR SWEETS

1   WWF. (2018, April 25). Top 10 facts about Adélie penguins. Retrieved 27 October 2021, from www.wwf.org.uk/learn/fascinating-facts/adelie-penguins.

2   McKeag, T. (2012). Auspicious forms: Designing the Sanyo Shinkansen 500-Series bullet train. *Zygote Quarterly,* Summer 2012. ISSN 1927-8314.

3   Ibid.

4   Pawlyn, M. (Personal Communication, 2019).

5   Biomimicry Institute. (n.d.). What is Biomimicry? Retrieved 27 October 2021, from biomimicry.org/what-is-biomimicry.

6   Sagarin (2012).

Additional Sources & Further Reading

Burnham, T. C. (2013). Toward a neo-Darwinian synthesis of neoclassical and behavioral economics. *Journal of Economic Behavior & Organization,* 90, S113–S127. doi.org/10.1016/j.jebo.2012.12.015.

Grant, B. R., & Grant, P. R. (2003). What Darwin's finches can teach us about the evolutionary origin and regulation of biodiversity. *BioScience,* 53(10), 965. doi.org/10.1641/0006-3568(2003)053[0965:WDFCTU]2.0.CO;2.

Leary, C. (2021, February 7). 8 Uncanny Examples of Convergent Evolution. Retrieved 26 October 2021, from www.treehugger.com/uncanny-examples-convergent-evolution-4869742.

Meijer, H. (2018, July 30). Origin of the species: Where did Darwin's finches come from? *The Guardian.* Retrieved from www.theguardian.com.

CHAPTER 2: INNOVATION IMPOSSIBLE

1   Genrich Altshuller: Father of TRIZ. By Leonid Lerner. Retrieved from rosetta.vn/triz/wp-content/uploads/sites/8/2019/01/Genrich_Altshuller_Father_of_TRIZ.pdf.

2   smithhn. (2007, March 30). *Genrich Altshuller Teaching TRIZ.* 1 of 6 [Video file]. Retrieved from www.youtube.com/watch?v=dawPn8neL-U.

3   Thomas, J. (2020, July 16). Heart Disease: Facts, Statistics, and You. Retrieved 27 October 2021, from www.healthline.com/health/heart-disease/statistics.

4   Naseem, R., Zhao, L., Liu, Y., & Silberschmidt, V. V. (2017). Experimental and computational studies of poly-L-lactic acid for cardiovascular applications: recent progress. *Mechanics of Advanced Materials and Modern Processes*, 3(1). doi.org/10.1186/s40759-017-0028-y.

Additional Sources & Further Reading

ICG Consulting. (2020). TRIZ Success Cases. Author. Retrieved (via Web Archive) from web.archive.org/web/20090106180503/http://www.xtriz.com/documents/TRIZSuccessCases.pdf.

ssabusiness. (2012, May 31). Triz Case Study – Dissolving Stent [Video file]. Retrieved from youtu.be/_1vNamfZ2qE.

Teplitskiy, A. (2007, July 2). Student Corner: Principle of Nesting. Retrieved 1 November 2021 (via Web Archive), from web.archive.org/web/20201124071224/ https://triz-journal.com/student-corner-the-principle-of-nesting.

TRIZ40 by SolidCreativity. (n.d.). The TRIZ 40 Principles. Retrieved 27 October 2021, from www.triz40.com/aff_Principles_TRIZ.php.

Wallace, M. (2000, June 30). The science of invention. *Salon.* Retrieved from www.salon.com.

Zeeman, A. (2020, July 19). Genrich Altshuller. Retrieved 27 October 2021, from www.toolshero.com/toolsheroes/genrich-altshuller.

CHAPTER 3: THE QUICK AND THE DEAD

1   Adelson, E. H. (1993). Perceptual organization and the judgment of brightness. *Science*, 262(5142), 2042–2044. doi.org/10.1126/science.82661.

2   Ibid.

3   Gilchrist, A. L. (2010). Lightness Constancy. In Goldstein, E. B. (Ed.), *Sage Encyclopedia of Perception.* London, UK: Sage.

4   Cherniak, C. (1990). The bounded brain: Toward quantitative neuroanotomy. *Journal of Cognitive Neuroscience*, 2(1), 58–68. doi.org/10.1162/jocn.1990.2.1.58.

5   Hofman, M. A. (2012). Design principles of the human brain. *Evolution of the Primate Brain*, 373–390. doi.org/10.1016/b978-0-444-53860-4.00018-0.

6   Wilson, T. D. (2004). *Strangers to Ourselves: Discovering the Adaptive Unconscious*. Cambridge, USA: Belknap Press: An Imprint of Harvard University Press.

7   Kahneman, D. (2013). *Thinking, Fast and Slow* (1st pbk. ed.). New York, USA: Farrar, Straus and Giroux.

8   Haidt, J. (2012). *The Righteous Mind Why Good People are Divided by Politics and Religion* (1st ed.). New York, USA: Pantheon Books.

9   Thaler, R.H. (1987). Anomalies: The January effect. *Journal of Economic Perspectives*, 1(1): 197–201.

10   Frederick, S., Loewenstein, G., & O'Donoghue, T. (2002). Time discounting and time preference: A critical review. *Journal of Economic Literature*, 40, 351–401.

11   Burd, M. (2010). Hunting, gathering, investing, globalizing: The biological roots of economic behaviour. *Systems Research and Behavioral Science*, 27(5), 510–522. doi.org/10.1002/sres.1055.

12   Mosley, M. (2011, May 5). Anatomical clues to human evolution from fish. *BBC News*. Retrieved from www.bbc.com.

13   Halpern, D. (2016). *Inside the Nudge Unit: How Small Changes Can Make a Big Difference*. London, UK: WH Allen.

14   Fehr, E., & Gachter, S. (2000). Fairness and retaliation: The economics of reciprocity. *The Journal of Economic Perspectives*, 14(3), doi.org/10.1257/jep.14.3.159.

15   Tversky, A., & Kahneman, D. (1986). Rational choice and the framing of decisions. *The Journal of Business*, 59(S4): S251. doi:10.1086/296365.

16   Cialdini, R. B. (2007). *Influence : The Psychology of Persuasion* (1st Collins Business Essentials ed.). New York, USA: Collins.

17   Kruger, J., Wirtz, D., Boven, L., & Altermatt, T. (2004). The effort heuristic. *Journal of Experimental Social Psychology*, 40, 91–98.

18   Quarmby, D.A. (1967) Choice of travel mode for the journey to work. *Journal of Transport Economics and Policy*, 273-314.

Additional Sources & Further Reading

Hines, N. (2016, March 24). Why Your Eyes Are Fooled by the Famous Checker Shadow Illusion. Retrieved 27 October 2021, from allthatsinteresting.com/checker-shadow-illusion.

Thomson, G., & Macpherson, F. (2017, July). Adelson's Checker-Shadow Illusion. Retrieved 27 October 2021, from www.illusionsindex.org/ir/ checkershadow.

CHAPTER 4: SEEING WITH NEW EYES

1   Pagel, M. (2017). Q&A: What is human language, when did it evolve and why should we care? *BMC Biology*, 15(1). doi.org/10.1186/s12915-017-0405-3.

2   TED. (2018, May 2). How language shapes the way we think. Lera Boroditsky [Video file]. Retrieved from youtu.be/RKK7wGAYP6k.

3   Winawer, J., Witthoft, N., Frank, M. C., Wu, L., Wade, A. R., & Boroditsky, L. (2007). Russian blues reveal effects of language on color discrimination. *Proceedings of the National Academy of Sciences*, 104(19), 7780–7785. doi.org/10.1073/pnas.0701644104.

4   Wu, K., & Dunning, D. A. (2019). Hypocognitive mind: How lack of conceptual knowledge confines what people see and remember. *PsyArXiv*. doi.org/10.31234/osf.io/29ryz.

5   Chen, M. K. (2013). The effect of language on economic behavior: Evidence from savings rates, health behaviors, and retirement assets. *American Economic Review*, 103(2), 690–731.

6   Lin, J. T., Bumcrot, C., Ulicny, T., Lusardi, A., Mottola, G., Kieffer, C., & Walsh, G. (2016). Financial capability in the United States 2016. Washington, DC: *FINRA Investor Education Foundation* – as referenced in Wu, K., & Dunning, D. (2018). Hypocognition: Making sense of the landscape beyond one's conceptual reach. *Review of General Psychology*, 22(1), 25–35. doi.org/10.1037/gpr0000126.

7   Cowie, C. C., Rust, K. F., Byrd-Holt, D. D., Eberhardt, M. S., Flegal, K. M., Engelgau, M. M., & Gregg, E. W. (2006). Prevalence of diabetes and impaired fasting glucose in adults in the U.S. population. *Diabetes Care,* 29, 1263–1268. 10.2337/dco6-0062 (in Wu & Dunning , 2018).

CHAPTER 5: PSYCHOLOGICAL TRIZ

1   Wansink, B., Kent, R. J., & Hoch, S. J. (1998). An anchoring and adjustment model of purchase quantity decisions. *Journal of Marketing Research*, 35(1), 71. doi.org/10.2307/3151931.

2   Goldenberg, J., Mazursky, D., & Solomon, S. (1999). The fundamental templates of quality ads. *Marketing Science*, 18(3), 333–351. doi.org/10.1287/mksc.18.3.333.

3   Boyd, D., & Goldenberg, J. (2013). *Inside the Box: The Creative Method that Works for Everyone.* London, UK: Profile Books.

4   Pisano, G. P. (2019). *Creative Construction: The DNA of Sustained Innovation.* New York, USA: PublicAffairs.

5   Radford, C., McNutt, J. W., Rogers, T. et al. (2020). Artificial eyespots on cattle reduce predation by large carnivores. *Commun Biol* 3, 430 doi.org/10.1038/s42003-020-01156-0.

6   Norton, M. I., Mochon, D., & Ariely, D. (2012). The IKEA effect: When labor leads to love. *Journal of Consumer Psychology,* 22(3), 453–460. doi.org/10.1016/j.jcps.2011.08.002.

7   Buell, R. W. (2019). Show Your Customers How Hard You're Working for Them. From the Magazine (March–April 2019), *Harvard Business Review.*

8   Ibid.

9   Nikiforuk, A. (2011). What saves energy? Shame: ENERGY & EQUITY: There's power in people caring what their neighbours do. *The Tyee* – accessed November 2021 from thetyee.ca/Opinion/2011/07/14/EnergyShaming.

10   Genrich Altshuller in Orloff, M. A. (2006). *Inventive Thinking through TRIZ: A Practical Guide* (2nd ed.). New York, USA: Springer.

11   Sutherland, R. (Personal communication, 2019).

12   Bill Bernbach cited in Young, J. W. (2003). *A Technique for Producing Ideas.* New York, USA: McGraw-Hill Education.

Additional Sources & Further Reading

Heath, C., & Heath, D. (2007). *Made to Stick: Why Some Ideas Survive and Others Die* (1st ed.). London, UK: Random House.

Orloff, M. A. (2006). *Inventive Thinking through TRIZ: A Practical Guide* (2nd ed.). New York, USA: Springer.

Sutherland, R. (2019). *Alchemy: The Surprising Power of Ideas That Don't Make Sense.* London, UK: WH Allen.

CHAPTER 6: TALK IS CHEAP

1   Kraus, M. W., Huang, C., & Keltner, D. (2010). Tactile communication, cooperation, and performance: An ethological study of the NBA. *Emotion* (Washington, D.C.), 10(5), 745–749. doi.org/10.1037/a0019382.

2   Uleman, J. (1999). Spontaneous versus intentional inferences in impression formation. In S. Chaiken & Y. Trope (Eds). *Dual-Process Theories in Social Psychology*. New York, USA: The Guilford Press. 141–160.

3   Stecher, K., & Counts, S. (2008). Thin Slices of Online Profile Attributes. Presented at the International Conference on Weblogs and Social Media, Seattle, USA: University of Washington & Microsoft Research.

4   McKnight, D. H., Choudhury, V. & Kacmar, C. J., (2002). The impact of initial consumer trust on intentions to transact with a web site: A trust building model. *Journal of Strategic Information* Systems, 11, 297–323.

5   Raine, L., & Fox, S. (2000, November 26). Section 2: Health Seekers. What health seekers want and how they hunt for it. Retrieved 27 November, 2021, from www.pewresearch.org/internet/2000/11/26/section-2-health-seekers.

6   Castledine, G. (1996). Nursing's image: It is how you use your stethoscope that counts. *British Journal of Nursing*, 5(14), 882–822.

7   McGlone, M. S., & Tofighnakhsh, J. (1999). The Keats heuristic: Rhyme as reason in aphorism interpretation. *Poetics*, 4(26), 235–244.

Additional Sources & Further Reading

Amerland, D. (2015). *The Tribe That Discovered Trust: How Trust is Created, Propagated, Lost and Regained in Commercial Interactions*. Mount Lebanon, Lebanon: New Line Publishing.

Carey, B. (2010, February 22). New Research Focuses on the Power of Physical Contact. *The New York Times*. Retrieved from www.nytimes.com.

Carter, G. G., & Wilkinson, G. S. (2013). Food sharing in vampire bats: Reciprocal help predicts donations more than relatedness or harassment. *Proceedings of the Royal Society B: Biological Sciences*, 280(1753). doi.org/10.1098/rspb.2012.2573.

Jaffe, D. (2018, December 5). The Essential Importance of Trust: How to Build It or Restore It. *Forbes*. Retrieved from www.forbes.com.

Kramer, R. M. (2009). Rethinking Trust. From the Magazine (June 2009), *Harvard Business Review*.

Okasha, S. (2013, July 21). Biological Altruism. *Stanford Encyclopedia of Philosophy*. Retrieved 27 October 2021, from plato.stanford.edu/entries/altruism-biological.

Waytz, A. [Northwestern University – Kellogg School of Management]. (01–01–01). The Importance of First Impressions and Trust. The Trust Project [Video file]. Retrieved from www.kellogg.northwestern.edu/trust-project/videos/waytz-ep-2.aspx.

CHAPTER 7: IF IT LOOKS LIKE A DUCK

1   Maan, M., Cummings, M., Associate Editor: Dean C. Adams, & Editor: Ruth G. Shaw. (2012). Poison frog colors are honest signals of toxicity, particularly for bird predators. *The American Naturalist*, 179(1), E1–E14. doi:10.1086/663197.

2   Parker, R. (2018, October 30). 'Red Dead Redemption 2' Breaks Records With $725 Million Opening Weekend. *The Hollywood Reporter*. Retrieved from www.hollywoodreporter.com.

3   Reid, C. (2018, September 23). 'Red Dead Redemption 2' Will Be So Realistic Horse's Balls Shrink In The Cold. Retrieved 27 October 2021, from www.ladbible.com/entertainment/gaming-red-dead-redemption-2-graphics-will-show-horses-balls-shrink-in-cold-20180923.

4   Ogilvy Consulting. (2018, June 13). Don Marti - Media Buying For Protozoa Nudgestock 2018 [Video file]. Retrieved from youtu.be/Q5vfuyWO2QI.

5   TEDx Talks. (2019, May 24). Designing For Trust. Dan Ariely | TEDxPorto [Video file]. Retrieved from youtu.be/k5MfuwMNcMo.

6   Perkin, N. (2015, July 17). David Lee Roth and Brown M & Ms. Retrieved 27 October 2021, from www.onlydeadfish.co.uk/only_dead_fish/2015/07/david-lee-roth-and-brown-m-ms.html.

7   Ogilvy Consulting (2018, June 13).

Additional Sources & Further Reading

Eschner, K. (2016, December 30). The Story of the Real Canary in the Coal Mine. *Smithsonian Magazine*. Retrieved from www.smithsonianmag.com.

Johnston, R. (2018, September 26). Red Dead Redemption 2 Is Set To Be Incredible, Because Of Horse Balls. Retrieved 27 October 2021, from junkee.com/best-thing-red-dead-redemption-horses-balls/176313.

McAndrew, F. T. (2018). Costly signaling theory. *Encyclopedia of Evolutionary Psychological Science*, 1–8. doi.org/10.1007/978-3-319-16999-6_3483-1.

Morrison, M. (2018, September 22). Red Dead Redemption 2: Horse Balls Shrink in Cold Weather. Retrieved 27 October 2021, from screenrant.com/ red-dead-redemption-2-horse-balls-shrink.

Raaphorst, N., & Walle, S. (2020). Trust, fairness, and signaling. *The Handbook of Public Sector Communication*, 59–70. doi.org/10.1002/ 9781119263203.ch3.

The Smoking Gun. (2008, December 11). Van Halen's Legendary M&M's Rider. Retrieved 27 October 2021, from www.thesmokinggun.com/ documents/crime/van-halens-legendary-mms-rider.

van Vugt, M., & Hardy, C. L. (2009). Cooperation for reputation: Wasteful contributions as costly signals in public goods. *Group Processes & Intergroup Relations*, 13(1), 101–111. doi.org/10.1177/1368430209342258.

CHAPTER 8: I 'LL BELIEVE IT WHEN I SEE IT

1   Kruger, J., Wirtz, D., Boven, L. V., & Altermatt, T. W. (2004). The effort heuristic. *Journal of Experimental Social Psychology*, 40(1), 91–98. doi.org/10.1016/S0022-1031(03)00065-9.

2   Buell (2019).

3   Ibid.

4   Buell, R. W., & Norton, M. I. (2011). The labor illusion: How operational transparency increases perceived value. *Management Science*, 57(9), 1564–1579. doi.org/10.1287/mnsc.1110.1376.

5   Norton, M. I., & Buell, R. W. (2011). Think Customers Hate Waiting? Not So Fast. From the Magazine (May 2011), *Harvard Business Review*.

6   Chalayut, C. (2012, June 30). *Sorry About the Twigs, Folks* [Video file]. Retrieved from youtu.be/_2chTI14FQQ.

7   Monteith's Crushed Cider: Sorry About the Twigs, Folks. Cannes Creative Lions, Creative Effectiveness Lions, 2013 (Downloaded from WARC).

8   Sutherland (2019).

9   Buell, R. (Personal communication, 2020).

CHAPTER 9: SAFETY IN NUMBERS

1   Cialdini, R. B. (2001). Harnessing the science of persuasion. *Harvard Business Review*, 79(9), 72–81.

2 Cialdini, R. B, Raymond, R. R., & Kallgren, C. A. (1990). A focus theory of normative conduct: Recycling the concept of norms to reduce littering in public places. *Journal of Personality and Social Psychology*, 58(6), 1015–1026.

3 Stewart-Williams, S. (2019). The Ape That Understood the Universe: How the Mind and Culture Evolve. Cambridge, USA: Cambridge University Press. doi.org/10.1017/9781108763516.

4 Parry, H. (2016, June 18). Expert claims mysterious "bent" trees were secret Native Americans trail markers. *Mail Online*. Retrieved from www.dailymail.co.uk.

5 Cialdini et al., (1990).

6 Martin, R., & Randal, J., (2008). How is donation behaviour affected by the donations of others? *Journal of Economic Behavior & Organization*, 67(1), 228–238.

7 Sagarin (2012).

Additional Sources & Further Reading

BBC Earth. (2017, February 3). Amazing Fish Form Giant Ball to Scare Predators Blue Planet | BBC Earth [Video file]. Retrieved from youtu.be/15B8qN9dre4.

Criscione, L. (2019, August 13). The Importance of Social Proof as a Trust Signal. Retrieved 27 October 2021, from online.wharton.upenn.edu/blog/the-importance-of-social-proof-as-a-trust-signal.

Eşanu, E. (2019, November 4). Norms Decide User Behaviour - UX Planet. Retrieved 27 October 2021, from uxplanet.org/behavioural-economics-descriptive-norms-97770a32a094.

The Trail Tree Project. (n.d.). Retrieved 1 November 2021 (via Web Archive), from web.archive.org/web/20190913102559/http://www.mountainstewards.org/project/project_trees.html.

Williams, D. (2018, October 14). Mysterious bent trees are actually Native American trail markers. *outdoorrevival*. Retrieved 27 October 2021, from www.outdoorrevival.com/news/mysterious-bent-trees-are-actually-native-american-trail-markers.html?safari=1.

Zara, C. (2019, December 18). How Facebook's 'like' button hijacked our attention and broke the 2010s. *Fast Company*. Retrieved from www.fastcompany.com.

CHAPTER 10: SPOILT FOR CHOICE

1   Fair, J. (2020, January 14). Apex predators in the wild: which mammals are the most dangerous? *Discover Wildlife (BBC Wildlife)*. Retrieved from www.discoverwildlife.com.

2   Gonzalez-Bellido, P. T., Peng, H., Yang, J., Georgopoulos, A. P., & Olberg, R. M. (2012). Eight pairs of descending visual neurons in the dragonfly give wing motor centers accurate population vector of prey direction. *Proceedings of the National Academy of Sciences*, 110(2), 696–701. doi.org/10.1073/pnas.1210489109.

3   Wiederman, S., & O'Carroll, D. (2013). Selective attention in an insect visual neuron. *Current Biology*, 23(2), 156–161. doi.org/10.1016/j.cub.2012.11.048.

4   Iyengar, S. (2011). *The Art of Choosing*. Zaltbommel, Netherlands: Van Haren Publishing.

5   Ibid.

6   Botti, S., & Iyengar, S. S. (2004). The psychological pleasure and pain of choosing: When people prefer choosing at the cost of subsequent outcome satisfaction. *Journal of Personality and Social Psychology*, 87(3), 312–326. doi.org/10.1037/0022-3514.87.3.312.

7   Haynes, G. (2009). Testing the boundaries of the choice overload phenomenon: The effect of number of options and time pressure on decision difficulty and satisfaction. *Psychology and Marketing*, 26, 204 - 212. 10.1002/mar.20269.

8   Inbar, Y., Botti, S., & Hanko, K. (2011). Decision speed and choice regret: When haste feels like waste. *Journal of Experimental Social Psychology*, 47(3), 533–540. doi.org/10.1016/j.jesp.2011.01.011.

9   Iyengar, S. S., & Lepper, M. R. (2000). When choice is demotivating: Can one desire too much of a good thing? *Journal of Personality and Social Psychology*, 79(6), 995–1006. doi.org/10.1037/0022-3514.79.6.995.

10   Chernev, A. (2003). When more is less and less is more: The role of ideal point availability and assortment in consumer choice. *Journal of Consumer Research*, 30(2), 170–183. doi.org/10.1086/376808.

11   Zak, H. (2020, January 21). Adults Make More Than 35,000 Decisions Per Day. Here Are 4 Ways to Prevent Mental Burnout - Don't let decision fatigue get the best of you. *Inc.* Retrieved from www.inc.com.

12   Sethi-Iyengar, S., Huberman, G., & Jiang, G. (2004). How much choice is too much? Contributions to 401(k) retirement plans. *Pension Design and Structure*, 83–96. doi.org/10.1093/0199273391.003.0005.

13   Schwartz, B. (2016). *The Paradox of Choice: Why More Is Less.* New York, USA: Ecco.

14   Parrish, A. E., Evans, T. A., & Beran, M. J. (2015). Rhesus macaques (Macaca mulatta) exhibit the decoy effect in a perceptual discrimination task. *Attention, Perception & Psychophysics,* 77(5), 1715–1725. doi.org/10.3758/s13414-015-0885-6.

15   Burd, M. (2010). Hunting, gathering, investing, globalizing: the biological roots of economic behaviour. *Systems Research and Behavioral Science,* 27(5). dx.doi.org.ezproxy1.library.usyd.edu.au/10.1002/sres.1055.

16   Stoffel, S. T., Yang, J., Vlaev, I., & von Wagner, C. (2019). Testing the decoy effect to increase interest in colorectal cancer screening. *PloS One,* 14(3), e0213668–e0213668. doi.org/10.1371/journal.pone.0213668.

17   Bateson, M., Healy, S. D., & Hurly, T. A. (2003). Context–dependent foraging decisions in rufous hummingbirds. *Proceedings of the Royal Society.* B, Biological Sciences, 270(1521), 1271–1276. doi.org/10.1098/rspb.2003.2365.

18   Thaler, R. H., Sunstein, C. R., & Balz, J. P. (2010). Choice architecture. *SSRN Electronic Journal.* doi.org/10.2139/ssrn.1583509.

19   Ibid.

Additional Sources & Further Reading:

Greenleaf, E. A., & Lehmann, D. R. (1995). Reasons for substantial delay in consumer decision making. *Journal of Consumer Research,* 22(2), 186. doi.org/10.1086/209444.

Kahn, B., Moore, W. L., & Glazer, R. (1987). Experiments in constrained choice. *Journal of Consumer Research,* 14(1), 96. doi.org/10.1086/209096.

CHAPTER 11: GO WITH THE FLOW

1   Rettner, R. (2009, July 13). Why Are Human Brains So Big? *Livescience. Com.* Retrieved from www.livescience.com.

2   Resnick, B. (2018, May 23). Why do humans have such huge brains? Scientists have a few hypotheses. *Vox.* Retrieved from www.vox.com.

3   Ibid.

4   Mergenthaler, P., Lindauer, U., Dienel, G. A., & Meisel, A. (2013). Sugar for the brain: the role of glucose in physiological and pathological brain function. *Trends in Neurosciences,* 36(10), 587–597. doi.org/10.1016/j.tins.2013.07.001.

5   Bellini-Leite, S. (2013). The embodied embedded character of system 1 processing. *Mens Sana Monographs*, 11(1), 239–252. https://doi.org/10.4103/0973-1229.109345.

6   Jachimowicz, J., Duncan, S., Weber, E., & Johnson, E. (2019). When and why defaults influence decisions: A meta-analysis of default effects. *Behavioural Public Policy*, 3(2), 159-186. doi:10.1017/bpp.2018.43.

7   Peters, J., Beck, J., Lande, J., Pan, Z., Cardel, M., Ayoob, K., & Hill, J. O. (2016). Using healthy defaults in Walt Disney World restaurants to improve nutritional choices. *Journal of the Association for Consumer Research*, 1(1), 92–103. doi.org/10.1086/684364.

8   Johnson, E. J., & Goldstein, D. G. (2004). Defaults and donation decisions. *Transplantation*, 78(12), 1713–1716. doi.org/10.1097/01. TP.0000149788.10382.B2.

9   Jachimowicz, J., Duncan, S., Weber, E. U., & Johnson, E. (2019, April 16). Defaults Are Not the Same by Default. *Behavioral Scientist*. Retrieved from behavioralscientist.org.

10   Lima, E. (Personal Communication, 2020).

11   Brownstone, S. (2014, April 23). This Hospital Door Handle Sanitizes Your Hands As You Pull On It. *Fast Company*. Retrieved from https://www.fastcompany.com.

12   Babiarz, L. S., Savoie, B., McGuire, M., McConnell, L., & Nagy, P. (2014). Hand sanitizer-dispensing door handles increase hand hygiene compliance: A pilot study. *American Journal of Infection Control*, 42(4), 443–445. doi.org/10.1016/j.ajic.2013.11.009.

13   Ogilvy. (n.d.). Savlon Healthy Hands Chalk Sticks. Retrieved 29 October 2021, from www.ogilvy.com/work/savlon-healthy-hands-chalk-sticks.

Additional Sources & Further Reading

Sloat, S. (2018, February 21). Human Brain Size Grew 200 Percent in 3 Million Years. Inverse. Retrieved from www.inverse.com.

Rettner, R. (2009, July 13). Why Are Human Brains So Big? Livescience. Com. Retrieved from www.livescience.com.

7, B. (2018, May 23). Why do humans have such huge brains? Scientists have a few hypotheses. Vox. Retrieved from www.vox.com.

Unicycle Creative. (2009, August 14). It's easy to pee green. In the shower, that is. Retrieved 29 October 2021, from unicyclecreative.com/2009/08/its-easy-to-pee-green-in-the-shower-that-is.

CHAPTER 12: EASY PEASY, LEMON SQUEEZY

1   *Facing History and Ourselves.* (2017). Holocaust and Human Behavior
- Chapter 7: Taking Austria (4th ed.). Retrieved from www.facinghistory.
org/holocaust-and-human-behavior/chapter-7/taking-austria.

2   Camargo, M. G. G., Lunau, K., Batalha, M. A., Brings, S., Brito, V. L.
G., & Morellato, L. P. C. (2019). How flower colour signals allure bees and
hummingbirds: A community level test of the bee avoidance hypothesis.
The New Phytologist, 222(2), 1112–1122. doi.org/10.1111/nph.15594.

3   Tsujimoto, S., & Ishii, H. (2017). Erratum to: Effect of flower
perceptibility on spatial-reward associative learning by bumble bees.
s00265-017-2354-9.

4   Springer. (2017, June 29). Bumble bees make a beeline for larger
flowers: Flower size matters when bumble bees learn new foraging routes.
ScienceDaily. Retrieved 27 October, 2021 from www.sciencedaily.com/
releases/2017/06/170629101711.htm.

5   Roberts, J. (2019, May 13). Brexit Party logo 'subconsciously manipulates
voters into backing Farage'. *Metro*. Retrieved from metro.co.uk.

6   Frearson, A. (2019, May 15). Brexit Party logo 'a very clever piece of
graphic design' says Design of the Year winner. *Dezeen*. Retrieved from
www.dezeen.com.

7   Paivio, A. (1971). *Imagery and Verbal Processes* (1st ed.). New York, USA:
Holt, Rinehart & Winston.

8   Binder, J. R., Westbury, C. F., McKiernan, K. A., Possing, E. T., &
Medler, D. A. (2005). Distinct brain systems for processing concrete and
abstract concepts. *Journal of Cognitive Neuroscience*, 17(6), 905–917.
doi.org/10.1162/0898929054021102.

9   Jortberg, P. G. (2015). Research Study Evaluating the Effectiveness
of Caution Signs and Cones. Retrieved from www.conney.com/
WEBSPHERE/PDFFILES/CAUTION%20SIGN%20RESEARCH%20
STUDY.PDF.

10   Statista. (2011–2018). United Kingdom: greeting card market value
2011–2018 [Dataset]. Retrieved from www.statista.com/statistics/500956/
greeting-card-market-value-united-kingdom-uk.

11   West, E. (2018). Understanding authenticity in commercial sentiment:
The greeting card as emotional commodity. *Emotions as Commodities*,
123–144. doi.org/10.4324/9781315210742-6.

12   NBC Universal. (2007, February 15). Chemo to coming out, Hallmark has the card. *NBC News*. Retrieved from www.nbcnews.com.

13   Arnold, K. C., Gajos, K. Z., & Kalai, A. T. (2016). On suggesting phrases vs. predicting words for mobile text composition. *Proceedings of the 29th Annual Symposium on User Interface Software and Technology*. doi.org/10.1145/2984511.2984584.

14   Apple. (n.d.). Apple - iOS 8 - QuickType. Retrieved 29 October 2021, from www.apple.com/my/ios/whats-new/quicktype.

15   Dohrmann, T., & Pinshaw, G. (2009, September). The roadmap to improved compliance: A McKinsey benchmarking study of tax administrations – 2008–2009. *McKinsey & Company*. Retrieved from www.mckinsey.com/~/media/mckinsey/dotcom/client_service/public%20sector/pdfs/road_improved_compliance.ashx.

16   The Behavioural Insights Team (BIT). (2014, April). EAST: Four simple ways to apply behavioural insights. *BIT*. Retrieved from www.bi.team/wp-content/uploads/2015/07/BIT-Publication-EAST_FA_WEB.pdf.

Additional Sources & Further Reading

Bettinger, E. P., Long, B. T., Oreopoulos, P., & Sanbonmatsu, L. (2012). The role of application assistance and information in college decisions: Results from the H&R Block Fafsa experiment. *The Quarterly Journal of Economics*, 127(3), 1205–1242. doi.org/10.1093/qje/qjs017.

Cavendish, R. (2015, September). Discovery of the Lascaux Cave Paintings. *History Today*, 65(9). Retrieved from www.historytoday.com.

Clean It Supply. (2015, November 24). The Banana Cone brings a recognizable awareness to wet floor safety. Retrieved 29 October 2021, from www.cleanitsupply.com/blog/the-banana-cone-brings-a-recognizable-awareness-to-wet-floor-safety.

Lombardi, L., & Hashi, H. (2014, May 15). Sampuru: Japanese Plastic Food Models. Retrieved 29 October 2021, from www.tofugu.com/japan/sampuru.

PwC Australia: Comms Lab. (2017, April). The Power of Visual Communication: Showing your story to land the message. *PwC Australia*. Retrieved from www.pwc.com.au/the-difference/the-power-of-visual-communication-apr17.pdf.

CHAPTER 13: ONE STEP AT A TIME

1   *Royal Mail PAF (Postcode Address File).* (2016, June 6). Postcodes are easier to remember than wedding anniversaries, birthdays, phone numbers and bank account details, Royal Mail reveals. Retrieved 29 October 2021, from www.poweredbypaf.com/postcodes-are-easier-to-remember-than-wedding-anniversaries-birthdays-phone-numbers-and-bank-account-details-royal-mail-reveals.

2   Miller. (1994). The magical number seven, plus or minus two: Some limits on our capacity for processing information. 1956. *Psychological Review*, 101(2), 343–352.

3   *gocognitive.* (2010, October 28). *alan baddeley postal codes* [Video file]. Retrieved from youtu.be/Jvoj4xwkdZM.

4   Williams, H., & Staples, K. (1992). Syllable chunking in zebra finch (Taeniopygia guttata) song. *Journal of Comparative Psychology*, 106(3), 278–286. doi.org/10.1037/0735-7036.106.3.278.

Additional Sources & Further Reading

Fox, M. (2008). *Da Vinci and the 40 Answers: A Playbook for Creativity and Fresh Ideas.* Austin, USA: Wizard Academy Press.

Huang, L., & Awh, E. (2018). Chunking in working memory via content-free labels. *Scientific Reports*, 8(1). doi.org/10.1038/s41598-017-18157-5.

Postal Heritage, & Sutton, P. (2010, October 6). Why are postcodes significant and where did they come from? Retrieved 29 October 2021, from postalheritage.wordpress.com/2010/10/06/why-are-postcodes-significant-and-where-did-they-come-from.

Smith, M. (2021, February 10). Why are UK postcodes so memorable? Retrieved 29 October 2021, from psychologymarc.medium.com/why-are-uk-postcodes-so-memorable-b0457e2e8a0d.

CHAPTER 14: INVISIBLE STRINGS

1   de Gelder, B., Tamietto, M., van Boxtel, G., Goebel, R., Sahraie, A., van den Stock, J., Pegna, A. (2008). Intact navigation skills after bilateral loss of striate cortex. *Current Biology*, 18(24), R1128–R1129. doi.org/10.1016/j.cub.2008.11.002.

2 Barratt, B. (2012). Attentional capture by emotional faces is contingent on attentional control settings. *Cognition and Emotion*, 26(7), 1223–1237. doi.org/10.1080/02699931.2011.645279.

3 Kawahara, J., Yanase, K., & Kitazaki, M. (2012). Attentional capture by the onset and offset of motion signals outside the spatial focus of attention. *Journal of Vision*, 12(12), 10. doi.org/10.1167/12.12.10.

4 Cosmides, L., & Tooby, J. (n.d.). Visual Attention. Center for Evolutionary Psychology – University of California Santa Barbara. Retrieved from www.cep.ucsb.edu/topics/attention.html.

5 Damasio, A. R. (2000). *Descartes' Error: Emotion, Reason and the Human Brain* (Repr.). New York, USA: Quill.

6 Soman, D. (2015). *The Last Mile: Creating Social and Economic Value from Behavioral Insights* (Rotman-Utp Publishing). Toronto, Canada: Rotman-UTP Publishing.

7 IDEC. (2012, May 9). Small change of habits, major contribution to the environment. *O Globo*. Retrieved from oglobo.globo.com

8 Ibid.

CHAPTER 15: FITS LIKE A GLOVE

1 Roos, D. (2021, June 16). Why Do We Get So Much Pleasure From Symmetry? *HowStuffWorks*. Retrieved from science.howstuffworks.com.

2 Bornstein, M. H., Ferdinandsen, K., & Gross, C. G. (1981). Perception of symmetry in infancy. *Developmental Psychology*, 17(1), 82–86. doi.org/10.1037/0012-1649.17.1.82.

3 Jones, B. C., & DeBruine, L. M. (2006). Why are symmetric faces attractive? *FaceResearch.org*. Retrieved from faceresearch.org/students/notes/symmetry.pdf.

4 Gollwitzer, A., & Clark, M. S. (2019). Anxious attachment as an antecedent of people's aversion towards pattern deviancy. *European Journal of Social Psychology*, 49(6), 1206–1222. doi.org/10.1002/ejsp.2565.

5 Wadhwa, M., & Zhang, K. (2015). This number just feels right: The impact of roundedness of price numbers on product evaluations. *Journal of Consumer Research*, 41(5), 1172–1185. doi:10.1086/678484.

Additional Sources & Further Reading

BBC News (Americas). (2004). 'Virgin Mary' toast fetches $28,000. BBC News (Americas). Retrieved from news.bbc.co.uk.

Canada Coin & Currency. (2013, January 24). The Devil's In The Details: The Story of the Devil's Face. Retrieved 29 October 2021, from canadiancoin.wordpress.com/2013/01/24/the-devils-in-the-details-the-story-of-the-devils-face.

Lightman, A. (2013). *The Accidental Universe: The World You Thought You Knew*. London, UK: Corsair Books.

Robson, D. (2014, July 30). Neuroscience: why do we see faces in everyday objects? *BBC Future*. Retrieved from www.bbc.com.

Shermer, M. (2008, December 1). Patternicity: Finding Meaningful Patterns in Meaningless Noise. *Scientific American*. Retrieved from www.scientificamerican.com.

CHAPTER 16: MARCO...

1   Anglin, D., Spears, K. L., & Hutson, H. R. (1997). Flunitrazepam and its involvement in date or acquaintance rape. *Academic Emergency Medicine*, 4(4), 323–326. doi.org/10.1111/j.1553-2712.1997.tb03557.x.

2   Ibid.

3   Clopton, J., & Bhargava, H. D. (2019, July 29). Not Just One Reason Kids Don't Drink Enough Water. *WebMD*. Retrieved from www.webmd.com.

4   Williamson, M. R., Fries, R., & Zhou, H. (2016). Long-term effectiveness of radar speed display signs in a university environment. *Journal of Transportation Technologies*, 6(3), 99–105.

Additional Sources & Further Reading

Burkley, M. (n.d.). A Psychologist's Perspective: Why Radar Speed Signs are Effective in Reducing Speeding. Retrieved 1 November 2021 (via Web Archive), from web.archive.org/web/20210128040823/https://www.speedpatrol.com/why-radar-speed-signs-are-effective-in-reducing-speeding.

LaCapria, K., & Mikkelson, D. (2014, August 15). 'Undercover Colors': A Rape Drug-Detecting Nail Polish. Retrieved 29 October 2021, from www.snopes.com/fact-check/undercover-colors.

Nestlé Waters. (n.d.). Jump in and swim with Tummyfish: Changing kids drinking habits in a fun way. Retrieved 1 November 2021 (via Web Archive), from web.archive.org/web/20201124152627/https://www.nestle-waters.com/our-stories/tummyfish-drinking-water-app-for-kids.

Smith, J. E. W. (2019, January 22). It's cold! A physiologist explains how to keep your body feeling warm. *The Conversation*. Retrieved from theconversation.com.

CHAPTER 17: DIG YOUR HEELS IN

1   Barbra Streisand v. Kenneth Adelman et al., Superior Court of California, County of Los Angeles, USA. 20 May 2003, Case no. SC077257. Retrieved from www.californiacoastline.org/streisand/slapp-ruling-tentative.pdf.

2   Brehm, J. W. (1966). *A Theory of Psychological Reactance.* San Diego, CA: Academic Press.

3   Wang, H. (2020). Ironic effects of thought suppression: A meta-analysis. *Perspectives on Psychological Science,* 15(3), 778–793. doi. org/10.1177/1745691619898795.

4   Callcut, R. A., Robles, A. M., Kornblith, L. Z., Plevin, R. E., & Mell, M. W. (2019). Effect of mass shootings on gun sales-A 20-year perspective. *The Journal of Trauma and Acute Care Surgery,* 87(3), 531–540. doi.org/10.1097/TA.0000000000002399.

5   Soules, M. (2015). *Media, Persuasion and Propaganda.* Edinburgh, UK: Edinburgh University Press.

6   Loewenstein, G. (1994). The psychology of curiosity : A review and reinterpretation. *Psychological Bulletin,* 116(1), 75–98. doi. org/10.1037//0033-2909.116.1.75.

7   Product Page: Barbie Colour Magic Surprise Reveal Doll Assortment. (n.d.). Retrieved 1 November 2021 (via Web Archive), from web.archive. org/web/20210123132457/https://www.argos.co.uk/product/7181135.

8   Guéguen, N., & Pascual, A. (2000). Evocation of freedom and compliance: The "but you are free of…" technique." *Current Research in Social Psychology,* 5(18), 264–270. Retrieved from crisp.org.uiowa.edu/sites/crisp.org.uiowa.edu/files/2020-04/5.18.pdf.

9   Carpenter, C. J. (2013). A meta-analysis of the effectiveness of the "but you are free" compliance-gaining technique. *Communication Studies,* 64(1), 6–17. doi.org/10.1080/10510974.2012.727941.

10   Gallagher, S. (2020, November 2). Burger King encourages people to eat at McDonalds and KFC ahead of second lockdown. *The Independent.* Retrieved from www.independent.co.uk.

Additional Sources & Further Reading

Cacciottolo, M. (2012, June 15). The Streisand Effect: When censorship backfires. *BBC News.* Retrieved from www.bbc.com.

McGinley, T. (2015, March 3). Bank of Canada urges 'Star Trek' fans to stop 'Spocking' their fivers. Retrieved 29 October 2021, from dangerousminds.net/comments/bank_of_canada_urges_star_trek_fans_to_stop_spocking_their_fivers.

CHAPTER 18: TOGETHER FOR THE KIDS

1 Than, K. (2006, November 20). Wild Sex: Where Monogamy is Rare. *Livescience.Com.* Retrieved from www.livescience.com.

2 Whiteman, L. (2013, February 13). Animal Attraction: The Many Forms of Monogamy in the Animal Kingdom. Retrieved 29 October 2021, from www.nsf.gov/discoveries/disc_summ.jsp?cntn_id=126932.

3 Sharp, B. (2010). *How Brands Grow: What Marketers Don't Know.* Oxford, UK: Oxford University Press.

4 Wollan, R., Davis, P., de Angelis, F., & Quiring, K. (2017). Seeing Beyond the Loyalty Illusion: It's time you invest more wisely. *Accenture Strategy.* Retrieved from www.accenture.com/_acnmedia/pdf-43/accenture-strategy-gcpr-customer-loyalty.pdf.

5 Sharp (2010).

6 Trivers, R. L. (1972). Parental Investment and Sexual Selection. In Campbell, B. G. (ed.), *Sexual Selection and the Descent of Man: The Darwinian Pivot* (1st ed.) (pp. 136–179). Chicago, USA: Aldine Publishing Company. doi.org/10.4324/9781315129266.

7 Carlisle, T. R. (1985). Parental response to brood size in a cichlid fish. *Animal Behaviour, 33*(1), 234–238. doi.org/10.1016/s0003-3472(85)80137-8.

Additional Sources & Further Reading

Gabbatiss, J. (2016, February 13). Why pairing up for life is hardly ever a good idea. *BBC Earth.* Retrieved (via Web Archive) from web.archive.org/web/20200201044713/http://www.bbc.com/earth/story/20160213-why-pairing-up-for-life-is-hardly-ever-a-good-idea.

Macdonald, D. W., Campbell, L. A. D., Kamler, J. F., Marino, J., Werhahn, G., & Sillero-Zubiri, C. (2019). Monogamy: Cause, consequence, or corollary of success in wild canids? *Frontiers in Ecology and Evolution, 7.* doi.org/10.3389/fevo.2019.00341.

CHAPTER 19: I AM MY WORD

1   Adweek. (2018, July 10). Palau Pledge – Interview With Host/Havas [Video file]. Retrieved from youtu.be/vmfTL6lTECw.

2   Meredith, M. (2013, October 21). Why Do We Raise Our Right Hands When Testifying Before the Court? Retrieved 29 October 2021, from nwsidebar.wsba.org/2013/10/21/raise-right-hand-court.

3   Rosefield, H. (2014, June 20). A Brief History of Oaths and Books. *The New Yorker*. Retrieved from www.newyorker.com.

4   Mazar, N., Amir, O., & Ariely, D. (2008). The dishonesty of honest people: A theory of self-concept maintenance. *Journal of Marketing Research*, 45(6), 633–644. doi.org/10.1509/jmkr.45.6.633.

5   Michaels, S. (2009, July 13). Oasis refund fans almost £1m. *The Guardian*. Retrieved from www.theguardian.com.

6   Chou, E. Y. (2015). What's in a name? The toll e-signatures take on individual honesty. *Journal of Experimental Social Psychology*, 61, 84–95. doi.org/10.1016/j.jesp.2015.07.010.

7   Martin, S. J., Bassi, S., & Dunbar-Rees, R. (2012). Commitments, norms and custard creams – a social influence approach to reducing did not attends (DNAs). *Journal of the Royal Society of Medicine*, 105(3), 101–104. doi. org/10.1258/jrsm.2011.110250.

8   Chou (2015).

9   Wertenbroch, K. (1998). Consumption self-control by rationing purchase quantities of virtue and vice. *Marketing Science*, 17(4), 317–337. doi.org/10.1287/mksc.17.4.317.

10   Schwartz, J., Mochon, D., Wyper, L., Maroba, J., Patel, D., & Ariely, D. (2014). Healthier by precommitment. *Psychological Science*, 25(2), 538–546. doi.org/10.1177/0956797613510950.

11   World Health Organization (WHO). (2020, September 8). Children: improving survival and well-being. Retrieved 29 October 2021, from www. who.int/news-room/fact-sheets/detail/children-reducing-mortality.

12   Gurnani, V., Haldar, P., Aggarwal, M. K., Das, M. K., Chauhan, A., Murray, J., & Sudan, P. (2018). Improving vaccination coverage in India: lessons from Intensified Mission Indradhanush, a cross-sectoral systems strengthening strategy. *BMJ*, k4782. doi.org/10.1136/bmj.k4782.

Additional Sources & Further Reading

Gye, H. (2013, July 7). Man in Turkey wears a cage on his head to stop himself having a cigarette. *Mail Online.* Retrieved from www.dailymail.co.uk.

Jani, J. V., de Schacht, C., Jani, I. V., & Bjune, G. (2008). Risk factors for incomplete vaccination and missed opportunity for immunization in rural Mozambique. *BMC Public Health,* 8(1). doi.org/10.1186/1471-2458-8-161.

Knight, K. (2013, July 9). Turkish man Ibrahim Yücel from Kütahya locks head in cage to stop smoking. *Metro.* Retrieved from metro.co.uk.

Pruden, J. G. (2019, November 17). Eagle feathers, like the Bible, now an option for swearing oaths in all Alberta courts. *The Globe and Mail.* Retrieved from www.theglobeandmail.com.

CHAPTER 20: SO CLOSE I CAN SMELL IT

1 Miller, D. T., & Gunasegaram, S. (1990). Temporal order and the perceived mutability of events: Implications for blame assignment. *Journal of Personality and Social Psychology,* 59(6), 1111–1118. doi.org/10.1037/0022-3514.59.6.1111.

2 Hull, C. L. (1934). The rat's speed-of-locomotion gradient in the approach to food. *Journal of Comparative Psychology,* 17(3), 393–422. doi.org/10.1037/h0071299.

3 Kivetz, R., Urminsky, O., & Zheng, Y. (2006). The goal-gradient hypothesis resurrected: Purchase acceleration, illusionary goal progress, and customer retention. *Journal of Marketing Research,* 43(1), 39–58. doi.org/10.1509/jmkr.43.1.39.

4 Nunes, J., & Drèze, X. (2006). The endowed progress effect: How artificial advancement increases effort. *Journal of Consumer Research,* 32(4), 504–512. doi.org/10.1086/500480.

CHAPTER 21: YOU WIN SOME, YOU LOSE SOME.

1 Ferster, C. B., & Skinner, B. F. (1957). Schedules of reinforcement. *Appleton-Century-Crofts.* doi.org/10.1037/10627-000.

2 Staddon, J. E. R. (2001). *The New Behaviorism* (2nd ed.). Amsterdam, Netherlands: Amsterdam University Press.

3   MacPherson, L. (2018, November 8). A Deep Dive on Variable Rewards and How to Use Them. Retrieved 29 October 2021, from designli.co/blog/a-deep-dive-on-variable-rewards-and-how-to-use-them.

4   Knutson, B., Wimmer, G. E., Kuhnen, C. M., & Winkielman, P. (2008). Nucleus accumbens activation mediates the influence of reward cues on financial risk taking. *NeuroReport*, 19(5), 509–513. doi.org/10.1097/wnr.0b013e3282f85c01.

5   Press Association. (2015, July 17). 'I thought I was going to die,' says girl who ate spicy Doritos. *The Guardian*. Retrieved from www.theguardian.com.

6   Kinder Surprise. (n.d.). *Wikipedia*. Retrieved 29 October 2021, from en.wikipedia.org/wiki/Kinder_Surprise.

7   Elgot, J., & Addley, E. (2015, April 22). Pret staff's free coffee for people they like: discrimination or a nice gesture? *The Guardian*. Retrieved from www.theguardian.com.

8   Saul, H. (2015, April 22). Pret A Manger staff give free coffee and food to customers they like or find attractive. *The Independent*. Retrieved from www.independent.co.uk.

CHAPTER 22: BRAIN TIME

1   Healy, K., McNally, L., Ruxton, G. D., Cooper, N., & Jackson, A. L. (2013). Metabolic rate and body size are linked with perception of temporal information. *Animal Behaviour*, 86(4), 685–696.

2   Eagleman, D. M., & Pariyadath, V. (2009). Is subjective duration a signature of coding efficiency? *Philosophical Transactions of the Royal Society B: Biological Sciences*, 364(1525), 1841–1851.

3   Cepelewicz, J. (2020, September 24). Reasons Revealed for the Brain's Elastic Sense of Time. *Quanta Magazine*. Retrieved from www.quantamagazine.org.

4   Wittmann, M. (2010). The neural substrates of subjective time dilation. *Frontiers in Human Neuroscience*. doi.org/10.3389/neuro.09.002.2010.

5   Kahneman, D., & Riis, J. (2005). Living, and thinking about it: Two perspectives on life. *The Science of Well-Being*, 284–305. doi.org/10.1093/acprof:oso/9780198567523.003.0011.

6   Kemp, S., Burt, C., & Furneaux, L. (2008). A test of the peak-end rule with extended autobiographical events. *Memory & Cognition*, 36(1), 132–138. doi.org/10.3758/MC.36.1.132.

7   TEDGlobal 2009. (2009, July). *Life lessons from an ad man. Rory Sutherland* [Video file]. Retrieved from www.ted.com/talks/rory_sutherland_life_lessons_from_an_ad_man#t-133475.

8   Quarmby, D. A. (1967). Choice of travel mode for the journey to work. *Journal of Transport Economics and Policy*, 273–314.

9   Nie, W. (2000). Waiting: integrating social and psychological perspectives in operations management. *Omega*, 28(6), 611–629. doi. org/10.1016/s0305-0483(00)00019-0.

Additional Sources & Further Reading

Galloway, R. (2017, September 17). Why is it so hard to swat a fly? *BBC News*. Retrieved from www.bbc.co.uk.

Lawton, G. (2016, September 6). What Is The Oddball Effect? This Psychological Phenomenon May Explain Why You Perceive Time Differently. *Bustle*. Retrieved from www.bustle.com.

Livni, E. (2019, January 8). Physics explains why time passes faster as you age. *Quartz*. Retrieved from qz.com.

Norman, D. (2008). The psychology of waiting lines. jnd. org/the_psychology_of_waiting_lines.

Press Association. (2013, September 16). Time passes more slowly for flies, study finds. *The Guardian*. Retrieved from www.theguardian.com.

Reas, E. (2014, July 1). Small Animals Live in a Slow-Motion World. *Scientific American*. Retrieved from www.scientificamerican.com.

TED. (2010, March 1). *The riddle of experience vs. memory. Daniel Kahneman* [Video file]. Retrieved from youtu.be/XgRlrBl-7Yg.

The University of Edinburgh. (2016, April 5). Time perception varies between animals. Retrieved 29 October 2021, from www.ed.ac.uk/news/2013/time-160913.

CHAPTER 23: BETTER THE DEVIL YOU KNOW

1   Piper, J. (Host). (2019, September 27). *John Piper's Most Bizarre Moment in Preaching* (no. 1374) [Audio podcast episode]. In Ask Pastor John. *Desiring God.* www.desiringgod.org/interviews/john-pipers-most-bizarre-moment-in-preaching.

2   TheologyJeremy. (2018, Feb 17). *John Piper gets Laughed at by 8000 Christian Counselors* [Video file]. Retrieved from www.youtube.com/watch?v=EI7KAOSFq2A.

3   Reynolds, R. F., & Bronstein, A. M. (2003). The broken escalator phenomenon: Aftereffect of walking onto a moving platform. *Experimental Brain Research*, 151(3), 301–308. doi.org/10.1007/s00221-003-1444-2.

4   DuBose, C.N., Cardello, A. V., & Maller, O. (1980). Effects of colorants and flavorants on identification, perceived flavor intensity, and hedonic quality of fruit flavored beverages and cake. *Journal of Food Science*, 45, 1393–1399.

5   McClure, S. M., Li, J., Tomlin, D., Cypert, K. S., Montague, L. M., & Montague, P. R. (2004). Neural correlates of behavioral preference for culturally familiar drinks. *Neuron*, 44, 379–387.

6   de Berker, A. O., Rutledge, R. B., Mathys, C., Marshall, L., Cross, G. F., Dolan, R. J., & Bestmann, S. (2016). Computations of uncertainty mediate acute stress responses in humans. *Nature Communications*, 7(1). doi.org/10.1038/ncomms10996.

7   Campbell, D. (2016, October 6). Time warp: why uncertainty affects how we perceive time. Retrieved 31 October 2021, from www.utoronto.ca/news/time-warp-why-uncertainty-affects-how-we-perceive-time.

8   van de Ven, N., van Rijswijk, L., & Roy, M. M. (2011). The return trip effect: Why the return trip often seems to take less time. *Psychonomic Bulletin & Review*, 18(5), 827–832. doi.org/10.3758/s13423-011-0150-5.

9   Ibid.

10   D. (2021, April 1). No Jokes It's Not Awful in the Parks – Disney World Wait Times for Thursday, April 1, 2021. Retrieved 31 October 2021, from touringplans.com/blog/no-jokes-its-not-awful-in-the-parks-disney-world-wait-times-for-thursday-april-1-2021.

11   van de Ven et al. (2011).

12   Kamat, P., & Hogan, C. (2019, January, 28). How Uber Leverages Applied Behavioral Science at Scale. Retrieved 16 November, 2020 from eng.uber.com/applied-behavioral-science-at-scale.

13   Whitson, J. A., & Galinsky, A. D. (2008). Lacking control increases illusory pattern perception. *Science*, 322(5898), 115–117. doi.org/10.1126/science.1159845.

14   Homans, G. C. (1941). Anxiety and ritual: The theories of Malinowski and Radcliffe-Brown. *American Anthropologist*, 43(2), 164–172. doi.org/10.1525/aa.1941.43.2.02a00020.

15   Whitson & Galinsky (2008).

16   Sales, S. M. (1973). Threat as a factor in authoritarianism: An analysis of archival data. *Journal of Personality and Social Psychology*, 28(1), 44–57. doi.org/10.1037/h0035588.

17   Keinan, G. (1994). Effects of stress and tolerance of ambiguity on magical thinking. *Journal of Personality and Social Psychology*, 67(1), 48–55 doi.apa.org/getdoi.cfm?doi=10.1037/0022-3514.67.1.48.

18   Mele, C. (2016, October 27). Pushing That Crosswalk Button May Make You Feel Better, but... *The New York Times*. Retrieved from www.nytimes.com.

19   The pros and cons of placebo buttons. *The Economist*. (2019, January 26). Retrieved from www.economist.com.

20   Paumgarten, N. (2014, July 28). Up and Then Down. *The New Yorker*. Retrieved from www.newyorker.com.

Additional Sources & Further Reading

Lewis, M. (2016, April 4). Why we're hardwired to hate uncertainty. *The Guardian*. Retrieved from www.theguardian.com.

CHAPTER 24: TIME FLIES WHEN YOU'RE HAVING FUN

1   Stone, A. (2012, August 18). Opinion Why Waiting in Line Is Torture. *The New York Times*. Retrieved from www.nytimes.com.

2   Bench, S., & Lench, H. (2013). On the Function of Boredom. *Behavioral Sciences*, 3(3), 459–472. doi.org/10.3390/bs3030459.

3   Stone (2012, August 18).

Additional Sources & Further Reading

Danckert, J. A., & Allman, A. A. A. (2005). Time flies when you're having fun: Temporal estimation and the experience of boredom. *Brain and Cognition*, 59(3), 236–245. doi.org/10.1016/j.bandc.2005.07.002.

Debczak, M. (2020, August 11). The Psychological Tricks Disney Parks Use to Make Long Wait Times More Bearable. *Mental Floss*. Retrieved from www.mentalfloss.com.

History.com Editors. (2009, November 24). Disneyland opens. Retrieved 1 November 2021, from www.history.com/this-day-in-history/disneyland-opens.

Jarrett, C. (n.d.). Why does time seem to go slower when we're bored? *BBC Science Focus Magazine*. Retrieved from www.sciencefocus.com.

Just Disney. (n.d.). Disneyland Opening Day. Retrieved 1 November 2021, from www.justdisney.com/Features/disneyland_opening/index.html.

Larson, R. C. (1987). Perspectives on queues: Social justice and the psychology of queueing. *Operations Research*, 35(6), 895–905. doi. org/10.1287/opre.35.6.895.

Merrifield, C., & Danckert, J. (2013). Characterizing the psychophysiological signature of boredom. *Experimental Brain Research*, 232(2), 481–491. doi.org/10.1007/s00221-013-3755-2.

CHAPTER 25: ALL'S WELL THAT ENDS WELL

1   Kahneman, D., Fredrickson, B. L., Schreiber, C. A., & Redelmeier, D. A. (1993). When more pain is preferred to less: Adding a better end. *Psychological Science*, 4(6), 401–405. doi.org/10.1111/j.1467-9280.1993. tb00589.x.

2   Ibid.

3   Eyal, N. (n.d.). Peak-End Rule: Why You Make Terrible Life Choices. Retrieved 1 November 2021, from www.nirandfar.com/peak-end-rule.

4   Kemp et al. (2008).

5   Hoogerheide, V., Vink, M., Finn, B., Raes, A. K., & Paas, F. (2017). How to bring the news… peak-end effects in children's affective responses to peer assessments of their social behavior. *Cognition and Emotion*, 32(5), 1114–1121. doi.org/10.1080/02699931.2017.1362375.

6   Heath, C., & Heath, D. (2017). *The Power of Moments: Why Certain Experiences Have Extraordinary Impact*. New York, United States: Simon & Schuster.

7   Magic Castle Hotel. (n.d.). Magic Castle Hotel – Our Anniversary Vacation. Retrieved 1 November 2021, from www.magiccastlehotel.com/ reviews/our-anniversary-vacation.html.

8   Strohmetz, D. B., Rind, B., Fisher, R., & Lynn, M. (2002). Sweetening the till: The use of candy to increase restaurant tipping. Journal of Applied Social Psychology, 32(2), 300–309. doi.org/10.1111/j.1559-1816.2002.tb00216.x.

9   Egan Brad, L. C., Lakshminarayanan, V. R., Jordan, M. R., Phillips, W. C., & Santos, L. R. (2016). The evolution and development of peak–end effects for past and prospective experiences. *Journal of Neuroscience, Psychology, and Economics*, 9(1), 1–13. doi.org/10.1037/npe0000048.

10   Freedman, D. H. (2013, July). How Junk Food Can End Obesity. *The Atlantic*. Retrieved from www.theatlantic.com.

11 Technical glitches mar Amazon's Prime Day, threatening $4.6b haul. (2018, July 17). *The Sydney Morning Herald.* Retrieved from www.smh.com.au.

12 Amazon Staff. (2019, July 30). How much does Amazon love dogs? Just ask one of the 7,000 pups that "work" here. Retrieved 16 November 2021, from www.aboutamazon.com/news/workplace/how-much-does-amazon-love-dogs-just-ask-one-of-the-7-000-pups-that-work-here.

13 Stevens, B. (2018, July 19). Amazon Prime Day loses $90m due to outage but still breaks records. Retrieved 1 November 2021, from www.retailgazette.co.uk/blog/2018/07/amazon-prime-day-loses-90m-due-outage-still-breaks-records.

Additional Sources & Further Reading:

Cherry, K. (2020, May 10). Biological Preparedness and Classical Conditioning. Retrieved 1 November 2021, from www.verywellmind.com/what-is-biological-preparedness-2794879.

Westfall, P. (2017, November 13). 16 Super Clever 404 Pages that are Totally On-Brand. Retrieved 1 November 2021, from www.pagecloud.com/blog/best-404-pages.

CHAPTER 26: NEW EYES

1 Goodyear, L., Hossain, T., & Soman, D. (2022). Prescriptions for Successfully Scaling Behavioral Interventions. In Mažar, N., & Soman, D. (2022). *Behavioral Science in the Wild.* Toronto, Canada: University of Toronto Press.

2 Martin, R. L. (2020). *When More Is Not Better: Overcoming America's Obsession with Economic Efficiency.* Boston, USA: Harvard Business Review Press.

3 Krijnen, J. (2018, September 18). Choice Architecture 2.0: How People Interpret and Make Sense of Nudges. *Behavioral Scientist.* Retrieved from behavioralscientist.org.

4 Smets, K. (2018, July 24). There Is More to Behavioral Economics Than Biases and Fallacies. *Behavioral Scientist.* Retrieved from behavioralscientist.org.

INDEX

ABOUT THE
AUTHOR

 SAM TATAM is Global Head of Behavioural Science at Ogilvy. His passion is understanding human behaviour, and his experience comes from organisational/industrial psychology and advertising strategy.

From New York to Nairobi, Sam has led behaviour change projects across virtually every category and continent. Today, he leads a global team of talented psychologists and behavioural economists to develop interventions and shape the communications of some of the world's most influential brands and organisations.